DEVELOPMENT AND PLANNING

DEVELOPMENT AND PLANNING

Essays in honour of Paul Rosenstein Rodan

edited by

JAGDISH BHAGWATI

and

RICHARD S. ECKAUS

THE MIT PRESS

Cambridge, Massachusetts

Printed in Great Britain

PREFACE

Having benefited for many years from his wit and wisdom, this group of Paul Rosenstein-Rodan's friends and colleagues is now pleased to offer him this *festschrift* The Rodan hospitality has been legendary. There have been aperitifs of stimulating conversation and fresh new ideas, robust courses of professionalism and desserts of frothy talk. All of it has been served with a humane vision of the world. The feast served here in his honour is not so varied a menu, but then there are few chefs to compare with Paul Rosenstein-Rodan.

The varied background of the contributors to this volume reflects Rosenstein-Rodan's own long and varied career, his professional influence and his friendships. He is a vigorous representative of the best of continental European culture and scholarship. Just as clearly he is Bloomsbury, he also reflects the liberal and progressive ideals of a civilised society.

For his first decade and a half as an economist, Rosenstein-Rodan was among the 'purest of the pure'. During this period he wrote seminal papers on utility and value theory and his interests extended into other fields such as monetary theory. He was also renowned as *the* authority on the history of economic thought and was a great bibliophile in that area. The Second World War was a watershed in his career, however. He anticipated the great struggle, participated in the economic policy-making that its exigencies required, and turned early to an examination of the pressing problems of the post-war world.

For thirty years Paul Rosenstein-Rodan has been a leader in the efforts of the economics profession to understand the problems of the poor nations of the world and to assist in their development. He has not merely been the doyen of development theorists; he has also dedicated much of his life to policy-making by international organizations for development and to domestic policy formation within many of the less developed countries. A clear and non-ideological concern for individual welfare has provided the credentials which continue to lead Prime Ministers and Presidents to seek and act on

7

his advice. He is one of those few persons without official position who are truly international civil servants.

The variety of the positions of the contributors to this volume reflects the range of the Rodan interests. There are men of affairs, theorists and empiricists. All, and many more, are pleased to have the occasion to express their esteem and affection.

M.I.T.   *Jagdish Bhagwati*

Richard S. Eckaus

CONTENTS

10 CONTENTS

I

GROWTH OF
DEVELOPMENT ECONOMICS

CHAPTER 1

Development Economics Before 1945

H. W. ARNDT

In his book, *On the Theory of Social Change*, Professor Everett Hagen refers to 'the surge of interest after the Second World War in the problems of growth in low-income economies' and adds in a footnote: 'Of course there was earlier interest in economic growth. . . . [But] interest specifically in the problems of low-income or technologically static economies became conspicuous only after the Second World War. One earlier article, a landmark in the analysis of those problems, is P. N. Rosenstein-Rodan's "Problems of Industrialization of Eastern and South-Eastern Europe", *Economic Journal*, June–September 1943.'[1]

What, if anything, did Western economists have to say before 1945 about the problems of the underdeveloped regions of the world? How did the post-1945 'surge of interest' in these problems come about? This volume in tribute to one of the pioneers of modern development economics seems a fitting occasion to ask and attempt to answer these questions.

THE CLASSICS, NEO-CLASSICS AND MARX

The classical economists, from Adam Smith to J. S. Mill and Marx, were intensely interested in economic development. But their concern was naturally with the capitalist development of their own Western world.

Adam Smith liked to illustrate his argument by occasional references to China and India, well aware that he had to rely largely on accounts 'generally drawn up by weak and wondering travellers,

[1] E. E. Hagen, *On the Theory of Social Change* (Dorsey Press, 1962), p. 36.

13

frequently by stupid and lying missionaries'.[2] To illustrate his proposition that 'it is not the actual greatness of national wealth but its continual increase which occasions a rise in the wages of labour', he cited the case of China, 'one of the richest, that is one of the most fertile, best cultivated, most illustrious, and most populous countries of the world'. Yet, because 'it has long been stationary', the wages of labour are so low that 'the poverty of the lower ranks of people far surpasses that of the most beggarly nations in Europe'.[3] To illustrate the advantage for export trade of a large domestic market he referred to India. 'The great extent of Hindostan rendered the home market of the country very great, and sufficient to support a great variety of manufactures. ... Bengal, accordingly, has always been more remarkable for the exportation of a great variety of manufactures, than for that of its grain.'[4] But all this was little more than the encyclopaedic stock-in-trade of the eighteenth-century philosopher.

Ricardo and his contemporaries kept their eyes firmly on England, Western Europe and North America, mentioning other parts of the world, if at all, only in the context of British commercial, colonial or migration policy, and this remained substantially true of English economists, and *mutatis mutandis* of Western economists, at any rate until 1914. J. S. Mill, who was for over thirty years an official of the East India Company and knew a good deal about India, committed himself to the statement that 'it is only in the backward countries of the world that increased production is still an important subject. In those most advanced, what is economically needed is a better distribution.'[5] But what concerned him was not the need for greater production in the backward countries but for better distribution in his own.

It was John Stuart Mill, Professor Hicks has pointed out, 'who killed the old Growth Economics and paved the way for the Static Epoch which was to follow'.[6] From about 1850 onwards, most Western economists took growth for granted and worried about other aspects of economic welfare – allocative efficiency, distribution and stability. Marshall has two 'really rather perfunctory' chapters on economic progress, Wicksell a chapter on capital accumulation

[2] Adam Smith, *The Wealth of Nations*, ed. E. Cannan (Methuen, 1950), vol. 2, p. 221.

[3] Ibid., vol. 1, p. 73.   [4] Ibid., vol. 2, p. 180.

[5] J. S. Mill, *Principles of Political Economy*, 5th edn, (London, 1862), vol. 2, p. 324.

[6] J. R. Hicks, 'Growth and Anti-Growth', *Oxford Economic Papers* (November 1966), p. 260.

'just tacked on at the end'. 'But the spotlight is not on them. And in Walras, Pareto and the Austrians there is even less.'[7] If there was little interest in growth, there was even less in underdevelopment.[8]

Karl Marx, of course, 'the last of the classical economists',[9] wrote a great deal about Asia. But as Shlomo Avineri has pointed out in his acute introduction to his collection of the writings of *Karl Marx on Colonialism and Modernization*, Marx was 'a European thinker, primarily interested in the impact of industrialization on Western society. . . . In the *Manifesto* Marx refers in an undifferentiated yet characteristic way to "barbarians", "semi-barbarians", "nations of peasants", "the East". Compared to Marx's careful analysis of European society and history, this is primitive and certainly unsatisfactory. It is even surprising within the context of the *Manifesto*, since its appeal is, after all, predicated upon a philosophy of history for whose universal applicability the strongest possible claim is made throughout the whole document.' 'Despite the explicit dynamism of Marx's dialectical model, it seems to be an uneasy combination of two sets of disparate elements: a sophisticated, carefully worked out schema describing the historical dynamism of European societies,

[7] Ibid., p. 258.

[8] Marshall is, as always, something of an exception. In the *Principles* and elsewhere, he referred to India and other parts of the East. But his chief motive was the belief, as he said in his reply to Cunningham, that much can be done 'in applying contemporary observation of the East to explain the economic past' of Europe (A. Marshall, *Principles of Economics*, 9th edn (Macmillan, 1961), vol. 2, p. 737). A more surprising exception is the greatest of the American neo-classics, J. B. Clark, whose efforts to expound and delimit economic statics led him into more imaginative thinking about economic dynamics than any of his contemporaries and who, in this connection, at least put the analytical problem of the relations between economically developed and underdeveloped parts of the world 'on the agenda of theory' (J. M. Clark on J. B. Clark, in H. W. Spiegel, *The Development of Economic Thought*. 1952). The flavour of his discussion may be indicated by two quotations from *Essentials of Economic Theory* (1907). There is a 'line of demarcation about the countries (Western Europe, America, etc.) which constitute the economic centre [of the world] and thus include an area within which economic causes produce speedy effects. . . . Across the boundary which separates this centre from the outer zone, economic influences act in a more feeble way and are unable to bring rates of wages and interest even to an approximate equality' (p. 231). 'Our studies have included, not the activities of the whole world, but those of that central part of it which is highly sensitive to economic influences . . . . This society *par excellence* is extending its boundaries and annexing successive belts of outlying territory; and as this shall go on, it must bring the whole world more and more nearly into the shape of a single economic organism. The relations of the central society to the annexed zones are attaining transcendent importance, and a fuller treatment of Economic Dynamics . . . would give more space to such subjects as the transformation of Asia and the resulting changes in the economic life of Europe and America' (p. 560).

[9] Hicks, op. cit., p. 263.

rather simple-mindedly grafted upon a dismissal of all non-European forms of society under the blanket designation of a mere geographic terminology of the "Asiatic mode of production", which appears static, unchanging, and totally non-dialectical.'[10] Marx saw the future of the underdeveloped countries entirely in terms of the triumph of capitalist colonialism. 'Since Oriental society does not develop internally, it cannot evolve towards capitalism through the dialectics of internal change; and since Marx postulates the ultimate victory of socialism on the prior universalization of capitalism, he necessarily arrives at the position of having to endorse European colonial expansion as a brutal but necessary step towards the victory of socialism. Just as the horrors of industrialization are dialectically necessary for the triumph of communism, so the horrors of colonialism are dialectically necessary for the world revolution of the proletariat since without them the countries of Asia (and presumably Africa) will not be able to emancipate themselves from their stagnant backwardness.'[11]

THE INTER-WAR YEARS I: THE MAINSTREAM

During the inter-war years, the problems of long-term economic growth all but disappeared from the mainstream of economics and, to a degree which is astonishing in retrospect, Western economists ignored the underdeveloped world. 'Economists generally have been too much concerned with static models and too culturally bound by a Western European framework of institutions to make the contribution to the subject of the economics of growth that might reasonably be expected from the profession.'[12]

In all the works of the leading economists of the inter-war period, there is hardly a reference to the problems of the underdeveloped regions of the world. Marshall, in his last major work, *Industry and Trade* (1919), refers to them only in the course of 'some slight speculations as to future homes of industrial leadership' . . . 'Passing away from European races, we find in Japan a bold claimant for leadership of the East on lines that are mainly Western. . . . India, though less agile, is developing renewed vigour and independence in

---

[10] Shlomo Avineri (ed.), *Karl Marx on Colonialism and Modernization* (Doubleday, 1968), p. 5.

[11] Ibid., p. 12.

[12] H. F. Williamson, in B. Haley, *A Survey of Contemporary Economics* (Irwin, 1952), vol. 2, p. 182.

industry as in thought. . . . Great futures may also await Russia and China. . . . but recent events obscure the outlook. . . . Up to the present time a tropical climate has been fatal to the best energies of races, however vigorous.'[13] Pigou in his great work on *The Economics of Welfare* (1920) never once referred to poverty outside Europe, while pointing out that 'in a great number of ways, and for a variety of reasons, poor people in civilized countries are given help, in the main through some State agency, at the expense of their better-to-do fellow-citizens'.[14] In Taussig's *Principles of Economics*, non-Europeans make an appearance only in a chapter on 'Some Causes Affecting Productiveness'. 'The Hottentot cannot use tools even of a comparatively simple kind because his brain power is not sufficiently developed. . . . Many of the operations of agriculture require nothing beyond delving and ditching. But the fruitful agriculture of advanced peoples calls for care, discrimination, intelligence and could not be practised by Indian ryots or Russian peasants.'[15] Irving Fisher refers once to differences between rich and poor countries but only to play down their importance: 'Although a whole nation may be rich or poor relatively to another nation, the widest differences between nations are small compared with the differences *within* any one nation.'[16]

Keynes, of course, as a young man wrote on *Indian Currency and Finance*. But in all his later works one searches almost entirely in vain for any signs of interest in or concern for the poor outside Europe. When, in 1930, to counter the 'bad attack of economic pessimism' from which 'we are suffering just now', he dazzled himself and his readers with 'the power of accumulation of compound interest', he predicted, with a Europocentrism that strikes us as grotesque, that 'assuming no important wars and no important increase in population, the *economic problem* may be solved, or be at least within sight of solution, within a hundred years. This means that the economic problem is not – if we look into the future – *the permanent problem of*

[13] Alfred Marshall, *Industry and Trade* (Macmillan, 1919), pp. 161f.
[14] A. C. Pigou, *The Economics of Welfare*, 2nd edn (Macmillan, 1924), p. 657. Marshall did visualize an age of international aid: 'This and other Western countries can now afford to make increased sacrifices of material wealth for the purpose of raising the quality of life throughout their whole populations. A time may come when such matters will be treated as of cosmopolitan rather than national obligation: but that time is not in sight' (op. cit., p. 5).
[15] F. W. Taussig, *Principles of Economics*, 2nd edn (Macmillan, 1916), vol. 1, p. 101.
[16] Irving Fisher, *Elementary Principles of Economics* (Macmillan, 1915), pp. 476f.

the human race.'[17] Schumpeter, for all his interest and insight into the process of economic development, shared Keynes's tastes and limitations in this respect.

The most likely place in which to find references to the underdeveloped countries in the treatises and textbooks of the period is in the chapters on population. Cannan, noting in 1931 the decline in the birth-rate in Western countries, optimistically predicts that 'the cause of it – birth control – will doubtless in time affect the rest of the world, so that while we may expect considerable increase . . . to take place among the more backward peoples for another half-century at least, there is no reason whatever for expecting the population of the world to "tread close on the heels of subsistence" in the future'.[18] Benham's single reference to the underdeveloped countries in his *Economics* (1938) is in the context of international migration: 'Emigration has had very little effect on the dense populations of Eastern countries. . . . Their populations remain much larger, relatively to their resources, than those of Western countries, and this is perhaps the main reason why their standards of living are so low.'[19]

Rather than further labour the obvious, let me drive the point home with two striking illustrations at the end of the inter-war period. In 1938, James Meade wrote the best of the *World Economic Surveys* of the League of Nations. The focus was on the state of world 'business activity'. Developments in the United States, Western Europe and Japan were covered in some detail in twenty-six pages; the 'primary producing countries' (Australia, Canada, New Zealand, Argentina, Brazil, Chile, Hungary, Rumania, Yugoslavia) rated one paragraph and a table; the Balkans, the Dutch East Indies one sentence each, South America one paragraph; all the rest, including all of Asia (except Japan), Africa and the USSR, were completely ignored.[20]

In 1948, Paul Samuelson published the first edition of his *Economics*. Of the theme of underdevelopment, which in the latest edition (1967) runs from the front flyleaf through chapter 6 on 'Affluence and Poverty' to many of the last 100 pages, there are only three traces:

[17] J. M. Keynes, 'Economic Possibilities for our Grandchildren', in *Essays in Persuasion* (Macmillan, 1933), pp. 358, 361, 365f.

[18] E. Cannan, *Economic Scares* (P. S. King, 1933), p. 92.

[19] F. Benham, *Economics* (Pitman, 1938), p. 418.

[20] League of Nations, *World Economic Survey 1937/8* (Geneva, 1938). In fairness it should be mentioned that two later economic surveys of the inter-war period also completely ignored the 'third world': H. W. Arndt, *The Economic Lessons of the 1930s* (O.U.P., 1944); and W. Arthur Lewis, *Economic Survey 1919–39* (Allen & Unwin, 1949).

a sentence comparing the steady improvement in Western living standards with 'more backward nations, two-thirds of whose inhabitants are badly undernourished';[21] a statement, in a paragraph on the International Bank, that 'South America, the Orient and other regions of the world could profitably use our capital for their industrial development';[22] and a reference to Chinese coolies in a rebuttal of the 'cheap-labour' argument for protection![23]

THE INTER-WAR YEARS II: THE SPECIALISTS

Almost wholly ignored by the mainstream of Western economics during the inter-war period, the economic problems of under-developed and developing countries were at the same time the subject of quite a large specialist literature. There were a) studies of special aspects of underdeveloped countries of interest to the developed countries, such as commodity problems, international investment, migration and industrialization; b) studies by Western specialists of the economic problems of dependent and semi-dependent territories; c) studies of the problems of underdeveloped countries by their own nationals; and d) statistical work which threw light on the facts of underdevelopment.

Problems of Interest to the West
The first group need not detain us long. World commodity problems were of interest as part of the wider problem of economic stability; Brazil, Malaya, West Africa and the East Indies were studied, because and to the extent that they were exporters of coffee, rubber, cocoa and sugar and as such part of the international trading system.[24] Similarly, studies of the collapse and chances of revival of international investment were generally undertaken from the point of view of the investing countries,[25] studies of international migration from that of the countries of potential emigration.[26]

Of greater interest are a series of studies of industrialization,

[21] P. A. Samuelson, *Economics*, 1st edn (McGraw-Hill, 1948), p. 67.
[22] Ibid., p. 377.   [23] Ibid., p. 563.
[24] Cf., for example, J. W. F. Rowe, *Markets and Men* (C.U.P., 1936); P. Lamartine Yates, *Commodity Control* (Cape, 1943).
[25] Cf., for example, H. Feis, *Europe, the World's Banker 1870–1914* (Yale University Press, 1920); Royal Institute of International Affairs, *The Problem of International Investment* (O.U.P., 1937); S. H. Frankel, *Capital Investment in Africa* (O.U.P., 1938).
[26] Cf., for example, I. Bowman (ed.), *Limits of Land Settlement* (Council on Foreign Relations, 1937).

especially in Asia. For although they derived their initial impetus from Western fears of Eastern competition, they produced a number of scholarly works which contain some of the most important analyses of this aspect of economic development and its effects on world trade written before 1945.[27] The theme of Eastern competition was prominent also in the early biennial conferences of the Institute of Pacific Relations.[28] But both through its conferences and the monographs it sponsored, the IPR contributed greatly during the inter-war years to scholarly study of problems of economic development in the Pacific region.

Colonial Economics

Since so large a part of the underdeveloped regions of the world consisted of colonial territories, it is not surprising that much of what development economics there was during the inter-war years was produced by specialists on colonial economics. What is surprising is that their often excellent work made virtually no impact on the profession at large before 1945. Two names stand out: among Dutch colonial economists, J. H. Boeke; among British colonial economists, J. S. Furnivall.

Boeke's theory of social dualism – 'the clashing of an imported social system with an indigenous social system of another style' – which he formulated during the 1930s as Professor of Eastern Economics at Leiden University, on the basis of his experience as a colonial administrator in the Dutch East Indies, has been one of the major influences on post-war thinking about underdevelopment.[29] Furnivall, with a similar background as a colonial civil servant in Burma, made no less important a contribution to understanding of the conditions from which economic development must start, especially in his two major works, *Netherlands India: A Study of Plural Economy* and *Colonial Policy and Practice: A Comparative Study of Burma and Netherlands India*.[30]

[27] See especially, G. E. Hubbard, *Eastern Industrialization and Its Effects on the West* (O.U.P., 1938); and Kate L. Mitchell, *Industrialization of the Western Pacific* (Institute of Pacific Relations, 1942).

[28] See, for example, Institute of Pacific Relations, *First Conference* (Honolulu, 1925); Second Conference: J. B. Condliffe (ed.), *Problems of the Pacific* (Chicago University Press, 1928).

[29] See especially J. H. Boeke, *The Structure of Netherlands Indian Economy* (Institute of Pacific Relations, 1942); cf. B. Higgins, *Economic Development* (Constable, 1959), chap. 12, and W. F. Wertheim *et al.*, *Indonesian Economics: The Concept of Dualism in Theory and Practice* (The Hague, 1961).

[30] Cf. F. N. Traeger, *Furnivall of Burma: An Annotated Bibliography of the Work of John S. Furnivall* (Yale University Press, 1963).

The work of Boeke and Furnivall is best known because both attempted to conceptualize the problem of underdevelopment, at any rate in relation to the colonial societies of South-East Asia. Many others contributed to the study of colonial economic development and economic policy.[31] While it is perhaps true that 'before the war the most intensive work in the underdeveloped world was done by cultural anthropologists ... in static terms',[32] there existed by the 1930s a large literature of colonial economics, in scholarly books and articles as well as in mountains of official reports, on which the profession at large could have drawn had the subject interested them. A lone attempt to 'analyse the economic metamorphosis that accompanies the extension of imperial rule over hitherto remote and self-sufficing communities ... to subsume these societies under the same analytical technique as is applicable to those more advanced' was made by Ida Greaves in her PhD thesis at the London School of Economics.[33]

Besides the Western specialists on colonial economics, there were others who studied the problems of independent underdeveloped countries. R. H. Tawney's *Land and Labour in China* (1932) and J. L. Buck's *Chinese Farm Economy* (1930) and *Land Utilization in China* (1937) come to mind, as does Doreen Warriner's *Economics of Peasant Farming* (1939).[34]

Non-Western Development Economics
Apart from Western specialists on the problems of colonial and other underdeveloped countries, a good deal of thinking about these problems must have gone on among nationals of these countries, among government officials and economists of independent States

[31] For bibliographies of Dutch colonial economics, see W. F. Wertheim *et al.*, op. cit., pp. 405–24, and J. S. Furnivall, *Netherlands India* (C.U.P., 1944), pp. 471–8; for an extensive bibliography of British and Indian writings on the economy of pre-independence India, see Vera Anstey, *The Economic Development of India*, 4th edn (Longmans, 1952), pp. 639ff.; two outstanding works of pre-1945 British colonial economics are Lord Hailey, *An African Survey* (O.U.P., 1938), and W. K. Hancock, *Survey of British Commonwealth Affairs*, vol. 2; *Problems of Economic Policy, 1918–39* (O.U.P., 1942); for a bibliography of French colonial policy, see R. F. Betts, *Assimilation and Association in French Colonial Policy, 1890–1914* (Columbia University Press, 1961).

[32] Gunnar Myrdal, *Asian Drama* (Dorsey Press, 1962), vol. 1, p. 9.

[33] I. C. Greaves, *Modern Production among Backward Peoples* (Allen & Unwin, 1935).

[34] For a bibliography of the extensive pre-1945 literature on the economic development and problems of Latin America, see W. C. Gordon, *The Economy of Latin America* (Columbia University Press, 1950), pp. 403–14.

in Latin America and elsewhere, among the leaders of the nationalist movements in the more advanced colonies, and among their own economists. Most of this literature is not easily accessible and may hardly repay the effort of research.[35] Indian economists wrote a great deal about their country's economic problems but the following comment by one of them, while jaundiced, is not entirely unfair: 'What is our contribution to Economics? Our contribution to pure economic thought is practically nil; and our contribution to the analysis and solution of Indian economic problems is, if we count the paper written, enormous; but if we dwell on its quality, it gives a taste as of some stale stuff. . . . We lack that "apparatus of mind" that makes the economist; we have not yet developed that "technique of analysis". . . . We argue in a vacuum. The economic policy of this country is a "set" policy. We have no say in it. . . . The views of the Indian economists are totally ignored. But we too are at fault. . . . We are bound up to the chariot-wheel of "English" economics. The sources of our inspiration are foreign.'[36]

A most striking contrast in the same category is presented by the brilliant industrialization debate among the first generation of Soviet economists during the years 1924–8. Schooled Marxists all, they found Marxist theory of little use when it came to tackling the immense practical problems of post-revolutionary Russia and working out a strategy of economic development. In the four years between Lenin's 'New Economic Policy' and Stalin's 'Revolution from Above' (in which all of them later perished), the leading theorists, especially Bukharin, Preobrazhenski, Bazarov and Rykov, produced what is without question the most realistic and profound discussion of the main issues of development strategy before 1945. 'Both the problems raised and answers given anticipate to an astonishing degree the work done in the same field, at a much higher level of sophistication and within a different conceptual framework,

[35] For economic development planning in China during the inter-war period, beginning with Sun Yat-Sen's *International Development of China* (1920), see H. D. Fong, *Towards Economic Control in China* (China Institute of Pacific Relations, 1936).

[36] D. H. Butani, 'The Quality and Perspective of Indian Economic Thought', *Indian Journal of Economics* (1941–2), p. 280. The author identified his own position by saying that 'Mr Gandhi is to me a greater economist than all the Indian economists bundled together' (ibid., p. 285). Two books which exemplify the better work of Indian economists during the 1930s are K. N. Sen, *Economic Reconstruction of India: A Study in Economic Planning* (University of Calcutta, 1937), and N. S. Subba Rao, *Some Aspects of Economic Planning* (Bangalore, 1935).

by economists outside the Soviet orbit during the last two decades.'[37]

Statistics of Underdevelopment

Contributions to development economics whose importance, though not at first obvious, should not be under-rated were made in the inter-war years by social scientists in various fields who provided statistical data on the facts of underdevelopment.

One of these, associated especially with the name of Colin Clark, emerged, almost as a by-product, from the development of national income estimates. As such estimates became available for an increasing number of countries, the way was opened towards quantification of international comparisons of living standards. It was Colin Clark who, on the suggestion of Bowley, embarked on the task with indefatigable energy, verve and imagination and in 1939 produced his monumental *Conditions of Economic Progress*. The book not only gave a considerable stimulus to the subsequent development of growth theory and models but also had an important effect on Western thinking about the underdeveloped world. For the first time, the gulf between living standards in the rich and the poor countries of the world was brought home in hard statistical terms. Well into the post-war years, until United Nations' data became available, almost every writer on development economics quoted Colin Clark's estimates.

A similar contribution was made by the international surveys of nutrition conducted by the League of Nations. Initiated by the League's health organization in the 1920s, the study of nutrition standards was given a new impetus after the abortive World Economic Conference of 1933 by a group of enthusiasts including the British agricultural scientist, Boyd Orr, and two Australians, the former Prime Minister, Stanley Bruce, and his economic adviser, F. L. McDougall. They induced the League to appoint a committee under Lord Astor whose report in 1935 gave the first systematic account of the extent of hunger and malnutrition in the world.[38]

Finally, mention should be made of the work of the ILO. Charged with the task of promoting industrial peace and social welfare through international co-operation, the ILO not only sponsored

[37] A. Erlich, *The Soviet Industrialization Debate, 1924–8* (Harvard University Press, 1960), p. xx.

[38] G. Hambridge, *The Story of the FAO* (New York, 1955); J. Boyd Orr, *The White Man's Dilemma* (Allen & Unwin, 1953), pp. 83ff.; C. Edwards, *Bruce of Melbourne* (Heinemann, 1965).

studies of social and industrial conditions throughout the world, including dependent and other less developed territories, but during the 1930s began to parallel the nutrition studies of the League of Nations by systematic international comparison of levels of consumption in such fields as food, clothing, housing, medical care and education.[39] It is no accident that several of the most influential voices in the awakening concern with world poverty during the war were those of former members of the ILO Secretariat.

WAR AIMS AND POST-WAR PLANS

Development economics as a major interest of the economic profession and branch of the discipline was born during the Second World War. It was the need of the Western Allies to formulate war aims, not least to counter Hitler's New Order and Japan's Co-Prosperity Sphere, and the characteristic reaction of British and American public opinion to the horrors of war through a wave of idealism about plans for a better post-war world, which in the span of a few years promoted development economics from the most neglected to the most written-about branch of economics. At the same time, by demonstrating the power of government action in mobilizing economic resources, the war itself generated a climate of optimism about what could be done to make a better world, abroad as much as at home.

Within a few days of the outbreak of the war in Europe, Cordell Hull, then Secretary of State, appointed an advisory committee in the State Department to deal with post-war problems.[40] The subcommittee on post-war international economic problems and policies did not at first go beyond the problems of the 1930s, such as regional blocs and international commodity markets, and appraisal of the economic capacity of various countries.[41] But a new note was injected into official thinking in the next few months. In January 1941, in his message to Congress, President Roosevelt proclaimed the Four Freedoms, including freedom from want, as the Allies' peace objectives; and in August 1941, Churchill and Roosevelt

[39] Cf. E. Staley, *World Economy in Transition* (Council on Foreign Relations, 1939), pp. 61ff. For an account of ILO studies of social conditions in colonial territories, see ILO, *Social Policy in Dependent Territories* (Montreal, 1944), especially p. iii.

[40] Cordell Hull, *Memoirs* (Hodder & Stoughton, 1948), pp. 1625ff.

[41] F. S. Dunn, *Peace-Making and the Settlement with Japan* (Princeton, 1963), p. 5.

signed the Atlantic Charter which, among its eight principles, promised equal access to trade and raw materials to all States and 'assurance that all the men in all the lands might live out their lives in freedom from fear and want'.[42] These broad aims, as well as the departure from orthodox international finance in the Lend-Lease arrangements between the Allies, became signposts to a new era of which governments were reminded again and again in the following years.

For two years after Pearl Harbor, post-war problems received little official attention in Washington. But as the tide of war turned, planning for post-war reconstruction was resumed. In 1943, the same group of 'nutrition fanatics' who had stirred the League of Nations in the 1930s to investigate the world nutrition conditions induced President Roosevelt to call the Hot Springs Conference on Food and Agriculture which led to the establishment of the FAO. In the following year, the Bretton Woods Conference created the IMF and IBRD; an International Labour Conference at Philadelphia re-defined the social objectives of economic policy for the post-war world; and at Dumbarton Oaks a draft charter for the United Nations was agreed upon which, in the final version adopted at San Francisco, included among its objects the promotion of 'higher standards of living, full employment, and conditions of economic and social progress and development'. By 1945, economic develop-ment of underdeveloped countries had become an accepted objective of national and international policy of the developed countries. For this, much of the credit is due to sustained emphasis on this objective in unofficial discussion of peace aims in Britain and the United States almost from the moment of outbreak of the war.

'The average citizen has been thinking a great deal about how to to win the peace. . . . The commonest symptom of this attitude of mind has been a strong demand for, and much controversy about, the formulation of "peace aims". Groups and societies for the study of the problems of the peace sprang up like mushrooms overnight. Pamphlets, broadsheets . . . burgeoned from every printing works. . . .'[43] This, though written about Britain, was as true of the United States. Indeed, the traditional American readiness to espouse causes, led by Cordell Hull's Wilsonian idealism and less hampered by the

[42] Cf. W. L. Neumann, *Making the Peace 1941–5* (Foundation for Foreign Affairs, Washington, 1950).

[43] Heather Harvey, 'War-Time Research in Great Britain on International Problems of Reconstruction', *Agenda* (London School of Economics, April 1942), p. 164.

immediate pressures of the war, ensured that public discussion of peace aims started there earlier than in Britain. The first phase did not advance much beyond the proclamation of liberal generalities. A symposium of distinguished names published in *The Annals* in July 1940 did not get closer to the issues of economic development than a statement by Gustav Cassel that 'the fundamental problem before us is to create such conditions as will secure the greatest possible progress', and such policy objectives as the principle of the 'open door' in trade, loosening the fetters on migration and condemnation of autarky.[44]

The man who more than any other brought the theme of economic development into the American discussion was Eugene Staley. In 1939, the Council on Foreign Relations had published his report on *World Economy in Transition*. Its central theme was the conflict between technological opportunities and political barriers to greater human welfare. Much of the book was inspired by a broad liberal concern for world welfare in the ILO tradition, for 'world federal union' and freer trade. But in one chapter, Staley moved from international investment to a discussion of a 'world development programme' with a thoroughly post-war flavour. Keynes's 'economic millennium . . . will not be brought about by hoping for it'.[45] 'In some areas, like China and India, the people live so near the margin of subsistence that rapid capital accumulation could take place only at a great cost in human deprivation.'[46] What is needed is 'an international long-term investment bank for financing world public utilities' and 'international transfer of knowledge and its industrial application'.[47] A beginning is already being made in the Americas.[48] This must be extended by 'bringing roads and schools and technical institutes and machinery to China and India and Borneo . . . education must go along with capital investment'.[49] When in 1941 the Commission to Study the Organization of Peace published a preliminary report, Staley developed this theme, demanding educational and technical assistance, as well as capital investment, organized through International Agencies. 'International assistance for this purpose should be a fundamental goal of the development programmes.'[50]

In the next two years, these ideas were taken up by many others.[51]

[44] *The Annals* (July 1940), p. 24.   [45] E. Staley, op. cit., p. 68.
[46] Ibid., p. 70.   [47] Ibid., p. 278.   [48] Ibid., p. 282.   [49] Ibid.
[50] *International Conciliation* (1941), no. 369, p. 414. See also Staley's later ILO Report, *World Economic Development* (Montreal, 1944).
[51] Cf., for example, H. P. Jordan (ed.), *Problems of Post-War Reconstruction* (Washington, 1942), especially Jordan's own chapter on Latin America; P. E.

A Canadian, R. B. Bryce, summed them up well in a 1943 symposium organized by Professor Seymour Harris: 'If indeed in the post-war world we are to apply the lesson the world has now learnt at so heavy a price, that no nation can live unto itself alone, then we must have substantial loans from the richer States to the poorer States of the United Nations. . . . These conclusions follow from the fact that most of the world and its inhabitants are woefully short of capital and unable to provide it from current income. . . . Billions upon billions of dollars must be invested in Asia, Polynesia, South America and Africa, if the great masses in these lands are to be made productive and eventually brought up to minimum standards of health and decency, let alone comfort.'[52]

In Britain, one of the first statements of similar ideas was the report of a conference organized by the National Peace Council. Once again it was a member of the ILO Secretariat, Wilfred Benson, who expounded the case for 'The Economic Advancement of Underdeveloped Areas'.[53] He was powerfully backed up by Evan Durbin, in perhaps his last published statement before his tragic death: 'Despite a very strong left-wing prejudice . . . the fact remains that international lending has been one of the most powerful engines of economic progress throughout the world, and that an immense task remains for it to do. Consider the position of the poorer part of the earth – the position of China, India or of our Colonies in Africa. What they require in order to raise their standard of living is the sort of changes in the techniques of production that we called the "Industrial Revolution" in our history, and that Russia calls a series of "Five-Year Plans" – that is, a wider programme of industrialization . . . [and] modernization of agriculture.'[54]

From 1941 onwards various organizations, among them the Royal Institute of International Affairs, Nuffield College and the Oxford Institute of Statistics, and Political and Economic Planning (PEP), embarked on programmes of research on post-war problems.[55]

Corbett, *Post-War Worlds* (Institute of Pacific Relations, 1942); S. E. Harris (ed.), *Post-War Economic Problems* (New York, 1943). The latter includes a striking statement by Professor Kindleberger: 'The desire for greater equality in standards of living and its continued frustration lie close to the basis of the international disequilibrium of the twentieth century' (p. 394).

[52] S. E. Harris, op. cit., p. 364.

[53] National Peace Council, *The Economic Basis of Peace* (London, 1942), p. 10. This may well be the first use of 'underdeveloped' in the post-war sense; in a more literal sense, it appears earlier in I. Bowman, op. cit., p. 1.

[54] Ibid., p. 26.

[55] See the various surveys of research on post-war reconstruction in *Agenda: A*

Partly because of the presence in London of several refugee governments and economists from Czechoslovakia, Poland and Yugoslavia, research on underdeveloped countries concentrated on
Eastern and South-Eastern Europe. PEP published a preliminary
report on 'Economic Development in South-East Europe' in 1944.[56]
The Oxford programme produced a planning model for the region
in K. Mandelbaum's *The Industrialization of Backward Areas*.[57]

At Chatham House, P. N. Rosenstein-Rodan in 1941 became
Secretary to the Committee on Post-War Reconstruction and in the
next two years, both at Chatham House and in a private study
group with Eastern European economists, including Bicanic, Rud-
zinski, Baranski, most of whom were old personal friends, he thought
about 'Problems of Industrialization of Eastern and South-Eastern
Europe'. The article with this title which was published in 1943 is
the landmark in development economics to which Hagen referred
and is too well known to need summarizing. Not so well known is a
lecture he gave in 1944 on 'The International Development of
Economically Backward Areas'.[58]

Here Rodan described the 'common characteristics of underdevelopment' in the 'five vast international depressed areas', the Far
East, colonial Africa, the Caribbean, the Middle East, and Eastern
and South-Eastern Europe. He contrasted the role played by the
State in the advanced countries in influencing the distribution of
income towards greater equality with the lack of any such mechanism in the international system. He warned that underdevelopment
has become a political as well as a moral problem because people
will prefer to die fighting when they see no prospect for a better life
– 'the development of the economically backward areas of the world
is, therefore, the most important task facing us in the making of the
peace'. He then went on to describe 'the common characteristics of
underdevelopment'. He explained the nature of 'disguised unemploy-

Quarterly Journal of Reconstruction (London School of Economics, 1942–4). The
last issue published (November 1944) includes a remarkable paper by W. Arthur
Lewis in which, in the course of a highly critical review of F. Benham's report as
chairman of the Jamaica Economic Policy Committee, he foreshadowed many of
his post-war contributions to development economics.
    [56] 'Economic Development in South-Eastern Europe', *Planning* (21 July 1944),
no. 223; PEP, *Economic Development in South-Eastern Europe* (London, 1945).
    [57] K. Mandelbaum, *The Industrialization of Backward Areas* (Blackwell, 1947);
mention should also be made of a similar study of the Middle East, A. Bonné,
*The Economic Development of the Middle East: An Outline of Planned Recon-
struction* (Kegan Paul, 1945, and of the 'Bombay Plan' for India, Sir P. Thakurdas
et al., *A Plan of Economic Development for India* (Penguin, 1944).
    [58] *International Affairs* (April 1944).

ment' in agriculture and the obstacles, in the form of inadequate capital and skills, to making use of this reserve of labour. He emphasized the importance of training facilities – 'by far the most important problem in backward areas' – and urged government provision of training since 'although not a good investment for a private firm, it is a sound investment for the State'. He outlined the great advantages of industrialization with the aid of large-scale international investment over attempts to 'go it alone', emphasizing that it is no more rational to expect repayment of capital by countries than by private corporations, and concluded with a reference to the Chatham House study group on Eastern and South-Eastern Europe, the area which 'provides a model presenting all the problems relevant to the reconstruction and development of backward areas'.

The lecture was at once a manifesto calling on the developed countries to wake up to the needs and demands of the underdeveloped and an example of the application of techniques of economic analysis to the problems of underdevelopment. In the latter sense, it may fairly be said to have formed, together with the *Economic Journal* article, the beginning of Development Economics as a distinct branch of the discipline.

CHAPTER 2

The World Bank's Concept of Development – An In-House *Dogmengeschichte*

J. H. ADLER

I INTRODUCTION

Observers of the World Bank (officially the International Bank for Reconstruction and Development – IBRD) and its Group affiliates, the International Development Association (IDA) and the International Finance Corporation (IFC), though ranging in their attitudes from warm praise to cold contempt, are likely to agree on one proposition: in the last twenty years, the World Bank Group has played an important role in economic development, chiefly as a source of long-term finance, but also as purveyor – though not necessarily originator – of ideas which bear on the analysis and interpretation of the development process and on the formulation of development policies; it also has undoubtedly influenced the size and direction of development finance. It may therefore be of some interest to record the evolution of the Bank Group's notions on the process of economic development.

It is of course conceivable that the Bank engaged in its business of development finance without having a definite concept of the development process and it is virtually certain that nobody speaking with authority for the Bank has ever come up explicitly with a 'development philosophy', or endorsed in so many words somebody else's concept of the development process. It is clear, however, that even a superficial (and unavoidably subjective) scrutiny of Bank operations and Bank pronouncements reveals certain preferences – in hues of emphasis rather than in crass assertions – and a certain selectivity in policy and policy approval which together form the component parts of what may be considered a comprehensive – though not necessarily internally consistent – concept of the development process.[1] It is equally clear that this concept has continuously changed, with some facets receiving more attention and others less, and, on occasion, some new 'radical' departures forcing revisions and modifications of some parts of what appeared to be firmly established doctrine. It is this constant change of ideas and attitudes which is, or at any rate should be, of special interest to the historian of economic thought because it is inevitably also a reflection of the evolution of development theory (in the broadest sense of propositions of general validity) over the last two decades.

Conversely, the Bank's operations, its institutional pronounce-ments in annual and special reports and statements by the Bank's Presidents may also be viewed as an important part of the 'develop-ment scene' in which the development process unfolds. For better or worse, the Bank's operations and its (mostly informal) advice to developing countries and, more recently, to Consortia and Consulta-tive Groups of 'aid donors', inevitably affected the *practice* of development; and in so far as development *theory* is concerned with the practice of development and the issues and conflicts which arise in it, the Bank also affected the theorists.

In order to give a picture of the evolution of the World Bank's 'doctrine' of economic development over time in an orderly fashion, it seems useful to divide the period from 1949, when the Bank's involvement in development as distinct from post-war reconstruction, began, to the present, in three unequal parts coinciding with the tenure of three presidents: 1949–62 when E. R. Black was President, 1963–8 with G. D. Woods as President, and the first three years of the Presidency of R. S. McNamara, who assumed office on 1 April,

---

[1] This chapter has been written as an essay in the original sense of the term, as a subjective attempt to interpret a flow of events and ideas underlying them. For that reason and because of the complexity of the 'evidence', no attempt has been made to document systematically the observations and evaluations presented here. I am certain that the assertions of this paper could be fully documented by an appropriate selection of quotations from official documents and quasi-official pronouncements such as speeches of the President of the Bank. However, because the Bank is an international organization and published Bank documents are supposed to reflect the views of all of its member countries, or at least not to offend their views (however divergent they may be), their language is inevitably bland and circumspect. Therefore quotations from Bank documents are rather unsatisfactory proof of anything. And even a full dossier of documentary evidence would reflect, at least to some degree, subjective selection and interpretation. For these reasons the standard disclaimer that the views expressed here are my own and in no way purport to reflect the views of the World Bank has special meaning and requires emphasis.

1968. The first period is presumably of the greatest interest because it began at a time when ignorance about economic development was encyclopedic and it ended just not long after a comprehensive picture of the developing world and its problems, some new tools of economic analysis (for example, capital/output ratio, linkages, shadow prices) and a host of policy prescriptions had emerged.

II   1949-1962: THE EVOLUTION OF A DOCTRINE

The Intellectual and Institutional Environment

In order to trace the gradual emergence of the Bank's views on development in its early years it is essential to recall first the state of the art in which development theory and policy found itself some twenty years ago, and the role that the Bank's statutes – its Articles of Agreement – had envisaged for it and the constraints which it imposed on it.

Although the development of underdeveloped, or backward, or less developed countries and territories[2] was clearly part of the agenda of the Brave New World which emerged from the Second World War and economic development was mentioned in the Preamble of the Charter of the United Nations[3] and, of course, in the Articles of Agreement of the World Bank[4] as well as in its formal name, the political good intention of the rich countries and the humanitarian inclinations of their people were not matched by knowledge of the state of underdevelopment and of the causes of backwardness. True, some books on development – by Buchanan and Ellis[5], by Mandelbaum[6], and Rostow[7] – had been published and were widely read, and made some contribution to the understanding of the development process. However, their aims were

---

[2] The diplomatic nicety of referring to them as developing countries had not been evolved—a fact which may be interpreted as a cultural lag; conversely, it may be argued that the subtle (and sometimes not so subtle) changes in terminology which have taken place are a reflection of the countries' growing political awareness and sensitivity. It is also worth noting that a large proportion of the group of countries which now consider themselves as 'developing', were in 1949 dependent territories.

[3] *Charter of the United Nations*, Preamble ('. . . to employ international machinery for the promotion of the *economic and social advancement* of all peoples . . .').

[4] *Articles of Agreement of the International Bank for Reconstruction and Development*, Article I, sub. 1.

[5] Norman S. Buchanan and Howard S. Ellis, *Approaches to Economic Development* (New York, 1955).

[6] K. Mandelbaum, *The Industrialization of Backward Areas* (Oxford, 1945).

[7] Walt Whitman Rostow, *The Process of Economic Growth* (New York, 1952).

essentially descriptive and analytic and not normative, that is, they did not tell what could and should be done to foster development. There were some notable exceptions to this failure to face up to policy problems that economic development posed: Rosenstein-Rodan's article on 'Problems of Industrialization of Eastern and South-Eastern Europe'[8] which dealt with a set of issues which subsequently were recognized as 'core problems' of development; Kahn's 'Investment Criteria in Development Programs'[9], Chenery's 'The Application of Investment Criteria',[10] and last but not least Nurkse's *Problems of Capital Formation in Underdeveloped Countries*[11]. And there were a number of official studies and reports dealing with development which, while they did not succeed in developing an analytic framework for the economics of development (or, at best, developed a very imperfect one), stimulated debate and controversy and thus indirectly made important contributions to the understanding of the process of development. The most important among them were the Report of the Economic Commission for Latin America of 1950[12] generally associated with the name of Dr Raul Prebisch, the first Secretary-General of the Commission, and the Report of a United Nations Committee of Experts, on Measures for Economic Development,[13] published in 1951. But it was not until the second half of the 1950s, when a steady flow of statistical data and descriptive material on developing countries became available and numerous articles on specific aspects of the development process appeared,

[8] Paul N. Rosenstein-Rodan, 'Problems of Industrialization of Eastern and South-Eastern Europe', *Economic Journal* (June-September 1943), pp. 202–11. Rosenstein-Rodan was a senior official of the Bank in its formative years, 1946–52. As Assistant Director of the Economics Department he was instrumental in steering the Bank's scant staff away from the narrow aspect of specific lending operations towards broader issues of policy, not only of the Bank but of its member countries as well. He was one of the very few staff members who had a clear idea of what economic development was all about. The impact of his ideas became an intangible long-term asset of the Bank.

[9] A. E. Kahn, 'Investment Criteria in Development Programs', *Quarterly Journal of Economics* (February 1951), pp. 38–61.

[10] H. B. Chenery, 'The Application of Investment Criteria', *Quarterly Journal of Economics* (February 1953), pp. 76–96.

[11] R. Nurkse, *Problems of Capital Formation in Underdeveloped Countries* (Oxford, 1953).

[12] United Nations Economic Commission for Latin America, *The Economic Development of Latin America and Its Principal Problems* (New York, 1950).

[13] United Nations Department of Economic Affairs, *Measures for the Economic Development of Under-Developed Countries* (New York, 1951). Report by a Group of Experts appointed by the Secretary-General of the United Nations. The members of the group were A. B. Cortez, D. R. Gadgil, G. Hamkin, W. A. Lewis and T. W. Schultz.

that the various facets of development theory and development
policy began to fall into place, and something akin to an intellectual
accord on the subject matter content of economic development and
on the magnitude and time dimension of the development process –
with much room for dissent and iconoclastic argument – began to
emerge.

In recording and evaluating the views of the World Bank on
development and on the role which it conceived for itself as a source
of development finance in the early 1950s, one must keep in mind the
state of underdevelopment which characterized the field of intellectual endeavour of development economics at that time. Moreover,
one must remember that the Bank was not completely free to develop
and define its own posture; its Articles of Agreement had been
drafted with a remarkably concise concept as to what its role, its
'business', was to be. Two constraints on its lending operations
which, for reasons which are not relevent in this context, were within
into its Articles of Agreement were of particular importance in
shaping the Bank's lending policy and influenced its concept of the
development process. They were the stipulation that Bank loans
could be made for specific investment projects only, and the limitations of Bank financing to the foreign exchange cost of projects. The
Articles did of course provide for some exceptions to these general
rules, but the primary intention of the Articles is abundantly clear.
Moreover, the Bank's capital structure, with its dependence for most
of its resources on borrowing operations in the capital markets of
the world, especially of the United States, also had a bearing on the
volume and direction of the Bank's operations and on its concept
of the development process.

Private Enterprise

The single most important component of the Bank's development
'philosophy' which emerged at the outset, was its firm and pronounced bias in favour of the advantages, not to say virtues, of a
market economy and a system of private ownership and enterprise.
By pronouncements at various levels of generalization and by
specific action it asserted that development is faster, 'sounder' and
altogether better if the market and price mechanism is allowed to
allocate resources, including resources available for investment.[14]

[14] The most explicit statement on the virtues of the market mechanism may be
found in the *Report on Cuba – Findings and Recommendations of an Economic and
Technical Mission Organized by the* IBRD *in Collaboration with the Government of
Cuba in 1950* (Washington, 1951): 'For, to date, none of man's efforts to repeal

This dogmatic preference – dogmatic in the sense that it was thought that there was no need for offering any proof for it, except perhaps by reference to the growth experience of the economies of Western Europe and of the advanced economies elsewhere – affected the Bank's attitudes and actions in a variety of ways.

In the first place, it led directly to an unqualified endorsement of the importance, not to say indispensability of private foreign direct investment and, wherever possible, of portfolio investment in the developing countries. Attempts to stimulate foreign investment by such devices as tax holidays – lower tax rates, rapid depreciation allowances or subsidies through loans at favourable terms, were considered desirable means of fostering development; conversely, limitation on the flow of foreign investment into some sectors of the economy of the host country, and restrictions on the transfer of dividends and principal were considered contrary to the best interest of the developing country.

As to the Bank's attitude regarding private portfolio investment, it adopted the policy that countries anxious to obtain loans must make reasonable efforts to come to terms with their creditors if they had defaulted on their obligations. It prided itself, with some justification, on the impact of this policy on the resumption of debt service and the settlement of debt disputes of a large number of member countries. Moreover, it made efforts to ensure that whenever possible Bank loans would be combined with, and ultimately replaced by, borrowing in the private capital market.

The Bank's concept of private foreign investment as the foremost means and the ultimate solution of development finance of course was not unique. It was accepted without question in the capital exporting countries and considered essential by those who spoke, or claimed to speak, for developing countries – though a certain lack of enthusiasm may be detected in the pronouncements of some of them.[15]

Support by the rich countries of development efforts of the poor was to take the form chiefly of technical assistance[16] and there was

the law of supply and demand have been successful' (p. 158). Technically, the report was to reflect the views of the Mission, which were not necessarily identical with those of the Bank; but the letter from the President of the Bank to the President of Cuba accompanying the report (pp. v/vi) in effect endorsed the recommendation of the mission and came close to identifying the Bank with the Mission's views.

[15] For example, various issues of the *Economic Bulletin for Latin America*, issued by the UN Economic Commission for Latin America.

[16] This was the essence of President Truman's Point Four of his inaugural speech of 1949.

the clear implication that loans by the World Bank (and presumably also by such bilateral sources of finance as the Export-Import Bank) were to be a temporary arrangement, to be superseded sooner or later by the resumption of lending from private sources through the purchase of bonds issued by the governments of developing countries themselves.[17]

The Bank's view that development was the result of private initiative and private enterprise had its corollary in the view that government had only a limited role in the development process. It took a dim view of any attempt by government to force the pace of development by setting up government-owned and government-operated industries, and therefore adopted a general policy not to make loans to government-owned industries, ostensibly not on philosophical grounds but on grounds of efficiency of administration and management. It rejected the argument that private capital and entrepreneurship was not available in the developing country by pointing out that, given adequate incentives and assurances, private foreign capital, technology and management would be forthcoming. As an extension of this policy it promoted the establishment of a large number of privately-owned and -operated development finance companies to finance industrial investment, although in virtually all cases it accepted, and even insisted, that private capital, which occasionally also included equity participations from abroad, be supplemented by loans from government.[18]

The Role of Infrastructure

The Bank's essentially *laissez-faire* notion of the development process was, however, perfectly compatible with its view of the proper function of government in the development process: it was to create the institutional framework for the effective functioning of the privately-owned productive units which make up the economy. This was to be accomplished chiefly by an adequate provision of infrastructure investment, generally referred to in the early 1950s as 'social overhead capital'.

---

[17] In the early 1950s, the IBRD, which rented its office space, received an offer to buy a plot of land on which it could erect its own building. Although the offer was attractive in many respects it was turned down on the advice of the Bank's New York bankers because, they argued, to build its own headquarters would not be compatible with the public image of a temporary institution!

[18] The policy of lending only to private industrial development banks and manufacturing enterprises was not revised until 1968. It should be noted, however, that the Bank made loans to state-owned agricultural credit institutions.

In the discussion of specific loan operations and even more so in the recommendations of the survey missions[19] the Bank stated its views in numerous variations but always with a clear *leitmotiv*: The advancement of the developing countries – to be sure, through private initiative – is hindered by the inadequate provision of the economy with economic infrastructure, chiefly of power and transportation. An adequate supply of power and providing new or improved means of transportation will stimulate productive effort, bring new sources of supply (and income) into the market, for sale at home and abroad, and start or sustain, through the creation of external economies, a cumulative process of growth.

It is not too difficult to determine the origin of the Bank's doctrine of the crucial and in some ways catalytic role of infrastructure investment. With investment in directly productive activities presumed to be financed by private capital, and with the provisions of the Bank's Articles of Agreement implying that Bank lending would be directed chiefly towards the public sector, the emphasis on economic infrastructure provided an excellent justification for the large majority of the Bank's operations. Moreover, investment in the public sector (and in the case of revenue-yielding activities such as power, railways and telecommunications in the private sector as well) was eminently suitable to be financed by long-term loans, and indirectly through the sale of bonds by the Bank.

Finally, public investment and investment in public utilities made it easy to follow the provisions of the Articles of Agreement in two important respects: it made it possible to provide financing for well-defined specific investment projects and to limit financing to the direct foreign exchange cost of the projects because in most cases the foreign exchange cost constituted a very substantial part – as much as two-thirds – of the total cost of investment.[20]

Lest the Bank's stress on the importance of infrastructure investment be interpreted as nothing but a 'rationalization of convenience' it must be recalled that the creation of economic infrastructure was generally considered in the early 1950s as an important ingredient of development strategy, applicable to virtually any developing

[19] Between 1949 and 1964, the Bank sponsored and organized twenty-five general survey missions which prepared reports of the development prospects of the surveyed countries. These reports contained advice on broad economic policies and detailed recommendations on specific infrastructure projects.

[20] The share of foreign exchange in *fixed* investment is also large for manufacturing industries, but much smaller than in utilities in total investment, including working capital.

country.[21] It was stimulated by the rediscovery of external economies as a driving and sustaining force in the development process. The stress on infrastructure investment also made it possible to assign an 'activist' role to government which somehow seemed desirable at a time when economic development as an issue of global political importance rapidly gained momentum.[22]

Resource Mobilization

The pre-eminent role which the Bank attributed to investment in infrastructure led directly to two other facets of the Bank's view of the development process and to the evolution of its ideas on development strategy. One was the importance of mobilizing sufficient domestic resources to finance infrastructure investment; the other was the need to formulate development programmes to determine infrastructure requirements and financial resources necessary to finance them. The Bank's concern with the mobilization of domestic resources was of course closely related to the provisions of the Articles of Agreement that generally Bank financing should be confined to the foreign exchange cost of investment projects. In the preparation of a large number of lending operations it was soon discovered that governments and government agencies (as well as privately-owned utilities) found it difficult to meet the domestic investment expenditures even when the Bank was ready to finance the foreign exchange cost.[23] Therefore it had to take an interest in the fiscal performance of borrowing governments, in the financial operations of revenue-yielding projects and in attempts to supplement fiscal revenues through borrowing operations by governments and government agencies.

The Bank showed concern with all these aspects either through

[21] Rosenstein-Rodan was among the first, perhaps the first, to stress the importance of investment in infrastructure, and the need to overcome the indivisibilities of infrastructure investment through external financing. Cf. P. N. Rosenstein-Rodan, 'Notes on the Theory of the Big Push', in Howard S. Ellis (ed.), *Economic Development for Latin America* (London and New York, 1961), pp. 57–82.

[22] The gradual shift from investment in infrastructure towards 'investment in human resources' and the broadening of the role of government which this implied started, as far as underdeveloped countries were concerned, only in the late 1950s, although the limited contribution of capital investment alone, as distinct from education, technological advancement, and improved organization had been suggested already in 1956 (John W. Kendrick, *Productivity Trends: Capital and Labour*. National Bureau of Economic Research, Occasional Paper No. 53 (New York, 1956)).

[23] This is true even today, notwithstanding the small fraction of total government expenditures which the local cost of any particular project involves.

technical assistance, frequently in the form of specific recommendations of the Bank's survey missions, or by provisions in loan agreements under which the borrower or the government committed itself
to measures to obtain an increase in domestic financial resources,
such as an increase in some taxes, the allocation of revenues for
certain purposes, or increases in rates charged by public utilities. On
numerous occasions the Bank stressed the importance of full-cost
pricing of public utilities as a means of assuring an adequate flow of
resources available for investment (and incidentally, to service debts
to the Bank) and of financial soundness and 'business-like' operations
of borrowers, to be achieved by setting up autonomous agencies
such as port authorities, power authorities, and regional multipurpose
agencies.

Development Programmes
The second consequence of the central role of infrastructure investment was the Bank's view that the formulation of development
programmes was an important task of government. The fact that as
early as 1951[24] the Bank endorsed development planning as an
important and perhaps even indispensable means of speeding
development may need underlining. At that time, with the Cold
War raging with new intensity and Senator Joseph McCarthy
beginning to look for Communists and their sympathizers, approval
of planning was considered by many as tantamount to embracing the
alien doctrine of socialism or, to say the least, as the reflection of mis-
guided and useless impatience. And to speak of priorities and priority
determination was readily interpreted as reflecting distrust of, and
dissatisfaction with, the efficiency of the market mechanism as a
method of allocating resources, and as a not-so-subtle way of
stupidly or maliciously interfering with private enterprise.

However, the objective of development planning, as the Bank saw
it, was not the creation of centrally planned economies – far from it.
Planning was necessary to assure that the limited resources available
for the financing of infrastructure investment would be put to their
best possible use so as to maximize the services which the public

---

[24] 'Since these [capital] resources will at best be limited, careful planning is
necessary to obtain the best result. If development is undertaken haphazardly it
stands little chance of success. It is a long-range process, which should rest on
investment programs designed for several years ahead.' Address of E. R. Black
before the United Nations Economic and Social Council, Santiago (Chile),
March 1951, in *Economic Development*. Statements by officials of the International Bank for Reconstruction and Development (Washington, 1951), p. 18.

sector and privately-owned utilities could render to the private sector, where resources allocation would be determined by private enterprise operating in a market economy. There was no indication that planning should be extended to the private sector by means of direct controls, or that there was need to supplement private initiative by enterprises established and operated by the government. On the contrary, there was unlimited faith that private initiative was ready to exploit whatever new opportunities were opened up by the expansion of infrastructure facilities.

Foreign Exchange Gap

There is one additional strand in the network of inter-related ideas which made up the Bank's concept of the development process in its formative years: that is the overriding importance of the availability of foreign exchange as a factor determining the performance of developing countries. The Bank was of course aware of the importance of the provision of foreign exchange to finance development because it was ostensibly established for the purpose of providing that foreign exchange. But the realization of the importance of foreign exchange earnings went beyond the Bank's own role as a source of foreign exchange and, it might be added, as a claimant of foreign exchange as a creditor. From the very beginning of its lending operations in developing countries the Bank was concerned about the policies of the developing, as well as the advanced, countries which would interfere with the growth of foreign exchange earnings by its borrowers. The Bank survey mission reports inevitably urged that close attention be paid to the export sector.[25] In official statements and more explicitly in (restricted) reports on individual countries, it warned against inflation, chiefly because of its adverse effects on their balance of payments prospects. It also stressed the importance of trade liberalization by the rich countries as a means of making it possible for developing countries to increase their foreign exchange earnings.[26] It did not, however, embrace the strategy of import substitution, which was actively promoted by the Economic Com-

[25] Cf. for example, *The Economic Development of Guatemala* (Washington, 1951), pp. 40–54. *Report on Cuba* (op. cit.), pp. 14–17.

[26] For example, '. . . no new mechanism for the administration of development aid can diminish the responsibility which is shared by all members of the international community to keep open and active the channels of international trade. Aid can never be an acceptable substitute for trade. And international investment can never prosper if it is not built upon a solid foundation of international trade.' Eugene R. Black, Address at the 1959 Annual Meeting of the IBRD Board of Governors. *Summary Proceedings*, p. 10.

mission for Latin America and widely accepted as offering a way out of the balance of payments dilemma posed by the low income and price elasticities of exports of primary products.[27]

It realized, however, that for many countries the foreign exchange requirements of accelerated development could not be met by loans on conventional terms and that foreign exchange would have to be provided on concessional terms. The need for development 'aid', as distinct from Bank loans, was recognized by the Bank in the early 1950s, at a time when aid for development was recommended also by many others.[28] It led subsequently to the establishment, in 1960, of the International Development Association (IDA). The argument for external capital on concessional terms was made by the Bank on the grounds that some developing countries had absorptive capacity for foreign capital in excess of the amounts which they could prudently borrow in view of their balance of payments prospects. No clear distinction was made, however, between a 'resources gap' and a 'balance of payments gap'.

III 1962–1968: THE REVISION OF CONVICTIONS

In the first years of the decade of the 1960s an unprecedented outburst of intellectual interest in the process of economic development occurred. It produced an avalanche of studies, new concepts and new methods of analysis. Many of them greatly enhanced the understanding of development and affected almost immediately development policies and policies of development assistance. In line with this general advancement in the analysis and understanding of the development process the Bank's approach to development problems became more variegated. As a consequence, the period of the tenure of office of George D. Woods was characterized by a number of policy changes which brought into the open the gradual modification in the Bank's views on development which had started several years before.

The most important change, which preceded the Presidency of

[27] It also did not accept the corollary proposition of the inevitability of an internal and external structural disequilibrium in the economies of developing countries. In the confrontation between the 'structuralists' and the 'monetarists' which developed in the late 1950s, its sympathies were clearly on the side of the 'monetarists'. Cf. W. Baer and I. Kerstenetzky (eds), *Inflation and Growth in Latin America* (Homewood, Ill., 1964).

[28] Gordon Gray, *Report to the President on Foreign Economic Policies* (Washington, 1950); United Nations Department of Economic Affairs, *Measures for the Economic Development of Under-Developed Countries* (op. cit.).

Woods, was the recognition that the resources which the Bank could mobilize, or could expect to mobilize, to finance development were too small to permit the Bank to play the leading role in development finance which it had assigned to itself. Moreover, the Bank realized that the debt servicing capacity of some countries was too small to service debt contracted on the terms on which Bank loans were typically made. The gradual recognition of the magnitude of the development 'problem' and of aid requirements on non-conventional terms had three important practical effects: the doubling of the Bank's subscribed capital (1959); the establishment of IDA (1960); and the setting up of the Aid Consortium for India (1958), which was followed by the Consortium for Pakistan (1960) and later by several Consultative Groups for other countries.

This important evolution in the Bank's view of the development process led also, in 1966, to the Bank's initiative in proposing a replenishment of the resources of IDA of $1 billion a year, compared with $250 million per year at the preceding replenishment. The Bank's proposal was based on the contention that the developing countries could readily absorb annually $3–$4 billion more than the net flow of capital, then of the order of $11 billion, as defined and reported by the Development Assistance Committee (DAC) of OECD.[29] Moreover, contrary to the pronouncements of spokesmen of bilateral aid agencies, the Bank's President emphasized the long-term character of the development process; he referred to the 'century of development', as against the notion of the Development Decade promoted by the United Nations.[30]

In 1963 important changes in the intended direction of the Bank's operations were announced: the Bank said that it would expand its lending for agriculture and industry – two 'directly productive' sectors as distinct from the 'indirectly productive' utility sectors which had been its main concern.[31] Since agricultural projects inevitably served a multitude of productive units, and lending to industry was chiefly to take the form of loans to financial institutions,[32] this amounted to a significant modification in the Bank's

[29] *Statement* of George D. Woods to the Ministerial Meeting of DAC (Paris, July 1965). See also IBRD, *Annual Report, 1964–5*, p. 62.

[30] *The Development Century*. Address before the Canadian Club by George D. Woods (Toronto, November 1968).

[31] *Summary Proceedings*. Address by George D. Woods at the 1963 Annual Meeting of the IBRD Board of Governors, pp. 8–14.

[32] And occasionally also of equity participation in them by the International Finance Corporation.

view on the development process and on the requirements of development. In the first place, the policy modifications constituted a move away from the Bank's traditional position regarding the pivotal role of infrastructure investment; it implied that the investment in directly productive facilities did not necessarily follow the provision of economic infrastructure – but that these investments may require additional stimulation on the supply side in the form of financial support. In the second place, loans and credits to agriculture and industry meant a substantial broadening of the scope of 'project' financing, substituting in effect an entire sector as the object of financial support for individual projects.

The recognition that agricultural and industrial development required active support and intervention by government – in the case of Bank loans at least in the form of guarantees – did not change the Bank's view that manufacturing enterprises should be privately owned and managed. The same somewhat ambivalent attitude was reflected in the Bank's insistence that equity ownership and management of institutions financing industrial investment must be private while it urged at the same time that public authorities should provide financial support for such institutions.[33]

While the singling out of agriculture and industry as sectors deserving more attention may be considered as only changes in emphasis, the announcement, in 1963, to the effect that the Bank and IDA would be willing to finance educational projects constituted indeed a new departure. It was an open modification of the Bank's development 'philosophy' which hitherto had called for activist intervention only in economic infrastructure and 'directly productive' activities, with heavy emphasis on the former. The change resulted from the – obviously belated – recognition that under some conditions acceleration of the growth rate required not only an increased supply of capital, but also of other factors, especially skills. The Bank's willingness to provide financial support for education also reflected the previously-mentioned view that development was

[33] The doubts about the efficiency of free market forces as a mechanism for the optimum allocation of resources were also the foundations in logic of another change in the Bank's view of the development process. In the early 1960s the Bank began to make use of accounting or shadow prices, especially of foreign exchange, instead of market prices, in the appraisal of lending projects, wherever market price appeared to be distorted by intervention or simply by market imperfections. The acceptance of this methodology, proposed, among others, by J. Tinbergen in *Design for Development*, a study written for, and published by, the Bank (Baltimore, 1958) was slow at first, but the use of shadow prices for foreign exchange, capital and wages has since become standard practice.

inevitably slow; investment in education was accepted as yielding net returns with a high present value even if its full benefits could be expected only after a long gestation period.

The limited availability of IDA resources made it necessary to devise criteria for determining which countries should receive IDA credits. This meant that the Bank had to concern itself with differences in the development process and requirements for development support between countries at various income levels. It recognized that by and large the poorer countries among the developing countries had less freedom of action in the setting of their economic policies and obviously a longer way to go on the arduous path of development than the better-to-do countries in the group, and therefore were more deserving of grant-type assistance. It therefore set as a prime determinant of 'IDA eligibility' an annual *per capita* income of $150 (which subsequently was raised to $200 and $300).

The suggestion that the 'discovery' that there was a difference between countries with a *per capita* income of $100, and, say, $600, constituted a change in the Bank's outlook may seem almost ridiculous. It must be remembered, however, that until the early 1960s, the theoretical writing on development and the practice of agencies providing development finance did not make that distinction; or the distinction was observed but nothing was made of it. Even today, for a variety of largely non-economic reasons and on the basis of quasi-economic rationalizations, grant aid is provided by bilateral as well as multilateral sources to countries with a *per capita* income that is a multiple of the *per capita* income of the very poor countries of Asia and Africa.

Another result of major practical significance of the search for an optimum allocation of limited resources was a radical departure from the standard practice of lending for investment in specific projects, preferably in infrastructure sectors, by using a large part of IDA funds for programme loans (to India and Pakistan) to provide imported inputs for industrial production and to supplement foreign exchange earnings. It reflected, at least in part,[34] a modification in the Bank's concept of the development process by recognizing that under some conditions, which were the result either of irreversible effects of earlier policies, or of a configuration of circumstances inevitable in a certain phase of development, the provision of im-

---

[34] In part the decision to engage in programme loans was motivated by the desire to provide as quickly as possible foreign exchange 'relief' in view of the depletion of foreign exchange balances.

ports of commodities other than capital equipment was more important than the financing of the foreign exchange content of infrastructure investment.

The need to 'ration' IDA resources brought about still another modification in the Bank's view of the development process. Since IDA resources were clearly inadequate to be 'squandered' on countries which failed to make effective use of their own resources, or resources obtained from abroad, growing attention was paid to the 'performance' of potential borrowers and aid recipients. This implied, in effect, concern with the difference between the 'objective' growth potential of a country and the actual results, or expected results, of its economic policies.[35] Again, there was nothing new in the recognition that economic policies, and not only the care in the selection and execution of individual investment projects, were the prime determinants of the rate of growth; but the emphasis on the developing country's own responsibility for its economic advancement, the recognition that in most developing countries foreign resources account only for a small fraction of total investment, and the position that the providers of aid and development capital should join forces in urging countries receiving capital on concessional terms to pursue policies conducive to an acceleration of growth, are clear indications that the Bank's concept of the development process had undergone major changes: the availability of foreign capital was no longer considered the prime determinant of growth but only a necessary, but by no means sufficient, prerequisite. The stress on the volume of investment continued but policy choices bearing on resource allocation and the growth of efficiency – commercial policies, interest policies, exchange policies – became more prominent in the Bank's concept of successful growth.

In retrospect – even from the short perspective of a few years – there can be no doubt that in the early and mid-1960s the Bank's view of the development process came to reflect more and more the growing general recognition, of analysts and policy-makers, of the complexity of the development process and the difficulties besetting it. In its public posture, the Bank continued to display self-assurance

[35] Cf. Andrew M. Kamarck, 'The Appraisal of Country Economic Performance', in *Economic Development and Cultural Change* (January 1970), pp. 153–65. 'One of the principal lessons that the World Bank has learned from twenty-three years of experience is that the economic development or growth of a country depends primarily on a continuing improvement in the effectiveness with which a country uses the economic resources it possesses.' (p. 153). Kamarck was for many years Director of the Bank's Economics Department.

– that it knew the answers to the key question to development. At the same time it took pride in its 'flexibility'. It was this latter trait which reflected its awareness of the analytic issues and practical problems of development for which no solutions, and certainly no simple solutions, were in sight.

IV 1968–: DEVELOPMENT AS A PROCESS OF SOCIAL CHANGE

While it was difficult to put the evolution of the Bank's development doctrine in the 1960s into a pattern in which its main features stand out clearly, the task of high-lighting the changes in the Bank's attitude and approach to the problems of development in the last three years is relatively easy – largely because of the sharpness of the break with earlier attitudes. On the other hand, as the next few paragraphs show, these changes are still very much going on and what appear to be their main features today may be overshadowed by new departures tomorrow. This high degree of uncertainty is caused not only by the absence of time perspective; it also reflects the uncertain state of the arts (of development): today's conventional wisdom, the latest edition of eternal verities, of development economists, and practitioners of development assistance, is under heavy attack by impatient optimists who urge bolder action to attain faster growth, and by equally impatient pessimists who are disappointed with the results of development efforts and development aid so far and point to the detrimental effects of mistaken policies and the waste of development aid.

Population Control

As on earlier occasions, the most important change in the Bank's development 'philosophy' was a change in emphasis rather than a new discovery: in a series of formal pronouncements,[36] followed by a minor institutional change, the Bank has gone on record that it considers a sharp reduction in the rate of population growth as an indispensable ingredient of any rational development policy. The thought that the rate of population growth in the last two decades the world over, but especially in the developing countries, threatens to undo whatever progress in the growth of production and wealth

[36] Robert S. McNamara, Address at the University of Notre Dame (Washington, May 1969); *Summary Proceedings*. Address to the Annual Meeting of the IBRD Board of Governors (September 1970), pp. 13–31.

has been made was nothing new either to economists and other social scientists, or to the Bank itself.

As long ago as 1956, when population growth generally caused little more than uncomfortable thoughts, the Bank sponsored a study on the economic effects of population growth which became, and has remained, a classic statement of the problem.[37] What is novel in the Bank's approach of the last three years is the insistence that the political leaders of the developing countries must face up to the problem, initiate those socio-cultural changes which are necessary to bring about acceptance of birth control, and provide public support for the use of the various techniques of birth control. To show its earnest the Bank announced that it would provide financial support for population control measures and that it had set up a Population Projects Department.

Social Dimensions of Development

While the explicit – and intentionally loud – recognition of the rate of population growth as a prime determinant and policy variable in development received much public notice, the other major change in the Bank's view on development and on the prospects of development received much less attention although it is likely to affect to some extent all Bank operations. It is the recognition that the chances of attaining an 'orderly' process of development are closely related to the effectiveness of measures to distribute the gains of development equitably, or at least reasonably equitably, among income groups, regions and sectors. That implies, for instance, that in the formulation of a strategy for agricultural development the makers of development policy and the providers of development finance must pay attention to the small and subsistence farmer and his participation in the development process, and not only to the increase in agricultural output; it implies growing concern with urban unemployment and slum-living as potential or actual threats to social and political stability and the continuity of development; it also implies concern with the choice (and development) of technology in the construction and operation of productive facilities in economies in which the labour force is growing and is likely to grow in the next several decades at a rate twice or three times as high as in advanced countries.

[37] Ansley Coale and E. M. Hoover, *Population Growth and Economic Development in Low-Income Countries: A Case Study of India's Prospects* (Princeton, 1958).

The new awareness of the social dimensions of the development process – which add immensely to its complexity and riskiness – has also led to a search for policy measures, or a combination of measures, which serve the two-fold objectives of accelerated growth and social balance to take the place of the conventional standard prescriptions to save more, consume less, export more and import less.

It would of course be a complete misreading of the sequence of events if the Bank were to take credit for the 'discovery' of the demographic and social aspects of the development process – they have been recognized for a long time in the descriptive and analytic literature as development 'problems'. But it is significant that the Bank, which is presumably closer to the practice of development than the theorists and analysts, has committed itself to pay attention to these aspects of development in its own operations and advisory activities.

At the same time, the Bank has come to recognize that many obstacles stand in the way of a practical application of the growing insight in the development process. For one, although the social objectives – of greater equality of income distribution, a wider distribution of the stakes in development among social classes, sectors and regions – are recognized and can be defined with some accuracy in specific instances, the practical measures of achieving them are by no means certain. And if there is consensus as to what ought to be done, the authorities may lack the will, or the political strength, to do what ought to be done. Thus, the social goals of development may be frustrated by ignorance or by the inclination to take all necessary measures short of effective action.

Secondly, even where it is clear beyond doubt what measures to spur social development should and can be taken, the (short-term) cost of solving the social problems must be provided. The pay-off of long-run prevention of social upheaval is hard to quantify; therefore it is difficult to mobilize the resources, domestic and external, to pay for it, especially if the supply of development finance is inadequate to begin with.

V   CONCLUSION

This concludes the attempt to trace over the short span of some twenty years the development of the World Bank's views on the process of economic development. Because development has so many facets and their relative importance changes, or appears to change, from time to time, it is exasperatingly difficult to single out the 'general' and 'basic' features of the development process; this explains, I feel, the apparent lack of focus of the preceding account and makes it impossible to summarize it. However, looking back – over twenty years rather than over twenty pages – several trends of thought emerge. They are:

1. The more social scientists probe, and the longer practitioners of development finance try to do the right things to stimulate and accelerate economic development, the more complex the processes and problems appear to be. The attempts to understand and foster development have become more circumspect – to avoid the term sophisticated with its connotation of superiority. This does not mean that we know better; it only means that we are better aware of the limitations of our knowledge.

2. There is no short-cut to development – neither via industrialization, nor via import substitution, nor via infrastructure investment, nor via education. To the contrary; the only firm conclusion that emerges from twenty years of observation, analysis and action is that the path to development is far longer and much more arduous than it appeared to be when the conscious drive towards development, and development aid, began some twenty years ago.

3. The social and political complications of the development process, and the riskiness of the global development venture make the process of development and the task of development assistance not only more difficult but also more expensive. And because of the difficulties and the risks involved, only part of the cost of development is 'bankable' and can be financed by private investment and public loans on hard terms; another part, perhaps a substantial part, must be provided through grants and concessional aid.

A final comment must be made on the question (which is substantively not really relevant, but interesting from the point of view of the Dogmen-historian) as to how much of the Bank's development 'philosophy' was original and how much of it was the result of conscious or osmotic acceptance of new ideas generated 'outside'. There is no clear-cut answer because there was of course continuous professional-intellectual intercourse between the Bank and other institutions in developing as well as advanced countries, and innovating ideas have a tendency of changing their shape, sometimes but little and sometimes beyond recognition, between their conception and their ultimate application. It may be a fair guess that in the very early days of the Bank's operations in development finance, the Bank derived little help from the 'outside' while it was groping for a consistent concept of development. As time went on, intellectual innovations conceived on the 'outside' undoubtedly did much to change the Bank's views and operating stance; but even then it contributed to the state of the art of development by sifting and choosing among the wide array of novel notions. But the very difficulty of disentangling what was original and what was derived in the evolution of the Bank's development 'philosophy' may make this *Dogmengeschichte*, focusing on one institution, an imprecise mirror reflection, frayed at the edges and blurred in the grey light of everyday reality and political feasibility, of the history of thought on the process of development at large.

II

DEVELOPMENT AND PLANNING

CHAPTER 3

Should Growth Rates be Evaluated at International Prices?[1]

J. BHAGWATI AND B. HANSEN

I THE PROBLEM

It is sometimes argued that growth rates of value-added, income, or GDP as measured by standard methods tend to be misleading when domestic market prices and factor costs are 'distorted' by tariffs, quotas, trade and price controls, and overvalued currencies.

For developing countries in particular, it has been argued that standard methods should tend to exaggerate growth rates because it is the fast-growing sectors, usually manufacturing industry, that are protected and hence 'overpriced' and 'overweighted'. Intuition suggests a simple method of adjusting the conventionally measured growth rates by weights equal to the shares of sectoral value-added in total value-added, estimated at international prices.[2] Thus the conventional formula for a two-sector economy, X and Y denoting sectors,

$$g = g_X w_X + g_Y w_Y$$

where g denotes growth rates, w denotes weights equal to the

[1] We are grateful for comments from, and discussions with, Maurice Scott and Tibor Scitovsky. They helped us much in understanding the methods of I. Little, T. Scitovsky, and M. Scott, *Industry and Trade in Some Developing Countries* (Oxford University Press, 1970) but we are, of course, responsible for the exposition and interpretation given in this paper. We had the opportunity of discussing the paper at Scitovsky's seminar at Stanford and acknowledge a number of valuable comments from the participants. Bhagwati's research has been supported by the National Science Foundation and the National Bureau of Economic Research.

[2] B. Hansen, *Economic Development in Egypt*, Rand Corporation and Resources for the Future, RM-5961-FF (October 1969), p. 16, n. 2; also suggested independently by Tibor Scitovsky in a public lecture at Berkeley in 1969.

sectoral shares in value added, $w_X + w_Y = 1$, all measured conventionally at domestic market prices, is replaced by

$$g' = g_X w'_X + g_Y w'_Y$$

where g' is the adjusted overall growth rate and w'_X and w'_Y are the sectoral shares measured at international prices, $w'_X + w'_Y = 1$.

The growth rate thus adjusted is of course a hybrid in the sense that it uses observed sectoral growth rates of value-added at domestic prices but weights them at shares in international prices. At constant prices, as generally assumed in this paper (to avoid the discussion of standard index-number problems and instead to focus on the new issues raised here), this Hansen-Scitovsky method is clearly equivalent to evaluation at international prices.

Another method for re-valuing value-added and growth contributions has been suggested by Little, Scitovsky and Scott[3] in an important, recent study of import substitution in semi-industrialized LDCs. Disregarding non-traded goods which give rise to special problems (see Section 4, below), their operational procedures imply in effect that growth rates be measured at international prices although the reader is not likely to grasp this implication of their methodology. They take it that 'the relative prices of the industry's product measure their relative marginal values to society . . .' (p. 411), and they '. . . want to measure the social *value* of the output, and not its social *costs*' (p. 411, no. 1). Efficiency considerations, on the other hand, seem to require evaluation at international prices because they represent, through foreign trade and the balance of payments (pp. 72–3 and 411–14), the true opportunity costs in production.

As a way out of this dilemma, Little, Scitovsky and Scott apparently (p. 73) first calculate value-added for all sectors at international prices, and then convert the value-added of each individual sector (thus calculated) to domestic values through a common 'multiplicative factor', ϕ, which expresses the average relation between international prices and domestic prices and (in the simplest case without non-traded goods) is taken as the ratio between aggregate value-added for all sectors at domestic market prices and at international prices (p. 416). The method thus consists of an evaluation of each individual sector's contribution to value-added and value-added growth at international opportunity costs, adjusted upwards to be

[3] Little, Scitovsky and Scott, op. cit., chap. 2 and Appendix to chap. 2, pp. 70–6 and 410–21.

expressed in terms of the average purchasing power (marginal utility) of the consumers' money (income) at domestic market prices.

Clearly this procedure, *as contrasted with the standard evaluation at domestic market prices*, implies that both the absolute and relative contributions (to value-added as also to change in welfare) of the relatively more highly protected sectors will become smaller, while the sum of *all* the sectors' contributions will remain equal to the value-added increase at *domestic* market prices.

At the same time, the relative contribution to value-added, by each sector, under this procedure, is readily seen to be independent of ϕ (which multiplies into *each* sector's value-added at international prices) and hence to be, in effect, measured purely at international prices. Furthermore, when we calculate a growth *rate* as the ratio between the sum of all sectoral value-added increments at international prices, each one multiplied by the common ϕ, and the sum of all sectoral value-added in a base year, at the same international prices and multiplied by ϕ (p. 417),[4] the common factor ϕ divides out, of course. This procedure therefore implies that relative sector shares, sectoral growth rates as also the total growth rate are measured exclusively at international prices, as with the Hansen-Scitovsky method.[5]

[4] For non-traded goods, Little, Scitovsky and Scott propose to multiply the value at domestic market prices by ϕ determined on the basis of the trading sectors.

[5] Our interpretation of the Little–Scitovsky–Scott methods is accurate in describing the *actual* method underlying their empirical estimates of growth rates in the countries these authors have studied. In terms of Figure 3.1 below, for example, their procedure is to estimate the increment in value-added at international prices (that is, JK), divide it by the base-year value of expenditure at domestic prices (that is, OH), and then multiply this ratio into ϕ which is estimated as the base-year ratio of expenditure valued at domestic prices to expenditure valued at international prices (that is, OH/OK), which yields a growth rate at *international* prices (that is, a negative growth rate: JK/OK). This result, of course, is to be expected as their procedure amounts then merely to dividing incremental value-added at international prices by base-year value-added (converted back) at international prices: which is the same thing as taking the same ratio and multiplying both the numerator and the denominator thereof by the same ϕ, which of course then cancels out no matter how ϕ is defined.

Maurice Scott has, however, pointed out that their desired *ideal* method (as distinct from their actual method, underlying their estimates) was to evaluate growth rates at *domestic* prices. According to him, the ratio JK/OH was to be multiplied into a ϕ which was to be estimated, *not* as the base-year ratio of expenditure at market prices to expenditure at international prices (that is, OH/OK), but as the *marginal* ratio of expenditure at market prices to expenditure at international prices (that is, GH/JK), thus yielding a growth rate at *domestic* prices (that is, a negative growth rate: GH/OK).

The two methods distinguished by Scott, in correspondence, as the actual and

Conventional methods, on the other hand, require measurement of growth rates at either domestic market prices or domestic factor cost. In addition, therefore, we now have measurement at international prices. Measurement at international prices certainly takes into account opportunity costs in international trade but with 'distortions' they do not express domestic consumer preferences. Measurement at domestic market prices expresses (by assumption) consumer or community preferences but seems to ignore international opportunity costs. It is clear also that we cannot evaluate at both international and domestic market prices at the same time (although this is, indeed, what the two methods described above appear to make a vain attempt to do). What shall we do then? Is there one method of evaluating growth that is preferable to all other methods? Or should all methods be applied because they illuminate different aspects of growth?

We shall examine this issue for the case of growth subject to a given tariff in the framework of the simplest conceivable model: the value-theoretic model of traditional international trade theory, with two traded goods, X and Y, produced by non-traded primary factors with exogenously determined terms of trade and a given, well-behaved community preference map. We then examine the same model for the case of growth subject to a given production subsidy. Finally, we discuss briefly complications implied by the existence of traded inputs, monopoly power in trade and non-traded goods.

II   THE WELFARE CRITERION

Assume that the economy, before growth, has a production possi-

the ideal Little–Scott–Scitovsky methods, thus lead to quite different estimates of growth rates. It may be useful to discuss more clearly why this is so. Thus, note that ϕ is different for the before-growth and after-growth situations; let therefore ϕ^b and ϕ^a represent the former and the latter respectively. Under the *ideal* method, these authors would divide the incremental value-added at international prices (that is, JK) by the before-growth expenditure at market prices (that is, $OH = OK.\phi^b$); then they would multiply it into what they call the marginal ϕ, whose definition is the incremental expenditure at market prices divided by the incremental value-added at international prices (and which therefore is: $\frac{OJ.\phi^a - OK.\phi^b}{JK}$). This then yields: $\left(\frac{OJ.\phi^a - OK.\phi^b}{OK.\phi^b}\right)$. This can then be rewritten as $\left\{-\frac{JK}{OK} + \frac{OJ}{OK}\left(\frac{\phi^a}{\phi^b} - 1\right)\right\}$.

If we now evaluate ϕ^b and ϕ^a correctly as OH/OK and OG/OJ respectively, it is easy to see that the growth rate will then reduce to $-GH/OH$. However, if a single, common ϕ is assumed, then $\phi^b = \phi^a$ and the growth rate reduces to $-JK/OK$.

bility curve, *AB*, while after growth it is *CD*; see Figure 3.1. In each situation there is a given, common tariff. In the pre-growth equilibrium, production, consumption, and welfare are at P_b, C_b and U_b, respectively. In the post-growth situation, equilibrium is at P_a, C_a and U_a. In each equilibrium situation we assume that tariff revenue is redistributed as an income subsidy to consumers; in the pre-growth equilibrium it is equivalent to *EH* units of X and after growth it is *FG*.

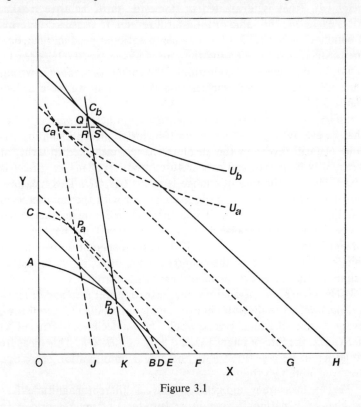

Figure 3.1

Note, first, that in this simple case with balanced trade and no factor payments to other countries, we need not distinguish between national and domestic product; and national expenditure and product (value-added, national income) are equal in size, provided that both are evaluated at either domestic factor cost or domestic factor prices or international prices. The difference between national expenditure (= national product) at domestic market prices and domestic factor cost represents clearly the total revenue from tariffs.

This is the standard national accounting terminology which we shall apply in what follows. In moving from pre-growth to post-growth equilibrium we may thus distinguish between three measures of the resulting change in national expenditure and product and ask which of these measures, if any, can measure (or at least indicate the direction of) the accompanying change in the level of welfare:

1. The change in national product (expenditure) at *domestic factor cost* (that is, evaluated at domestic, tariff-inclusive market prices excluding the value of total tariff revenue): measured in terms of commodity X, the absolute change in national product (expenditure) at factor cost is EF; and the rate of change is EF/OE. Clearly, to use this measure as an indicator of the change of welfare is wrong when we actually have immiseration ($U_a < U_b$) as we have drawn Figure 3.1.[6]

2. The change in national expenditure (product) *at market prices* (that is, evaluated at domestic, tariff-inclusive prices, including the value of tariff revenue): the absolute change, measured in terms of commodity X, in national expenditure (product) at market prices is *minus GH*, and the rate of change is *minus GH/OH*. This measure, showing a reduction in welfare, is consistent with the immiseration that has occurred. Besides, it is a 'natural' measure of the actual change in welfare because it may be construed in the Hicksian compensating-variational sense: if domestic expenditure worth GH units of X were given to the country after growth, it would restore welfare to the same level as before growth occurred.

3. The change in national product (expenditure) *revalued at international prices*: the absolute change in national product (expenditure), revalued at international prices, would show a decline (in terms of X) of JK; and the rate of change would be *minus JK/OK*. This measure would again be consistent with the actual immiseration ($U_a < U_b$). However, note two things:

i. This measure would generally have a different magnitude than the change in national expenditure (product) at market prices. In Figure 3.1, $JK \neq GH$ and $JK/OK \neq GH/OH$; hence it is *not a*

---

[6] The discussion here centres, of course, upon the 'odd' cases. For if both the production point and the expenditure point move to the north-east there is no doubt that both production and expenditure have increased. No matter what constant prices we use for evaluating the growth rate of production and/or expenditure, we come out with a positive growth rate. Although the measured growth rates will depend upon the prices, their signs will always be positive. It is when one or both of the expenditure and production points have moved to the north-west or south-east that problems of sign appear.

matter of indifference as to which measure is adopted for measuring either absolute growth or growth rates.

ii. Furthermore, this measure, at international prices, makes sense in the following way. If a net transfer (say, aid flow) equal to $C_a R = JK$ units of X were made to this country, starting out from the after-growth situation, the economy would clearly move from C_a to C_b, that is, from U_a to U_b, with $C_a O$ units of the inflow held in the form of X and QR units transformed into QC_b units of Y. But, note that national expenditure would have increased by $C_a R$ units of the transfer and RS units of tariff revenue. It follows that $C_a R = JK$ units of X represent the net transfer from abroad that would take the tariff-ridden economy back to the pre-growth level of welfare (U_b); it is thus a compensating-variational measure of the inflow of resources from abroad that would be required to restore the economy to its pre-growth level of welfare. Note that this measure is fully consistent conceptually with the preceding measure in terms of change in national expenditure at market prices: given the tariff, national expenditure must necessarily increase, to the extent that tariff revenue increases, by more than the net transfer. Hence, both measures are different evaluations of the same measure (that is, of the Hicksian compensating variation) and both would therefore seem 'natural' measures of the actual change in economic welfare.

We may therefore be tempted to conclude that the change in national product (expenditure) either at market price or revalued at international prices would correctly indicate the shift in *actual* welfare and that the choice between the two is essentially arbitrary.

However, we can conclude something a little stronger. Thus, take Figure 3.2 where we have a case, based on recent analysis of tariffs by Bhagwati, Kemp and Vanek,[7] where the growth leads to an improvement in the availabilities-locus from $P_b C_b$ to $P_a C_a$ but immiseration nonetheless occurs ($U_b > U_a$).[8] This case requires inferiority in social consumption of the exportable good; and the Pareto-superiority of the availability-locus $P_a C_a$ over $P_b C_b$ implies that a superior equilibrium exists in the after-growth situation which, if chosen, would lead to $U_a > U_b$.

[7] See J. Bhagwati, 'The Gains from Trade Once Again', *Oxford Economic Papers*, vol. 20 (1968), pp. 137–48; M. Kemp, 'Some Issues in the Analysis of Trade Gains', *Oxford Economic Papers*, vol. 20 (1968), pp. 149–61; J. Vanek, *General Equilibrium of International Discrimination* (Harvard University Press, 1965).

[8] An analogous case with a deterioration of availability and increase of welfare may also occur, but the implications are, of course, the same.

Now, in this situation, our analysis of Figure 3.1 goes through but with a new twist. We see that, starting from the after-growth situation, a *net transfer out*, worth RC_a units of X, will lead to a net increase in national expenditure of C_aS units of X (the tariff-revenue increase being RS, the transfer outflow being RC_a, the difference then being C_aS). Thus, we have the paradox: the measure in terms

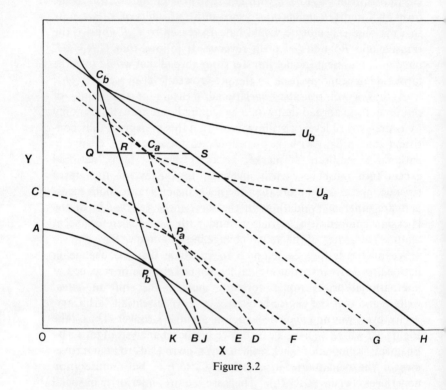

Figure 3.2

of market prices will show a *negative* growth rate of GH/OH, which is consistent with the *actual* immiseration; the measure in terms of international prices will show, on the other hand, a *positive* growth rate of JK/OK, which would contradict the fact of the immiseration that has actually occurred.

We can thus conclude that:

1. As an index of the direction of change in *actual* welfare, the conventional measure of expenditure (product) at market prices will be correct invariably; the measure at international prices will work in the absence of inferiority in social consumption; and the measure

at factor cost is both conceptually unsuitable and would be treacherous (in the presence of immiseration).

On the other hand, noting that in Figure 3.2 the availability-locus P_aC_a dominates P_bC_b and therefore potential or feasible welfare at the actual production vector will have improved even though actual welfare has reduced after growth, we can conclude that:

2. As an index of *potential* or *feasible* welfare at the *actual* production vector, the measure of national product (expenditure) at international prices will be correct invariably; the measure at market prices will work in so far as, if inferiority in consumption is present, it does not lead to choice of 'inferior' equilibria in the Pareto-superior situation;[9] and the measure at factor cost would again be both conceptually inappropriate and treacherous (in the presence of immiseration).

III THE 'PRODUCTIVE CAPACITY' CRITERION

So far we have chosen to evaluate the different national product (expenditure) measures by reference to whether they suitably indicate welfare-change. Suppose instead that we are interested in measuring changes in 'productive capacity'. Would the revaluation of actual production at international prices be correct in that case? Unfortunately, it fails here; and the correct measure (in a sense to be shortly defined) would be national product (expenditure) at factor cost – that is, the production vector evaluated at the domestic, tariff-inclusive price ratios but excluding tariff revenue.

For, if we aim to measure changes in 'productive capacity', we are essentially measuring the shift, in Figures 3.1 and 3.2, in either the production possibility curve from AB to CD or the availability-locus defined inclusive of the trade possibility.

1. In the former case, it only makes sense to measure the shift in the production possibility curve by positing a price-ratio and competitively choosing the production vector by reference to it: measuring the change in national product at domestic factor cost would do precisely this. Both production vector and price ratio would then be observable. Evaluating the production vector, which has been chosen by reference to the tariff-inclusive price ratio, at the international

---

[9] As Kemp (op. cit.) has shown, plausible stability conditions can be established which rule out the 'inferior' equilibria as unstable. Hence, the distinction between actual and potential welfare may not be terribly important in practice; in which case, the two measures, at international prices and at market prices, are both equally 'legitimate'.

price ratio would for this purpose be a meaningless hybrid and could, indeed, show a decline in productive capacity, as in Figure 3.1, when in fact the productive capacity has increased (that is, the production possibility curve has been pushed outwards).

2. In the latter case, where the shift in the availability-locus, inclusive of the trade opportunity, is sought to be measured, however, the international price vector does become relevant: but it should be used to evaluate a production vector which is chosen by reference to it – in Figures 3.1 and 3.2, the production bundles must be chosen, in our competitive economy, by putting the international price-ratio tangent to AB and to CD successively. In that case, evaluation at international prices measures both productive capacity and *maximal* feasible welfare; but this production point is not directly observable. When the production possibility curve has shifted outward, implying increase in productive capacity in the trade-augmented sense as well, the measure of increment in national product at factor cost will, however, be directionally correct as it must show an increase in productive capacity.[10] On the other hand, a measure which merely revalues the given production vector (chosen by reference to the tariff-inclusive prices) could, as we have just argued via Figure 3.1, show a reduction in 'productive capacity' and hence be directionally incorrect as well.

IV   GROWTH SUBJECT TO A PRODUCTION SUBSIDY

If, however, we consider the case of a production subsidy – which differs from the tariff in not causing a consumption distortion as well – then the revaluation at international prices yields a measure of welfare-change which is identical with that yielded by evaluation at domestic market prices; both, therefore, indicate correctly the actual and potential change in welfare resulting from growth. (The inappropriateness of either for measuring the change in 'productive capacity', however, continues.)

Thus, in Figure 3.3, assume that commodity Y enjoys a subsidy on production at rate RS/QR. Production is therefore at P_b before growth, and at P_a after growth, at the subsidy-inclusive price-ratio equal to the slope of P_aW or P_bS. RS is the subsidy actually paid out, measured in terms of commodity X, in the situation before growth: it is assumed that it is collected by lump-sum taxation from the earnings

[10] Assuming, of course, that the old and the new production possibility curves do not intersect. This could happen if natural resources upon which the production of one of the commodities depends were exhausted, for instance.

at factor cost. The measure of national product (expenditure) at factor cost is therefore OS and OW, before and after growth, respectively.

Clearly, therefore, the increment in national product at factor cost is an erroneous measure of welfare change: it shows positive increment at rate SW/OS, whereas immiseration has occurred ($U_b > U_a$).

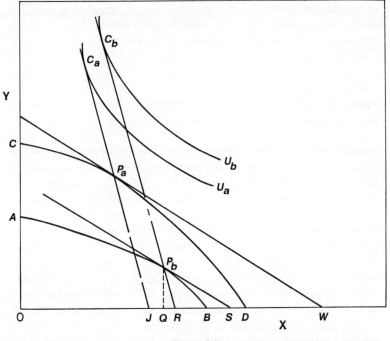

Figure 3.3

But the increment at market price correctly shows immiseration at rate JR/OR; and so does valuation at international prices. Thus the revaluation at international prices yields the correct measure of welfare-change: but note that it reduces, in view of the equality between the domestic prices at which consumption occurs and the international price vector, to the same measure as the measure in terms of domestic market prices.

V   SOME COMPLICATIONS

Our analysis clarifies the issues in relation to a highly simplified value-theoretic, trade model. This simplicity of the model helps us to focus on the important issues. At the same time, however, it masks a number of difficulties.

Some of these difficulties are well known and common to all methods of evaluating growth rates: for example, price changes between the pre-growth and the post-growth situations, the presence of externalities and non-marketed output such as government services, the treatment of investment goods, and so on. We focus now rather on the problems, if any, arising from introducing multiple goods and intermediates; and the differential effect on our different measures of the presence of monopoly power in trade and of non-traded goods.

Multiple goods. Clearly our analysis is not conditional on the assumption of only two goods; it would readily carry over into a multi-good model, holding the other features of the model unchanged.

Intermediates. Our model disregards the use of produced or imported inputs in production, but abandoning this simplification does not really upset our conclusions. For such commodities are either used by both consumers and industries (for example, gasoline) or they are only used by industry (aluminium). Unless there are special consumer taxes that industry does not pay, produced or imported inputs are indeed evaluated at domestic market (consumer) prices in the first case. In the second case there is no direct consumer evaluation; the value of the inputs to the consumer is then equal to the value of the marginal product of the input at domestic market prices for the output. Profit maximization should make sure that in equilibrium the value of the marginal product is equal to the domestic market price of the input. Thus produced inputs do not present us with any new problems as far as measuring the growth rate is concerned.

Monopoly power in trade. Falling demand and rising supply curves abroad (monopoly) imply that export and import prices do not express marginal opportunity costs. The marginal revenues and costs that should be substituted for prices in such circumstances are not directly observable, and this fact immediately deprives international price evaluation of one of its major advantages. Little, Scitovsky and Scott[11] mention this possibility in the case of exports but express the hope that export taxes may have been optimal.

---

[11] Little, Scitovsky and Scott, op. cit., p. 418.

Should this hope be fulfilled, market prices would clearly be identical with marginal revenues, and evaluation of production at 'international opportunity costs' would be identical with evaluation of production at factor cost. On the other hand, evaluation at domestic market prices would remain the correct method if an index of actual welfare is sought.

To assume that actual export taxes are optimal would, of course, be to beg the question of measuring marginal revenues (and costs) in foreign trade. But quite apart from whether tariffs actually are optimal or not, there are a number of problems when we attempt to measure at international prices, making it necessary to take a careful look at our criteria when monopoly power in trade obtains.

i. Our first criterion was actual welfare. Given our general assumptions, the introduction of monopoly power in trade is consistent with the existence of a unique expenditure point with an associated utility level in each situation before and after growth, whether actual tariffs are optimal or not; and the change of this point is still to be measured in terms of domestic market prices to obtain a measure of the change in actual welfare.

ii. But our second criterion, feasible or potential welfare *at given production*, may break down. Feasible expenditure at given production can no longer be expressed uniquely at the observed, given international price because the price itself depends upon the volume of trade. And, in any case, international prices no longer measure opportunity costs. Hence we may shift to evaluation at marginal revenue. But generally speaking, marginal revenue also depends upon the volume of trade. Feasible expenditure at given production now takes place along a non-linear offer curve superimposed à la Baldwin[12] on the production point. Evaluating each point of the offer curve at the corresponding marginal revenue (the slope of the offer curve at that point), we find now that the value of expenditure in terms of the exportable good in the simple two-good model will be larger the larger is the volume of trade. And there is no one-to-one correspondence between the value of expenditure thus evaluated and the utility level obtained. As trade increases along the offer curve from the production point, utility will increase up to a point and then decrease while the value of expenditure in terms of X will continue increasing. We could then ask if there is any particular point on the offer curve which could be singled out. If we are looking for feasible

[12] R. E. Baldwin, 'The New Welfare Economics and Gains in International Trade', *Quarterly Journal of Economics*, vol. 64 (1952), pp. 99–101.

welfare, this point would naturally be the point of highest utility – that is, the point of tangency between the offer curve and the utility curves. Should the tariffs happen to be at optimum, this point will be identical with actual expenditure and what we measure is identical with expenditure at domestic market prices. If tariffs are not at optimum, evaluation of expenditure at marginal revenue in trade *at the highest utility level* (as defined here) is indeed an independent measure, but to make this evaluation we would have to work with quantities and marginal revenues, neither of which is directly observed and would require knowledge not only of the offer curve but also of the preference map for their (econometric) estimation.

iii. Our third criterion, 'production capacity', may now be interpreted as either the production possibility curve or the efficient Baldwin-envelope. What we said in Section II about the production possibility curve applies here, too, *mutatis mutandis*: only one set of related prices and quantities can be directly observed, viz., actual production and factor costs, and measurement at factor cost is a correct solution. Concerning the Baldwin-envelope, on the other hand, the actual expenditure point (the only directly observable point) will be on the Baldwin-envelope only if tariffs are optimal, and we are then back to evaluation at domestic market prices. If tariffs are not optimal, however, no point on the Baldwin-envelope (with the corresponding marginal revenue) will be directly observable. And even if the envelope could be econometrically estimated, we would have to evaluate the 'capacity' with respect to the preference map if we wish to come out with econometrically meaningful *single* numbers.

Thus, the existence of monopoly in trade seems to imply that evaluation at the 'correct' quantities and related *international* 'prices' (that is, marginal revenues) is generally impossible without resort to econometric estimation of the foreign offer curve – and not just of marginal revenue around the observed trade point alone – and specification of the country's own preference map. In the very special case of optimal tariffs, evaluation of international 'prices' simply coincides with one of the conventional methods, evaluation at market prices or at factor costs. The *conventional* methods, on the other hand, make sense in the same way as they did in the case where the country had no monopoly power in trade.

Non-traded goods. Conceptually, we may further modify the model to allow for non-traded goods by *either* introducing a sector which is non-tradable (for example, services) *or* assuming that all 'goods' are in principle tradable but that each good has an f.o.b. and a c.i.f. price and that, in equilibrium, one or more goods may become non-traded (with their prices lying between the c.i.f. and the f.o.b. price).

In either conceptualization, the measure of change in domestic expenditure at market prices should continue to provide an idea of the change in actual welfare. However, serious difficulties arise in revaluation of the production vector at international prices. In the former model, the non-*tradable* sector has no 'international' price by assumption; whereas, in the latter case, the equilibrium allocation of resources is likely to involve the presence of non-*traded* goods whose price is between the c.i.f. and the f.o.b. prices and hence which do not have a single, identifiable 'international' price.[13] Hence, these non-traded goods have to be perforce evaluated at other-than-international prices and the international-price-valuation approach is just not applicable in the presence of non-traded goods – as literally stated.

These problems can be fairly serious in practice. Two examples may suffice as illustrations. In Egypt, the c.i.f. price for fertilizer (15·5 calcium nitrate) was LE 18·53 per hkg in 1960 at an f.o.b. price of LE 14·95. In Afghanistan (average for 1964/5 – 67/8), at a wheat price of 7·3 USc/kg f.o.b. US port, the price c.i.f. Kabul was 10·9 USc/kg, implying a hypothetical price f.o.b. Kabul for shipment to US port of 3·7 USc/kg. Similarly, the proportion of non-tradable services in LDCs is often a large fraction of total GNP and cannot be dismissed lightheartedly.

VI CONCLUSIONS

Not surprisingly we come out with the result that the answer depends upon the question. It is best to try to specify what is meant by growth and then to look around for adequate yardsticks. We find then that:

1. If we are looking for an indicator of the development of actual welfare, granted the existence of a well-behaved community preference map, the correct measure is the conventional growth rate at domestic market prices.

2. If we seek, however, an indicator of feasible, potential welfare

---

[13] We may also note that no matter which method of evaluation is used, a commodity that is exported or non-traded in the pre-growth situation may be imported in the post-growth situation even at given c.i.f. and f.o.b. prices and tariffs; this will also generally lead to price changes and hence index number problems.

at actual production, the growth rate of national product or expenditure evaluated at international prices is the correct measure. But in the latter case there are serious problems arising from the existence of non-traded tradables and non-tradables; and with monopoly power in trade, the measure at international prices breaks down (in the sense discussed earlier).

3. In either case, the measures are at best ordinal; thus we cannot tell whether a particular measure 'exaggerates' the growth rate – this is an issue that seems intractable.

4. If we are interested, however, in productive capacity, the growth rate as conventionally evaluated at factor cost is a correct ordinal measure and the only one that is based on directly observable quantities and prices. If we allow for the possibility of using non-observable, estimated production, international prices may be used for obtaining a measure of capacity at optimal production, and maximum feasible welfare; but when monopoly power in trade prevails, the 'correct' quantities and 'prices' (that is, marginal revenues) have to be estimated, and this would require knowledge not only about the production possibility and offer curves, but also about the social preference map.

We do not exclude the possibility, finally, that growth may be defined in ways other than those discussed here; other measures may then be the correct ones.

CHAPTER 4

Economic Growth with Unlimited Foreign Exchange and No Technical Progress

E. E. HAGEN

I

In some and probably all of the world's economies in which petroleum extraction generates a significant fraction of gross national product, a continuing rise in value productivity and a higher rate of rise in real income is occurring in the non-petroleum sector without (or in excess of) technical progress in that sector. In some of these economies, the rise in money income and even in real income is at as high a percentage rate as or an even higher rate than the rate of increase in value-added in the petroleum sector. Table 4.1 illustrates the process in the case of Saudi Arabia.

The process is the familiar one of a transfer of resources from low productivity to high productivity employment plus the less familiar one of a partial divorce of incomes and costs. No analyst has presented a model that incorporates both aspects. This method of 'sowing the petroleum' may account for a good deal of rising income that has been assumed to be the result of technical progress. A model that describes this phenomenon has implications not only for the petroleum economies but also for a few economies whose only 'oil' is American economic aid and perhaps also for many other economies which during some period of their histories have had some type of resource available at low cost in almost unlimited amounts.

This essay examines the process and considers its duration.

II

Let us define an 'oil economy' by stating a set of hypothetical empirical conditions from which by only moderate simplification we

69

derive our model. The statement is made with no specific country in mind. The hypothesized conditions are sufficiently typical of a group of countries to serve an analytical purpose.

TABLE 4.1 *Estimates of the Gross National Product of Saudi Arabia by Industrial Origin, at Factor Cost, 1382/83–1388/89**

Sector	Millions of Saudi Riyals of Year 1386/87 1382/83	1388/89	Average Annual Growth Rates (%)
Agriculture, forestry, fishing	879·2	923·9	0·8
Mining and quarrying:			
Crude petroleum and natural gas	3,843·1	6,972·1	10·4
Other mining and quarrying	17·5	39·3	14·4
Manufacturing:			
Petroleum refining	553·2	961·4	9·6
Other manufacturing	157·0	299·0	11·3
Construction	380·6	753·8	12·1
Electricity, gas, water and sanitary services	87·1	208·3	15·6
Transport, storage and communications	537·3	1,172·1	13·9
Wholesale and retail trade	559·0	1,151·7	12·8
Banking, insurance and real estate	47·3	95·7	12·5
Ownership of dwellings	413·4	577·9	5·7
Public administration and defence	778·9	1,099·4	5·9
Services:			
Education	213·3	391·9	10·7
Medical and health	91·9	129·0	5·8
Other services	191·5	307·6	8·2
Gross Domestic Product	8,750·3	15,083·1	9·5
Factor income payments abroad	2,154·8	3,331·3	7·5
Gross National Product	6,595·5	11,751·8	10·1

* 1963/1969 A.D.

Source: Saudi Arabian Monetary Agency, *Annual Report*, 1389–90 AH (1970).

Workers constituting between 0·1 and 1 per cent of the labour force extract and refine petroleum. The annual gross product is $100,000 per man. One-fifth of the value of petroleum production goes abroad as profit and return to capital to the foreign oil companies that hold the petroleum concession. One-eighth to one-quarter of the remainder, or 10 to 20 per cent of the total value of production, consists of costs (other than profit and return to capital), and the balance – 60 to 70 per cent of the gross value of petroleum output – becomes (foreign exchange) revenues to the government. Other governmental revenues and other foreign exchange earnings are small. The country levies no customs duties. No immigration is permitted.

The country as a whole has a population between 100,000 and 10 million. It is a desert country. The non-petroleum productive sectors are agriculture and a fabricating and service sector which I shall refer to as sector three. Sector three is divided into government and private sub-sectors. Between 60 and 80 per cent of the labour force is engaged in agriculture. There is little cereal or textile production; agriculture consists almost wholly of nomadic goat and camel herding. The goats and camels provide food and materials for clothing and shelter. Goats are also sold for meat and the proceeds used to buy commodities from sector three; few other agricultural products are marketed.

The government sub-sector purchases the construction of economic infrastructure, educational and medical facilities, other public buildings, and most urban housing; produces education, medical care, and general governmental administration; and trains workers for these activities. The government makes no transfer payments. There is little private capital formation in sector three.

Now for the model. We simplify the hypothetical empirical conditions in certain respects. Assume a petroleum sector small in manpower but large in value-added, as in the hypothetical empirical case. There is no value production in agriculture (the agricultural population subsisting on zero income), no private capital formation in sector three, no government revenue and no foreign exchange earnings except from oil. There is full employment throughout the economy, at low value productivity except in the petroleum sector.[1] Population and the labour force are constant in size. As the model progresses physical productivity per worker in each non-petroleum sector remains constant, but petroleum output can be increased without increase in employment. There exists a monetary authority in which the treasury deposits the foreign exchange revenues accruing to it. The monetary authority disburses them to pay for foreign purchases by the government, and issues local currency which it sells to the treasury in exchange for foreign exchange. With this local

---

[1] Dudley Seers, 'The Mechanism of an Open Economy', *Social and Economic Studies*, vol. 13 (1964), no. 2, pp. 233–42, presents a model in which petroleum revenues determine the level of employment.

currency the government finances its domestic expenditures. The monetary authority then has the foreign exchange available to sell to private importers or for private transfers to abroad. There is no other currency issue or credit creation. (We ignore the fact that the petroleum concessionaire sells foreign exchange to the monetary authority to obtain local currency with which to pay its local salaries and other domestic expenses. We could if we wished make assumptions concerning expenditures out of this income identical to those we make concerning the expenditure of government revenue, and lump the two together in operating the model.)

There is no other government revenue. There is no food or textile production in agriculture; all food and textiles consumed in the non-agricultural sectors are imported. The marginal consumer propensity to import is 0·4, and the marginal consumer propensity to save is 0·1. There is no saving but consumer saving; government expenditures equal its revenues. World prices of petroleum are constant.

III

Let us designate output in the petroleum sector, less that share which flows abroad as return on capital plus profit, as 'national' value-added in that sector, and use the following symbols:

Subscript T refers to the non-petroleum sector.

P = output in the petroleum sector.

P_d = national value-added in that sector.

G = government expenditures, and C_d domestic government expenditures.

Y = aggregate money income and Y^* aggregate real income, in the economy as a whole without subscripts and within sectors with appropriate subscripts.

y = per capita money income and y^* per capita real income.

C = consumer expenditures, C_d consumer expenditures within the country, and C_M consumer imports.

S = saving.

K = the Keynesian multiplier.

We assume that an increase in petroleum production is accomplished with no additional domestic cost, so that the entire increase in national value added in the petroleum sector accrues to government. (We could if we wished assume increases in wage and salary rates in the petroleum sector, and incorporate them in the model without complicating it by the procedure referred to in the preceding parentheses.)

We begin the operation of the model by assuming an increase in petroleum production to a new higher level and thereby in the level of government expenditures both within the country and abroad. An increase in Y_T results. The Keynesian multiplier applies:

$$(1) \qquad \Delta Y_T = K\Delta G_d.$$

The leakages are saving and importing, and with the propensities to import and to save given above,

$$(1a) \qquad \Delta Y_T = 2\Delta G_d.$$

There is no foreign exchange constraint, regardless of the share spent domestically. For by familiar Keynesian analysis money income will rise only to the level at which the leakages, in this case increases in G_d financed by the sale of foreign exchange by the treasury to the monetary authority, equal the foreign exchange revenues accruing to the treasury. If all of the increase in saving is invested abroad, the incremental quantities of foreign exchange supplied and demanded will be equal. If part of saving is held domestically (hoarded), the monetary authority will accumulate foreign exchange.

IV

Let us assume for the moment that there is no migration from agriculture to sector three, so that the entire increase in income in sector three consists of an increase in *per capita* money income. In a closed economy at full employment, the entire increase in money income would be inflationary; the aggregate increase in money income would be equalled by an increase in money costs. However, in an 'oil economy', real income will increase by a fraction of the increase in money income, for a fraction of the increase in expenditure out of the increased incomes in sector T (all of which are consumer expenditures) is for imports, the price of which is not affected by the increase in money incomes. These costs do not increase. The increase in exports that pays for them was costless. Even if *per capita* money incomes increase without increase in productivity, only a part of the increase in incomes causes an increase in costs.

$$(2) \qquad \Delta Y_T^* = (\Delta C_M/\Delta C)\,\Delta Y_T.$$

Since there is no population increase, equation (2) also holds for *per capita* income.

This result, however, may be regarded as occurring in the third phase of increase in income in sector T rather than in the first. To introduce the first phase, assume that before the increase in government domestic expenditures the differential in real income *per capita* between agriculture and sector three was the maximum under which there would be no migration, and that over a considerable range the elasticity of intersector migration with respect to the real income differential is infinite.

The increase in G_d would then instantaneously induce a flow of migration such that neither *per capita* money incomes nor the price level in sector three would rise, the entire increase in Y_3 flowing to an increased labour force in sector three. The money and real increases in aggregate income in the sector and in the economy as a whole would then be identical.

If, alternatively, an increased differential induced only a low rate of intersector migration, then prices, money income *per capita*, and real income *per capita* in sector three would rise temporarily, money income *per capita* proportionately more than the price level. The increases in the three magnitudes would, however, be only temporary, given price flexibility, for the continuing inflowing of labour would gradually reduce all three to their initial level.

Without population increase, the agricultural labour pool would gradually dry up. Assume that after a certain flow of migration, further increments of migration would occur only at successively greater real income differentials. Term this transitional period phase two. After some total amount of migration, migration would cease, thus ushering in phase three. During phase two, the relationship between the rise in *per capita* money income and that in *per capita* real income in sector three is that shown in equation (2) for aggregate income, but the Keynesian effect is divided between increasing *per capita* money (and thereby real) income, and expanding the size of the sector three labour force. When that expansion ceases, assuming that ΔG_d is sufficient to carry the economy to this point, the process will enter phase three, in which the entire impact of income expansion is on *per capita* incomes. During phase two as well as phase three, some degree of inflation accompanies any increase in aggregate (and *per capita*) real income.

v

Whether the proportionate rate of rise in *per capita* real income in the non-petroleum sector is greater than that in national value-added in the petroleum sector depends on the share of domestic to total incremental government expenditures, the magnitude of the multiplier, and the relative size of the two sectors. If there is no population change and no migration between the petroleum and non-petroleum sectors, $\Delta Y_T / Y_T$ and $\Delta y_T / y_T$ are equal, and we can treat them interchangeably.

(3) $$\Delta Y_T = K \Delta G_d > \Delta P_d \text{ if } \frac{1}{K} < \Delta G_d / \Delta G$$
$$1/K = (\Delta C_M + \Delta S)/\Delta Y_T.$$

Therefore

(3a) $$\Delta Y_T > \Delta P_d \text{ if } (\Delta C_M + \Delta S)/\Delta Y_T < \Delta G_d / \Delta G.$$

That is, if ΔY_T is to be greater than $\Delta P_d(= \Delta G)$, the multiplier effect must more than offset the fact that part of the increment in government revenue is spent abroad.

$\Delta Y_T > \Delta P_d$ if, for example, $\Delta C_M / \Delta Y_T = 0.4$, $S/\Delta Y_T = 0.1$, and
$$\Delta G_d / \Delta G > 0.5.$$

These inequalities of course refer to absolute increases in money income in the non-petroleum and petroleum sectors. The relative magnitude of $\Delta Y_T / Y_T$ and $\Delta P_d / P_d$ depends, in addition to the ratios above, on Y_T / P_d. If the two sectors are equal, then equation (3a) states the conditions for $\Delta Y_T / Y_T > \Delta P_d / P_d$. Any decrease in the ratio Y_T / P_d of course increases the ratio of $(\Delta Y_T / Y_T)/(\Delta P_d / P_d)$, *ceteris paribus*.

The sector in which money income (or national value-added) is increasing at the faster proportionate rate is of course growing in size relative to the other, thus reducing the inequality in the proportionate rates of growth. Hence we arrive at the law: *In a country with an important petroleum sector and no technical progress in the non-petroleum sector, the relative rates of growth of aggregate money income in the latter sector and of national value-added in the petroleum sector will tend towards equality. If the relative population (labour force) of the two sectors remains constant, the statement also applies to* per capita *money income and national value-added.*

The absolute difference between $\Delta Y_T^* / Y_T^*$ and $\Delta Y_T / Y_T$ is of course smaller, the less the degree to which the multiplier effect bids up the price level in sector three and the greater the degree to which, conversely, it expands the work force by means of migration from agriculture. Hence a second law of petroleum economies: *The relative rates of growth in aggregate real income in the non-petroleum sector and of national value-added in the petroleum sector will tend the more strongly to approach equality, the greater the elasticity of migration from agriculture to non-agriculture with respect to the income differential between them.*

The trends in sectoral and aggregate gross product in Saudi Arabia during the 1960s illustrate both laws, though the migration into sector three was largely from abroad rather than from agriculture.

VI

When a continuing rise in the demand for labour in sector three has exhausted the làbour pool in agriculture, output in the non-petroleum sector will cease to rise, but real income will continue to rise as money incomes rise. This rise will be accompanied by inflation. Hence law three: *In the absence of technical progress and labour shifts,* real *per* capita *income in the non-petroleum sector of the economy can rise only during a process of inflation.* (This statement of course disregards transfer income.) Hence if real *per capita* income is continuing to rise secularly in the non-petroleum sector of a petroleum economy without inflation, this is evidence that technical progress is occurring in that sector. To prevent price rises as added money income per worker is pumped in, the rate of rise in physical productivity per worker must be $(\Delta C_d/\Delta C)(\Delta Y_T/Y_T)$.

This model of an 'oil economy' portrays no more faithfully than do other models the details of the actual situations from which it is derived. In the desert petroleum producing countries, there is population increase, production in agriculture, private capital formation in the non-petroleum sector, government revenue other than that from petroleum, technical progress though typically at a very slow rate, etc. These divergences from reality do not lessen the usefulness of the model.

The model applies to countries other than the petroleum – producing desert countries. To suggest this wider applicability, let us summarize the essential qualities of an 'oil economy'. Petroleum production is not one of them. Neither is the role of government that is a part of the model as delineated above.

The economy and its setting consist of five parts: the Fount, the Farm, the Market, the Bank, and the Rest of the World. The Fount has extremely high productivity in the production of a commodity for the world market, and the Farm and the Market low productivity, that in the Farm being much below that in the Market.

The Fount trades its foreign exchange earnings at the Bank for local currency, which it spends in the Market, either through the intermediary of the government or directly. The process bids up money incomes of the productive factors in the Market, who exchange the income, in part, for foreign currency at the Bank and import goods at unchanging world prices. So long as the expenditures by the Fount rise, real factor income in the Market will rise without change in technology.

This is the oil economy. In the oil economies of the period since the Second World War, the Fount – the major source of the 'oil' – has been either petroleum production or the United States government.

At this point, the reader's mind may turn to South Vietnam. No doubt there has been a spectacular rise in real factor incomes in South Vietnam since the major inflow of American resources into that economy began, precisely because of the operation of the 'oil economy' mechanism. However, there are other cases.

The rapid rises in real income in South Korea and Taiwan have been conspicuous features of post-Second World War economic growth in the world. One may suspect that these rises began with the 'oil economy' mechanism, which in these cases benefited persons who were interested in seizing the opportunities and able to do so and used the inflow of resources to finance continuing technical progress.

The 'oil economy' model explains other incidents in economic growth. The rise in real incomes in Argentina during the last decades of the nineteenth century and the first two of the twentieth attracted the notice of economic historians. A commentator in 1920 listed Argentina among the five countries of the world with the most promising economic prospects. Then suddenly, Argentina's progress became slow, and fifteen or twenty countries of the world passed her by. The reason, in the terms of the model, is that Argentina's growth was propelled by the explosion of her beef and wheat sales to the world market. Presently the flow from this Fount ceased to increase, and since very little technical progress occurred in other sectors, the rise in income slowed to a crawl.

The rapid rise in urban *per capita* income in the United States during the early decades of the country's history as a nation may be due in considerable part to a process analogous to that in Argentina before 1920. Here, too, agriculture was the Fount. But here of course technical ferment elsewhere in the economy carried economic growth forward simultaneously.

At this point, if it has not already happened, the relationship between the oil economy model and other models of economic growth becomes clear. It is made clearer if we eliminate the Rest of the World from the model, and assume that the Fount, in addition to pumping income into the Market, performs the function of the Rest of the World, that is, provides both a market for its own goods and also an expanding flow of goods at constant cost to the Market, which thus shares in the fruits of rising productivity in the Fount, even though it does not share in the technical advance. It is then seen that the oil economy model is, after all, only a special case of the general model of diffusion of the fruits of technical progress among the various sectors of an economy.

CHAPTER 5

Absorptive Capacity as a Constraint Due to Maturation Processes

R. S. ECKAUS

The formulation of the concept of absorptive capacity and the examination of its implications for foreign aid have been closely associated with Paul Rosenstein-Rodan.[1] The concept has appeared to be so eminently plausible that it has become a significant part of the literature on economic development. Yet there have been few intensive discussions of the origins and consequences for development of absorptive capacity limits. It remains something of a 'black box'. Its emanations apparently are recognizable to experienced development practitioners but their sources and characteristics are still not completely understood.

In this paper the existing interpretations of the absorptive capacity concept will be reviewed and assessed. Then a new interpretation will be advanced. This will then be embodied in a multi-sectoral, intertemporal linear programming model in order to examine its significance.

THE MEANINGS WHICH HAVE BEEN GIVEN TO ABSORPTIVE CAPACITY

According to Paul Rosenstein-Rodan: 'Absorptive capacity relates to the ability to use capital productively . . . total investment must not only cover its costs but must also yield a reasonable increase in income.

While the capacity to absorb capital is a limiting factor, it can, within a few years, be stepped up. There are, however, narrow limits

---

[1] Paul N. Rosenstein-Rodan, 'International Aid for Underdeveloped Countries', *Review of Economics and Statistics*, vol. 43 (May 1961), no. 2, pp. 107–38.

to the pace and extent at which a country's absorptive capacity can be expanded.'[2]

John Adler, in his monograph on absorptive capacity, says that: 'Absorptive capacity may then be defined as that amount of investment . . . that can be made at an acceptable rate of return, with the supply of co-operant factors considered as given.'[3]

In the Rodan quotation there is the suggestion that the decline in the marginal productivity of new capital may, at some level, become rather abrupt. This is the implication found in other discussions as well.[4] On the other hand, Adler draws a picture which shows the expected rate of return on new investment falling at a constant rather than at an accelerated rate as the level of new investment rises. Likewise the discussion in Benjamin Higgins's textbook suggests that absorptive capacity limits cause the marginal productivity of new investment to decline steadily but not necessarily in a discontinuous or accelerating manner as the rate of investment increases.[5]

These formulations of the absorptive capacity concept are not inconsistent with the familiar technological hypothesis of diminishing returns to a single factor, capital, with other factors held constant. If only conventional diminishing returns were implied by the absorptive capacity arguments, then, presumably, careful scheduling of increases in the availability of all factors would eliminate the constraint. With careful programming a country could plan its investment programme and the increase of 'co-operant factors' so as to move from one long-run equilibrium position to another with factor productivities remaining constant from one position to the next.

But the statements of the absorptive capacity hypothesis appear to go beyond the conventional diminishing returns relationship. They seem to claim that declining marginal productivity of new investment cannot be avoided by proportionate increases in other factors. There is a kind of inevitable decreasing returns to the scale of investment

[2] Ibid., p. 108.

[3] John Adler, *Absorptive Capacity and Its Determinants* (The Brookings Institution, Washington, 1965), p. 5.

[4] For example, in the United Nations, ECAFE, *Programming Techniques for Economic Development, Report of the First Group of Experts on Programming Techniques* (Bangkok, 1960), it is argued that 'absorptive capacity sets a limit to the amount of efficient investment physically possible' (p. 9). Likewise B. Horvat has written '. . . the capacity of absorbing productive investment is absolutely limited in every economy'. 'The Rule of Accumulation in a Planned Economy', *Kyklos*, vol. 21, no. 2, p. 242.

[5] Benjamin Higgins, *Economic Development*, rev. edn (New York, Norton, 1968), p. 579.

whose sources do not appear to be technological. What essential influences, missed by the conventional theory of production, could create such constraints?

There are a number of rationalizations provided in the development literature, not all of them fully consistent or with their implications worked out in detail. According to Albert Waterston, '. . . lack of absorptive capacity . . . essentially reflects an inability to invest in soundly conceived development programmes and projects that can be carried out well and operated economically upon completion. . . .'[6] In Waterston's view the difficulty appears to be one of identifying projects and drawing up plans. Adler has a list of sources of absorptive capacity limitations which includes most of the influences which have been mentioned in this connection. It includes lack of knowledge of resources and technology, lack of skills, lack of management expertise, institutional limitations such as civil disorder and cumbersome and inefficient government bureaucracies, and cultural and social constraints which induce an unwillingness to accept industrial discipline and supervision.[7]

These references are suggestive but finally are not a satisfactory way of describing the manner in which the conditions cited may cause a decline in productivity with increasing levels of investment. It is undoubtedly true that inadequate information about new projects often delays investment. It may also decrease the productivity of new investment.[8] But this need not be accepted as a continuing source of relative inefficiency in investment but rather an obstacle to be overcome in making investment policy. It is possible to exercise foresight about the education and training requirements associated with new investment projects. It is also possible to be foresighted and

[6] Albert Waterston, *Development Planning* (Baltimore, Johns Hopkins Press, 1965), p. 30.

[7] Adler, op. cit., pp. 31–5. A similar view is expressed by Salvatore Schiavo-Campo and Hans W. Singer in *Perspectives of Economic Development* (Boston, Houghton Mifflin, 1968). For example, 'This term [absorptive capacity] can be broadly interpreted as including all economic, social, institutional, political, cultural and psychological factors which are thought to have an influence on the attainable rate of economic growth but which are not explicitly taken into account because they cannot be subjected to quantitative measurement or analysis' (p. 34). See also Ravi Gulhati, 'The Need for Foreign Resources, Absorptive Capacity and Debt Servicing Capacity', J. H. Adler (ed.), *Capital Movements and Economic Development* (St Martin's Press, 1967), p. 249.

[8] That such conditions can prevail in advanced countries as well is noted by Waterston (op cit., p. 300). Horvat claims to have observed the phenomenon in Yugoslav growth experience as well as in the Soviet Union. See B. Horvat, 'The Optimum Rate of Investment', *Economic Journal*, vol. 68 (December 1958), pp. 750, 752.

lay in a stock of blue-prints for new projects so that projects need not be held up for lack of such advance planning. Such foresight should permit expansion without loss in productivity unless there is some inherent reason why there are diminishing returns to the allocation of resources to such advance planning.

It is often pointed out in the discussions of the aborptive capacity phenomenon that construction of new investment projects, education, training and planning themselves require time. There is a gestation period, often substantial, between inputs and outputs. Increasing the rate of investment within any one period will not result in immediate increases in output, but those increases will be forthcoming in some future period. This, in itself, however, need not be a cause of the falling productivity of new investment projects which is the heart of the absorptive capacity phenomenon. Again careful advance scheduling would make it possible to achieve any level of investment in any period without suffering a reduction in the productivity of that investment.

The technical progress function of Kaldor may also have been intended at least in part as a reflection of absorptive capacity constraints. However, it refers not only to new investment projects with unchanged technology but to new investments which embody technical changes. In the technical progress function the rate of growth of output is a function of the rate of increase of the capital stock which rises but at a declining rate and reaches some maximum. According to Kaldor: 'The height of the curve expresses society's "dynamism" . . . but the convexity of the curve expresses the fact that it is possible to utilize as yet unexploited ideas . . . more or less fully; and it is always the most profitable ideas . . . which are exploited first.' Kaldor does not go further than this in providing a rationale for the relationship.[9]

The references cited above refer to the many ways in which various institutional limitations and cultural and social constraints can limit the productivity of new investment projects. It is not just the anthropology and sociology books which are full of such anecdotes. Economists trying to explain the differentials in labour productivity

[9] N. Kaldor, 'Capital Accumulation and Economic Growth', in F. A. Lutz and D. C. Hague (eds), *The Theory of Capital* (London, Macmillan, 1961), p. 208. The suggestive terminology is consistent with Horvath's description '. . . absorptive capacity may now be defined to mean the ability of individuals and of the society as a whole to manipulate the stream of output increments'. See B. Horvat, 'The Optimum Date of Investment', *Economic Journal*, vol. 68 (December 1958), p. 753.

within and among relatively advanced countries as well as in less developed countries frequently fall back on this type of explanation.[10] But the absorptive capacity hypothesis goes beyond the recognition that labour and other factor productivities vary from country to country for reasons which have their sources in the general social milieu. The absorptive capacity hypothesis is that the effect of the social milieu, broadly speaking, is to reduce the productivity of new investment projects as the level of investment increases in any period. The rationale of that relation has not yet been clearly demonstrated.

THE EMBODIMENT OF ABSORPTIVE CAPACITY CONSTRAINTS IN OPTIMIZING MODELS

Application of the absorptive capacity concept has been most effective in some optimizing models which are designed to provide insights into the development process and to help formulate development policy. The embodiment of absorptive capacity constraints in these models serves a dual purpose. First of all, the simulation of absorptive capacity limitations can be regarded as an appreciation by the model builders of the practical significance of such limitations and an improvement in the descriptive quality of the models. Secondly, however, the constraints provide a means of remedying one of the most strikingly unrealistic features of the solutions of most such models. The linear programming models for development planning produce solutions with 'bang-bang' or 'flip-flop' characteristics unless they are otherwise constrained.[11] That means the solutions tend to extremes in time or in whatever dimension they can find which will permit the maximization of the objective or criterion function of the model. For example, the objective function of a planning model typically calls for the maximization of consumption over some plan period. If there is a choice between raising consumption in nearer or more distant time periods, the model solution will generally tend to delay any increase in consumption. It will plough back as many resources as possible until the latter part of

[10] H. Leibenstein has identified 'motivational' and 'non-market input efficiency', as sources of differences in the productivity of resources. These influences overlap with some of those commonly cited as sources of absorptive capacity limits. See H. Leibenstein, 'Allocative Efficiency v. "X-Efficiency"', *American Economic Review*, vol. 56, no. 3, pp. 392–415.

[11] This is a result of the thorough-going linearity in the models. The objective function and the constraints are linear. In effect, therefore, the simplix algorithm, searching along the feasible set of solution points for an optimum position ends up at a vertex, that is, at an extreme position.

the plan period. Then, near the end of the plan period, as much of the available resources as are divertible will be put into the kinds of output and the uses of output which increase the objective function most rapidly, consistent with all the constraints on the problem.

In effect, in the solutions of the models in each period a calculation is made of the marginal advantage of diverting resources to increasing the objective function in that period or of devoting resources to further accumulation of capital. The latter allocation will make it possible to increase the objective function in some future period.

Given the usual set of parameters, the constant marginal productivity of capital and with constant marginal utility of consumption implied by the linear objective function, the future usually wins. If the future did not win, the model solution would 'flip' and do its best to concentrate consumption in early periods. One of the attractions to model builders of constraints which simulate the limitations imposed on investment by absorptive capacity is that these constraints tend to limit the amount of investment in any period. They restrict, therefore, the freedom to embody extreme results.[12]

The model constructed by Hollis B. Chenery and Arthur MacEwan is an excellent example of the simple simulation of absorptive capacity constraints.[13] In this model, investment in any period, t, is constrained to be no more than investment in the previous period, $t-1$, times an exogenously stipulated growth rate $(1+g)$. Thus, the absorptive capacity constraint takes the form of an absolute limit on the amount of investment in any period rather than of the declining productivity of new investment as a function of the rate of investment. The limit is a sliding one, however, and will rise if the rate of investment rises. On the other hand, if, for some reason, the rate of investment should fall in any year, the absorptive capacity constraint in the succeeding year would also be at a lower level. Chenery and MacEwan provide no rationale for this formulation beyond the statement that it incorporates absorptive capacity limits.

[12] K. J. Arrow calls the temporal concentration of consumption and investment a 'wildly implausible' result in pointing out the significance of absorptive capacity constraints. He refers to the views of B. Horvat on Yugoslav experience and E. Penrose and R. Marris and some operations research analyses that there are [increasing] 'costs to the rate of change of capital'. K. J. Arrow, review of I. Adelman and E. Thorbecke (eds), *Theory and Design of Economic Development* (Baltimore, Johns Hopkins Press, 1966), in the *Journal of Economic Literature*, vol. 7 (September 1969), no. 3, p. 875.

[13] Hollis B. Chenery and Arthur MacEwan, 'Optimal Patterns of Growth and Aid: The Case of Pakistan', in Adelman and Thorbecke, op. cit., pp. 149–78.

They do indicate in a footnote, however, a preference for a formulation in which investment, rather than being absolutely stopped by the absorptive capacity constraint, could 'be carried out but only at higher capital-output ratios and with longer time lags'.[14]

In the linear programming model constructed by Irma Adelman and Frederick Sparrow and based on Argentinian data there is a constraint structure which is somewhat similar to that in the Chenery–MacEwan model.[15] There are both upper and lower limits to the level of investment. Unlike the Chenery–MacEwan model, however, the upper limit is set as a proportion (150 per cent) of investment in the model's base period. The upper limit, therefore, does not grow over time or with the previously achieved level of investment in each period. Neither does it contract if the level of investment should fall in any period.[16]

David Kendrick and Lance Taylor embody absorptive capacity limits in a form suggested by Robert Dorfman in an elegant dynamic programming model.[17] In this formulation, 'as the increase in capacity, Δk, approaches some fraction, m, of existing capacity, k, investment, δ, becomes less and less effective in increasing Δk'.[18] The sources of this constraint are not discussed by Kendrick and Taylor but the effects are clear. The addition to productive capacity by new investment is a declining function of the total amount of new investment and the effect is a permanent one. It is as if materials of

[14] Chenery and MacEwan also specify minimum levels of investment in each period. It is clear from their descriptions of the solutions to their model that the absorptive capacity upper limit on investment is effective in preventing flip-flop solutions which concentrate investment in the early part of the plan period and consumption in the latter part. The absorptive capacity constraint is the binding constraint for more than the first half of the planning period. Chenery and MacEwan in, ibid., p. 169.

[15] Irma Adelman and Frederick Sparrow, 'Experiments with Linear and Piece-Wise Linear Dynamic Programming Models', in I. Adelman and E. Thorbecke (eds), *Theory and Design of Development* (Baltimore, Johns Hopkins Press, 1966), pp. 291–316.

[16] Still other methods have been used to control the flip-flop tendencies of inter-temporal programming models. Eckaus and Parikh (R. S. Eckaus and K. S. Parikh, *Planning for Growth* (Cambridge, Mass., MIT Press, 1968)) imposed minimum growth requirements for consumption in one version of their models and maximum savings rates in other versions. The first type of constraint may be interpreted as an elaboration of the objective function in the form of a constraint. The second may be also interpreted in this way or as technical constraint because investment cannot of course exceed the available savings.

[17] David A. Kendrick and Lance J. Taylor, 'A Dynamic Non-Linear Planning Model for Korea', in I. Adelman, *Practical Approaches to Development Planning* (Baltimore, Johns Hopkins Press, 1969), pp. 213–40.

[18] Ibid., p. 218.

less and less good quality were used in the investment projects or the designs became more and more inferior as the rate of investment increases in any period. It will be argued below that this is not implausible but neither is it entirely persuasive as a description of the effects of the absorptive capacity limitations.

The embodiment of the absorptive capacity phenomenon in the inter-temporal programming models raises explicitly a number of questions touched on but not considered in depth in previous discussions. First, what is the effect of this constraint on new investment over time and with increased investment and output? Does it change with respect to any of these variables as has been suggested? If so, is there a causal relation or is this the result of the association of these variables with others which are more fundamental? If absorptive capacity constraints reflect the social milieu, are drastic or difficult changes in this milieu necessary in order to relax this constraint or can it be relaxed by relatively minor reorganizations? In the Chenery–MacEwan model described above, the constraint is related directly to prior investment and becomes tighter or more relaxed depending on what happens to that investment. In the Adelman–Sparrow model there is no change in the constraint over time or with investment. In the Kendrick–Taylor model the effect of the constraint depends on the ratio of new investment to the existing stock. This suggests that the underlying basis of the constraint might be an experience or learning relationship which depends on previous investment – an idea which will be pursued later.

The possible effects of absorptive capacity constraints on the productivity of new investment and previous investment have been noted before. According to Rosenstein-Rodan additional investment, education, improvements in the administrative capacity of the government and changes in work habits may all increase the capacity to absorb new projects.[19] Adler distinguishes short-run, medium-run and long-run absorptive capacity constraints and refers to the possibility of mobilizing the scarce co-operant factors which are their source.[20] The UN Expert Group on Programming Techniques suggests that absorptive capacity constraints can be relaxed by means of investment.[21] Presumably, however, they did not mean that it was possible to create capital which would relax the absorptive capacity constraints. If that were the case, then these constraints would be-

[19] P. N. Rosenstein-Rodan, op. cit., p. 108.
[20] Adler, op. cit., p. 28.
[21] United Nations ECAFE, op. cit., p. 12.

come just another resource limitation which could be removed by capital accumulation.

The second question which is raised explicitly in the model formulations of the absorptive capacity constraints is: what happens to the productivity of a particular investment project over time or with experience or the level of production? The Kendrick–Taylor model is clear on this point. As the level of investment increases in any period, the productivity of the new capital is decreased, not just in the period in which the new capital becomes effective but for the entire lifetime of the investment project. That is because the constraint is formulated so that resources become less and less effective in creating new capacity and that capacity once created, never changes. The other models cited do not face up to the issue because in them the absorptive capacity constraint simply prevents all new investment above a certain amount.

The discussion so far establishes the agenda for the next part. There have been notable accomplishments in identifying the effect of absorptive capacity limitations and in modelling them. Yet much remains to be done in achieving an understanding of the nature and effects of a widely recognized phenomenon. The social and economic mechanisms which create the constraint need to be identified and their operation explained. From this explanation it should then be possible to deduce the consequences of absorptive capacity constraints for investment projects undertaken at different points in time and for a particular project over time.

AN INTERPRETATION OF ABSORPTIVE CAPACITY AS A LEARNING AND ADAPTATION PHENOMENON

The interpretation of absorptive capacity which is proposed here has three components. These will first be set out briefly and then elaborated. First, it will be argued that each investment project has elements of uniqueness or novelty in its use of new technology, in its arrangement of known technologies, in the managerial staff used and in the labour force employed. Secondly, and closely related, such uniqueness implies that some time is required for the project to achieve its full capacity and potential productivity of the resources which it uses. The capital equipment must be 'shaken down', 'run in', and 'tuned up'. The managerial staff and labour force must also be 'seasoned', must learn new methods or at least new routines with old technologies.

These features of new investment projects imply that a gestation period for every new project includes the time for the adaptation and learning processes to work themselves out. Part of the gestation period for investment projects is the length of time required for construction. Yet even before construction is finally completed on certain types of projects, production or at least the tuning of some parts of the equipment and the training of the managerial staff and labour force can begin. So the adaptation and learning phase of the gestation period may overlap with the construction phase and during the adaptation and learning phase production may take place at increasing rates. For the sake of brevity but also to emphasize the next element in the absorptive capacity hypothesis which is advanced here, the adaptation and learning phase of the gestation period will be called the 'maturation' period. In spite of a natural tendency to think of economics in rather anthropomorphic terms, gestation has received more attention from economists than has maturation.

The third element in the absorptive capacity hypothesis presented here identifies the consequences of the two previous elements in the argument. It, in turn, has three parts. The first argues that the length of the maturation period is an increasing function of the amount of new investments. The second part hypothesizes that the difference between the initial productivity of new investment projects and the final productivity achieved at the end of the maturation period is also an increasing function of the level of investment. The last part of the hypothesis suggests that the final productivity achieved by new investment projects is itself a function of the rate of total investment. Thus, there may be a 'permanent' reduction in the productivity of new investment projects below their rated productivity.

In this interpretation of the absorptive capacity hypothesis the initial productivities of the resources used in new investment projects are below the levels which are achieved after some period of time. The time period, the final level of productivity achieved and the difference between the initial and final productivity levels all depend on the total amount of investment being undertaken.

These hypotheses will be justified by a simple characterization of the determinants of the maturation period and initial and final productivity levels. This is that the speed of adaptation of managerial staff and the labour force in production and the initial and final levels of proficiency both in production and in the 'tuning' of the new capital depend, among other things, on the previous experience gained on other new investments. That experience is a limited and wasting 'resource' which can be created only by the act of investment itself and is the source of a kind of diminishing returns to new investment.[22] This is the skeleton of the interpretation of the absorptive capacity hypothesis advanced here. It will now be elaborated in more detail.

The degree of uniqueness or novelty associated with new investment projects is an empirical issue which *a priori* argument may clarify but cannot resolve. It can be noted that there is an element of novelty whenever there is some technological change associated with investment projects. New processes and new products almost by definition imply new tasks to be performed by equipment and/or labour. Sometimes the novelty is profound and clear; sometimes the technical change is restricted to rearrangements of existing equipment and changes in the sequence of processing material. Yet it is hard to imagine technological changes without such novelty. As to the pervasiveness of technological change, it is, presumably, not necessary to argue the case now. It is also generally accepted that even in the process of replacement of worn-out capital there is frequently some technological change involved. So that such replacement might also involve elements of novelty. This, of course, is an argument as to the existence of unique elements, not an assessment of their significance.

It can also be argued that even when there is no change in processing or in product technology, new investment projects typically involve new arrangements and organizations of equipment, new combinations of existing methods of productions, and new flows of materials and output within and to and from the plant. The plausibility of this argument might be strengthened by reference to the well-known problems of 'starting up', new projects. The 'shaking down', 'tuning up', and 'running in' phrases are common parts of the language of production. They refer to processes during which the 'bugs' or 'mistakes' are worked out of the capital and the labour force and the managerial staff are trained in the particular set of operations involved. There may be a trade-off between the costs

---

[22] Though this hypothesis has an obvious relation to Kenneth Arrow's formulation of the learning-by-doing phenomenon, it is none the less different. It argues that there is some amount of learning-by-doing required to achieve the rated, full productivity of an investment project and that this amount increases with the level of investment in any period. The Arrow hypothesis is really an argument as to the evolution of the full or 'rated productivity with accumulated output or investment'. See K. J. Arrow, 'The Economic Implications of Learning by Doing', *Review of Economic Studies*, vol. 29 (3) (June 1962), no. 80, pp. 155–73.

imposed by the process to which these phrases refer and the costs of the new capital itself. To some extent, however, parturition pain cannot be avoided by improvements in the manufacturing process. This is clearest for those types of capital which are manufactured on the site and can be tested by actual operation in production. But it may be true to some extent of all types of capital that there is an ageing or 'curing' process like that in the production process of wine and cheese.

It is also plausible that there may be a trade-off between the costs of maturation and the final productivity of the resources in production. Presumably the smaller the difference between new plants and old plants, the smaller will be the costs of maturation. But also, the smaller will be the increase in the productivity of new plants over the old plant. While there may be abrupt changes in the productivity of capital plant and equipment during the maturation period, it appears more plausible to assume at least for a project as a whole that there is a gradual increase in its productivity. This may be the result of averaging of discontinuous improvements in the productivity of particular pieces of equipment.

It is convenient for many purposes to assume that there are types of capital and labour such that within the categories productivities are constant. Yet in reality it is difficult to separate the effectiveness of the managerial and labour force from the particular pieces of equipment and production organization in which they are associated. Thus, there are improvements which occur in the effectiveness of the managerial and labour force with time and experience in new investment projects. Changes in process or product technology or even changes in the sequencing of operations with given technology and products require adjustments.

This is not the occasion to review the role of learning and adaptation phenomena in economic life. Only a few main points will be mentioned. It is clear that, with a few notable exceptions, the phenomenon of learning – a phenomenon with which most economists are intimately familiar in their daily work – has not been included in the theory of production.[23] True, the learning-by-doing phrase has entered the economist's jargon. But the form in which the learning-by-doing has been embodied in production models is as if

[23] For important exceptions see, Armen Alchian, 'Costs and Output', in *The Allocation of Economic Resources* (Stanford, Stanford University Press, 1959), pp. 23–40, and Arrow, op. cit. The literature on 'learning curves' is well known and often cited but not related to production theory.

it were a source of technical change improving the productivity of all resources rather than as a source of improved productivity of labour with some specific set of equipment.[24]

Economists should be no more blamed for the neglect of learning effects on production than the professionals most familiar with and responsible for the details of production: the engineers. Production engineers are, of course, knowledgeable about the requirements for adjustment and tuning of capital equipment and for the on-the-job learning by managers and labour force. Yet the technical literature on the subject of learning in production and the adjustment of new capital is, at best, thin. Studies of changes in labour productivity with experience and/or time have oddly enough been concentrated on airframe production and are mainly descriptive in character with few generalizations.[25] The literature on training tends to be programmatic rather than analytical.

The psychological literature on learning is rich and extensive but seldom directed specifically towards production situations. The author is not qualified to review it but several relevant generalizations can be drawn readily from that literature. The increasing level of performance with repetition, in the terminology of economics, becomes increasing productivity of labour. Most of the learning literature suggests that the productivity increases associated with training and experience are bounded. The well-known learning curves pass through successive plateaux and end in one. The rate of acquisition of skill has been associated with age in some experiments on learning. In general the learning rate appears to rise with age up to, say, the middle thirties and then to decline somewhat before levelling off. There is, however, substantial variation and it would be reasonable to expect that learning rate would depend on the particular type of skill involved.

Skill transfer describes the carry-over of effectiveness in the performance of one type of task to other tasks. The conditions affecting this type of transfer have also been investigated by psychologists. However, there are few generalizations which appear to be useful

---

[24] This might be justified by arguing that learning-by-doing is in fact a general factor augmenting process. However, that argument has not been made, at least not in explicit detail and with empirical justification. Neither Alchian nor Arrow indicate whether the reduction in cost, which they ascribe to the learning process with a somewhat similar reasoning, is due only to labour augmentation as the result of learning or more general factor augmentation.

[25] See N. Baloff, 'The Learning Curve – Some Controversial Issues', *Journal of Industrial Economics*, vol. 13 (March 1965), pp. 122–8.

for economists other than the one that for certain kinds of tasks the rate of improvement of performance in the new task depends on the level of performance achieved in the original task. However, the degree of carry-over certainly depends on the character of the tasks involved.

Another kind of relationship for which generalizations appear to be difficult is the degree of substitutability among different kinds of education and between education and job experience in the achievement of particular job skill levels. While it is plausible that substitutions are possible, presumably there are limits to the trade-offs. Unfortunately there appears to be little organized empirical information on the subject.

If the argument that there are unavoidable elements of novelty in new investment projects is accepted, then the need for learning and adaptation processes follows. Those, in turn, require a maturation period and have associated 'costs'. The costs, it is argued here, depend on the time and the degree of adjustment required for the capital and the amount of learning and adaptation required in the managerial staff and labour force. There is a distribution of 'adaptable' and 'transferable' skills in the labour force. Unless managerial and labour skill differentials are fully reflected in salary and wage quasi-rents, at low levels of investment there will be tendencies to use the most readily adaptable managers and labour first. Then, as the level of investment increases, less and less adaptable and/or knowledgeable managerial staff and labour force must be used and the length and costs of maturation will increase. The skills which reduce the costs of maturation may, to some extent, be created by formal education but, it is argued here, they require to some minimum degree the experience of new investment itself for their development. They cannot be measured by the amount of capital stock in existence, however, because the skills are wasting. Both retirements from the labour force and loss of knowledge through disuse will lead to such depreciation.[26]

The particular hypothesis being advanced may, perhaps, be appreciated by contrasting it with the learning-by-doing formulation of K. J. Arrow. In the latter the effect of past investment and production is to create knowledge which permanently improves the efficiency

---

[26] It might be noted that forgetting, or the loss of skill, is the converse of learning, and, to some extent, the result of not using the skill. It has been pointed out in another context that this is one of the characteristics of human capital which distinguishes it from physical capital. R. S. Eckaus, 'On the Estimation of the Relations Between Education and Income' (March 1970), unpublished.

with which factors are used. Arrow advances 'the hypothesis that technical change can be ascribed to experience', and 'at any moment of time, the new capital goods incorporate all the knowledge then available'.[27] By comparison the hypothesis proposed here is that experience in the installation and starting up of new investment projects creates a stock of skills that facilitate installation and start up. These skills can be augmented by formal education but only at marginal rates of substitution between education and experience which are limited by the requirement for some minimum amount of experience. There is also some degree of transfer of other production skills to this particular type of skill.[28] Again, however, the trade-off rates are decreasing. Finally, there are diminishing returns to this stock of specialized skills which assist in bringing new investment projects to new maturity. It is hypothesized that these generate the absorptive capacity limits.

ABSORPTIVE CAPACITY AND MATURATION PHENOMENA IN A LINEAR PROGRAMMING MODEL

A little modelling will help to clarify the nature and significance of the absorptive capacity hypotheses advanced above. The model to be used for this purpose is a multi-sectoral, inter-temporal programming model developed for long-term economic policy investigations. As pointed out above, there has been a particular concern with absorptive capacity constraints by linear programming model planning builders because of the potential of such constraints for controlling the extreme flip-flop behaviour of the solutions to such models. The investigation in a linear programming model of the hypotheses proposed above is, therefore, an extension of that intellectual impetus. The structure of the entire linear programming model is relatively complex. None the less it will turn out that the aspects of the absorptive capacity hypotheses which have been proposed here can be formulated in a relatively simple manner in this context.

The linear programming model used to illustrate the maturation version of the absorptive capacity hypothesis is an extension of one previously constructed by Eckaus and Parikh.[29] Since it has been

[27] Arrow, op. cit., pp. 156, 157.

[28] It might also be argued that individuals vary in their potential effectiveness in bringing new projects into production because that type of activity demands particular personality attributes of adaptability and judgement with which individuals are endowed in different degrees.

[29] Eckaus and Parikh, op. cit. The particular model used from the Eckaus-Parikh book is the Guidepath Model presented in chapter 5.

described extensively before, it will be outlined here with detail provided only in the formulation of the absorptive capacity constraints. The model maximizes an objective function subject to a variety of technical and behavioural constraints intended to reflect the economic structure. The scarce factors are capital, foreign exchange, and, in one sector, land. The time horizon of the model is eighteen years divided into six periods of three years each. There are eleven separate producing sectors. The objective function of the model is the discounted sum of aggregate consumption over the plan period. The sectoral composition of the aggregate consumption is determined by arc elasticities relating sectoral consumption and aggregate consumption. The fundamental distribution constraint requires that the total supply as determined by output and imports in each period be greater than or equal to the total uses of each sector's product.

Intermediate input requirements are determined by a conventional, fixed coefficient input-output technology with one exception. The exception is the agricultural sector in which there are two alternative activities, each of which has its own fixed coefficient vector of input coefficients. Deliveries for inventory stocks in each sector are determined in each period as fixed proportions of the actual increase in output which will take place in the subsequent period. Only a few sectors deliver output which can be used for capital formation and those deliveries must take place one period (three years) in anticipation of the availability of the capital to subsequently produce output. Deliveries of each sector for government consumption and exports are specified exogenously.

Since capital is a composite good in the model, its components can and do depreciate at different rates. Depreciation is assumed to be of the one-horse shay type and the capital lifetimes are specified exogenously to be greater than the planning period for all components. Depreciation is, therefore, exogenous to the model but the decision is made within the model as to whether or not the depreciation will be made good. As with new capital stock it is assumed that capital produced in one period for replacement purposes becomes productive only in the next period.

Imports are required in some sectors. The amounts of 'non-competitive' imports are determined by fixed import coefficients multiplying sectoral output levels. Competitive imports can substitute for domestic production to some extent as limited by constraints. There is a balance of payments constraint which must be met in each period which requires that total imports be less than total exports plus a specified amount of net foreign capital inflow.

The initial conditions are the amounts of capital stocks available and in process at the beginning of the plan period. The terminal conditions require that enough capacity be on hand and in process at the end of the plan period to maintain an exogenously specified rate of growth of consumption from the level achieved in the last plan period. In addition capacity must be on hand and in process at the end of the plan period to maintain exogenously specified rates of growth of output for each of the exogenously specified vectors of government consumption and exports. The post-terminal requirements for imports are determined by a fixed coefficient relation with output.

The capital capacity constraints, which are one of the central features of the model, were originally formulated in the conventional manner:

$$(1) \qquad b(t) X(t) \le K(t), \qquad \text{for } t = 1, \ldots T,$$

where $b(t)$ is a diagonal matrix of capital-output ratios, $X(t)$ is the vector of sectoral outputs, $K(t)$ is the vector of sectoral capital stocks in each sector and t indicates the period. The accumulation of capital is recorded by the accounting relation:

$$(2) \quad K(t-1) = K(t-1) + Z(t) + R(t+1) - V(T), \quad \text{for } t+1, \ldots T+2.$$

In this relationship $Z(t+1)$ is a vector composed of the new additions to capital capacity in each sector in period $(t+1)$. $R(t+1)$ is a vector of depreciated capital capacities which have been restored and become effective in period $(t+1)$, and $V(t+1)$ is a vector of the capacities lost in each sector due to the depreciation of some component of the capital stock.

The solutions to the model unless constrained appropriately show the typical flip-flop behaviour previously described. Exogenously stipulated constraints were used to prevent this behaviour. One set of constraints required monotonic growth in consumption during the plan period from a specified initial level, and in some versions the growth was required to be at increasing rates. This tended to discourage the delaying of consumption to the end of the plan period and, thus, to prevent extreme behaviour. The constraint could be rationalized as an expression of a form of social preference. Another type of constraint used to control the flip-flop tendency was a linear

savings constraint with a fixed marginal propensity to save. This has
a stronger appeal as a behavioural relation. It effectively offset the
flip-flop tendency as it prevented the relatively high rates of new
investment which are associated with extreme results.

A Piece-wise Linear Approximation to a Non-linear Absorptive Capacity Constraint

A set of piece-wise linear constraints were formulated to approximate
a non-linear relation which would embody the previous rationalization of absorptive capacity constraints as a reflection of maturation
processes. It was also necessary to modify the production constraints
and output and capital accounting constraints. A distinction is now
made between 'old' capital which is assumed to be fully-seasoned

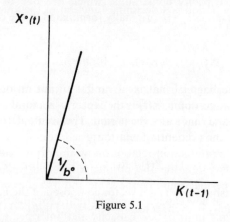

Figure 5.1

and to be operated by a fully-trained labour force and 'new' capital
which requires tuning and is operated by a labour force which has
not completely adapted to its new functions. In fact, there are several
types of new capital each distinguished by a successively lower
productivity. The amount of each type of new capital is constrained
so that as investment increases in each period the productivity of
successive increments falls. The output from the old capital and from
each type of the new capital in each sector is the same though it
is related by a different coefficient to the capacity which generates it.

The production constraints are embodied in the inequalities (3.0)
through (3.3) and are shown in Figure 5.1 and Figure 5.2. Figure 5.1
shows the constant productivity of the 'old' capital and Figure 5.2
embodies the assumption that the productivity of new capacity

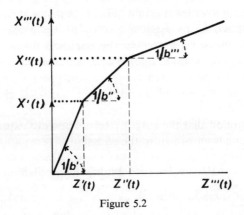

Figure 5.2

installed in any period is a declining function of the amount of new capacity which is created.

(3.0) $b^\circ X^\circ(t) \leqslant K(t-1)$ $\qquad$ (3.2) $b'' X''(t) \leqslant Z''(t)$

(3.1) $b' X'(t) \leqslant Z'(t)$ $\qquad$ (3.3) $b''' X'''(t) \leqslant Z'''(t)$.

Units of new capacity installed up to $Z'(t)$ have an output-capital ratio of $1/b'(t)$. Units of installed new capacity in amounts above $Z'(t)$ and less than $Z''(t)$ have an output-capital ratio of $1/b''(t)$, and so on. This formulation is different from the usual non-linear diminishing returns to scale production relation in an important way, however. In the customary relation the productivity of all the capacity installed in any period would be the same and its value would depend on the amount of new capacity created. In this formulation there are, so to speak, 'first' units of new capacity and 'intermediate' units and 'last' units and each has a successively lower productivity. Unlike some previous formulations of the absorptive capacity constraint there are no absolute limits to new investment in any period. But the greater the amount of new investment, the lower its overall initial productivity.

The bounds, $\overline{Z'(t)}$ and $\overline{Z''(t)}$, determine the range over which each of the capital-output ratios b', b'', and b''' hold. Their stipulation is shown in inequalities

(4) $\qquad\qquad\qquad Z'(t) \leqslant \overline{Z'(t)}$

(4.1) $\qquad\qquad\qquad Z''(t) \leqslant \overline{Z''(t)} - \overline{Z'(t)}$.

There is an important and substantive question as to the manner in which these boundaries should be set. It might be argued that the maturation processes are laws of nature which makes these boundaries constants. It would be more appealing to make the boundaries vary with output or time. The last approach was the one adopted in the solutions to be reported upon below. But it would not be argued that the particular device used was more than an expedient which was adopted to take account of the likelihood that some change in the bounds do occur.

The assumption that the output from all units of capacity new or old is the same is embodied in the equation

$$(5) \qquad X(t) = X^\circ(t) + X'(t) + X''(t) + X'''(t).$$

This requires some justification as it is not in general likely to be true. New capacity will often differ in the quality of its product as well as its productivity. Newly-installed steel-rolling mills, for example, will not only have a lower rate of output during their tuning-up period and while their labour force is being trained, but the quality of their output will generally be lower than will be achieved later. There will be a higher proportion of output with surface defects, for example, and other quality deficiencies which force sales at lower prices than first quality products.

The total amount of new capacity installed in any period is $Z(t)$ and that is the sum of the amounts of the capacity which are assigned to each of the productivity ranges. This is shown in equation

$$(6) \qquad Z(t) = Z'(t) + Z''(t) + Z'''(t).$$

This formulation guarantees that the same inputs are required to produce the new capital whatever the productivity range in which it falls. There is no specification in the model that new capacity should 'first' be assigned to the $Z'(t)$ range and finally to the $Z'''(t)$ range. But the optimizing principle in the model will automatically take care of that assignment as it will want to obtain the maximum productivity from the newly-installed capacity in each period and only that assignment will permit this to be achieved.

Finally, it is necessary to specify what happens to the productivity of the new capacity as it ages or is used. In this model it is assumed that one period is required for the new capacity to become 'seasoned' and to acquire the higher productivity of the older capacity. In the background of the model and completely undescribed are the patterns of change in the productivity of the labour force. Implicitly it is assumed that labour is never a constraint and will always adjust as it must, so that only capital is constraining in the production relations.

The time required for the seasoning of the new capacity is also assumed to be the same for the first, intermediate and last units of the new capacity created in each period. This is shown in equality

(7) $$K(t) = K(t-1) + Z(t-1) + R(t) - V(t).$$

There are several unique and important aspects of these relationships. First, it means that the relatively low productivity of new capacity is not a permanent feature of it as is the case in the Dorfman production relationship embodied in the Kendrick–Taylor model. The learning and adaptation requirements of new investment mean that new projects have a relatively low productivity. But, as the 'tuning' and 'seasoning' proceed, productivity rises. There are, in effect, short-run diminishing returns to the scale of new investment even though all factors may expand in the same proportions. There are also long-run constant returns to scale and there are no 'permanent' effects on productivity due to the fact that some capacity is created during a period of a high rate of investment and some capacity is created during periods of lower investment rates. This is probably more consistent with the weight of the available information as to the prevalence of constant or even increasing returns to scale. However, the evidence has not been examined with this effect in mind and should not be interpreted as by any means conclusive.

The formulation in (7) is probably deficient as a description of reality, however, in that the time required for seasoning is the same for all of the new capacity. The rationalization of this formulation of the absorptive capacity constraints would be followed more consistently if the time required for seasoning of the best of the new capacity were shorter than the time required for the seasoning of the least productive of the new capacity. Partial justification for the formulation chosen, however, is that the length of the time period, at three years, is relatively long.

It might also be argued persuasively that the gain in productivity of new capacity over time should be a function of its use rather than of time. That would also be more consistent with the learning rationale. It would also be a more complex specification. Moreover, since in general new capacity will not be created unless it is to be used, the alternative formulations may not lead to substantially different results in the solution of the model.

There are elements of truth in the Dorfman production relation, however. As pointed out above, if the argument as to the importance of learning is extended to the process of designing new capacity, that process may also deteriorate with the rate of new investment. That could result in permanently lower productivity of new capacity as the investment rate increases. It would be possible to extend the constraint and accounting relations above to embody the Dorfman effect in the production function. To do that, however, it would be necessary to add a permanent accounting of each type of capital in each sector with each different level of productivity.

THE SIGNIFICANCE OF THE ABSORPTIVE CAPACITY CONSTRAINTS IN LINEAR PROGRAMMING MODEL SOLUTIONS

In this section some illustrative characteristics of solutions to the multi-sectoral inter-temporal linear programming model will be presented which embody the effects of absorptive capacity constraints described in the relations (3) to (7) above. Only a few alternative solutions were computed for the model with these particular constraints as a computational budget constraint limited the range of the explorations which could be carried out. In any case no empirical research results were available on the absorptive capacity constraints and no new research was carried out to estimate the parameters of the absorptive capacity constraints. So the only feasible objective was to generate a few alternative patterns which would illustrate the range of results possible.

The data used in the model solutions are the same as employed in the Guidepath Models presented in Eckaus and Parikh.[30] Reference can be made there for details should the reader be interested. The data, though taken from Indian sources, has limited relevance to India's current situation. The model solutions, therefore, should not be interpreted as if they indicated realistic development alternatives for India. To emphasize this point the results will be presented in the form of index numbers rather than in Indian rupees.

Solutions were calculated for six alternative specifications of production and required consumption growth and savings constraints with a linear objective function. The alternative specifications were:

S—1 Linear production constraints, no constraints on consumption growth path, post-terminal growth requirements on consumption of 8% per year.

[30] Eckaus and Parikh, op. cit.

S—2 Linear production constraints, consumption required to grow between successive periods at least at 5%, 6%, 7%, 8%, 9%, post-terminal consumption growth at 12·5% per year.

S—3 Linear production constraints, uniform minimum consumption growth constraints of 5% per year, marginal savings rate constrained to be less than 30%, post-terminal growth at 8% per year.

S—4 Non-linear absorptive capacity constraints, no consumption growth constraints, capital output ratios (b's) determined in relation to originally specified ratios, b°, as follows (see Figure 5.2):

$b' = b^\circ$, for all sectors;

$b'' = \left(\dfrac{1}{0\cdot8}\right) b^\circ$ for all sectors, except

$b''_6 = \left(\dfrac{1}{0\cdot9}\right) b^\circ_6$

$b''_9 = \left(\dfrac{1}{0\cdot9}\right) b^\circ_9$

$b''_{10} = 1\cdot0\, b^\circ_{10}$

$b''_{11} = 1\cdot0\, b^\circ_{11}$

$b''_{12} = 1\cdot0\, b_{12}{}^\circ;$

$b''' = \left(\dfrac{1}{0\cdot6}\right) b^\circ$ for all sectors except

$b'''_6 = \left(\dfrac{1}{0\cdot9}\right) b_6 \qquad\qquad b'''_{11} = 1\cdot0\, b_{11}$

$b'''_9 = \left(\dfrac{1}{0\cdot8}\right) b_9 \qquad\qquad b''''_{12} = 1\cdot0\, b_{12}$

$b'''_{10} = 1\cdot0\, b_{10}.$

The boundaries, $\overline{Z'(t)}$ and $\overline{Z''(t)}$, (see Figure 5.2) were set in each sector by calculating the levels of capital stock which could be reached in each period by 6% and 9% annual growth rates from the original capital endowments.

S—5 Specifications as for S—4, except that:

$b' = \left(\dfrac{1}{0\cdot8}\right) b^\circ$ for all sectors;

$$b'' = \left(\frac{1}{0.6}\right) b° \quad \text{for all sectors;}$$

$$b''' = \left(\frac{1}{0.4}\right) b° \quad \text{for all sectors.}$$

The boundaries, $\overline{Z'(t)}$ and $\overline{Z''(t)}$, are set in each sector by calculating the levels of capital stock which would be reached in each period by 2% and 4% annual growth rates from the original capital endowments. Post-terminal consumption growth set at 4% per year.

S—6 Specifications as for S—4, except that

$$b' = \left(\frac{1}{0.9}\right) b° \quad \text{for all sectors;}$$

$$b'' = \left(\frac{1}{0.8}\right) b° \quad \text{for all sectors;}$$

$$b''' = \left(\frac{1}{0.7}\right) b° \quad \text{for all sectors.}$$

The boundaries, $\overline{Z'(t)}$ and $\overline{Z''(t)}$, are set in each sector by calculating the levels of capital stock which would be reached in each period by 3% and 5% annual growth rates from the original capital stock endowments.

One of the salient and striking features of the multi-sectoral inter-temporal linear programming models is the abundant detail in which the optimal solution is described. Not only are the objective function values provided but also the sectoral output levels and investment levels are determined period by period. From this information a complete set of annual national income accounts which are consistent with the optimal solution can be developed for the economy. Since the general character of these solutions and their detail has been described elsewhere, only the time path of aggregate consumption will be presented here as well as a few other salient features of the alternative solutions.

The solutions to the model unless effectively constrained show the typical flip-flop behaviour previously mentioned. The time path of consumption generated by solution S—1 with linear objective and production functions and without growth or savings constraints is shown in Figure 5.3 by the line S—1. In this solution the model was

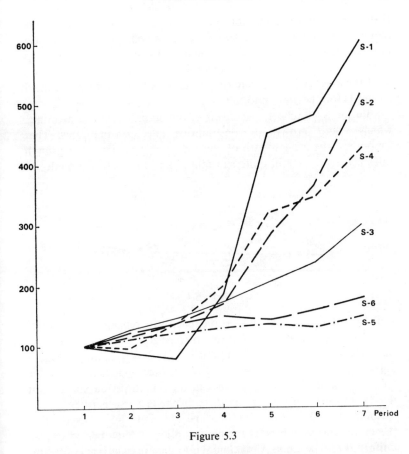

Figure 5.3

not even constrained to maintain consumption above some minimum level. In the solution, advantage is taken of the freedom to lower consumption in any period. This is done from period one to two and from two to three in order to devote more resources to investment accumulation. The great increase in consumption comes in the fifth period rather in the last period. That reflects the burden placed on the last period by the requirement that the solution provide enough capital to maintain the post-terminal growth of consumption at a rate of at least 8 per cent over that level of consumption achieved in the last period. If the solution had delayed the great increase in consumption until the last period, the investment requirements for post terminal growth would have been even more onerous.

Solution S—1 is the archetype of the extreme and 'wildly implausible' results which can emerge from linear programming models unless they are otherwise constrained. One other aspect of this type of result is shown in Figure 5.4 which traces the savings rates which are generated by the solutions over time. In solution S—1 the average savings rate rises as high as 54 per cent in the third period before beginning to fall.

Solution S—2 reflects the effects of the 'monotonicity constraints' which require growth in consumption at increasing rates. That 'smoothes' the growth path of consumption over time. The growth rates achieved are still quite substantial and the system provides as

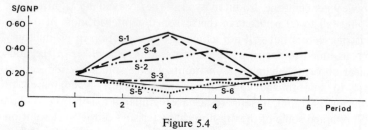

Figure 5.4

well for the creation of domestic capacity to replace the complete loss of foreign aid at the end of the third period. There may well still be elements of implausibility in Solution S—2 as indicated in Figure 5.4 which traces the savings rates. The average savings rates for this solution rise to almost 40 per cent in the fourth period and do not decline by very much from that level in the last two periods.

Solution S—3 has the same set of specifications as S—3 except that the minimum growth rates for consumption in each period are set uniformly at 5 per cent. A maximum marginal savings rate constraint is imposed which was set at 30 per cent, still relatively high by historical standards. The effect of the savings constraint as shown in Figure 5.3 is to smooth and lower the consumption growth path as compared to S—1 and S—2. The inter-period consumption growth rates are lower, too; the highest is achieved between the fourth and fifth period when the annual rate of growth of consumption reached 7·5 per cent.

A savings constraint, though realistic and justifiable as a behaviour relationship, is also a 'black box'. It is the net effect of the interaction of some more fundamental set of preferences and production possibilities. The stipulation of absorptive capacity constraints is an attempt to stimulate the production possibilities in a more realistic manner.

In solution S—4 the productivity of new capital in its first period of availability falls in successive tranches to different levels depending on the sector. It was assumed that in all sectors capital stocks could grow as much as 6 per cent per year with no fall in the productivity of newly-available capital stock as compared to the older seasoned capital. However, the productivity of the additional capital provided by growth from 6 to 9 per cent per year would be only 80 per cent of the seasoned capital in most of the industrial sectors. In the service sectors the fall in productivity with the growth of capital would be less as specified above. If the capital stock should grow at a rate above 9 per cent, the productivity of the newly available capital stock would fall to 60 per cent of the seasoned capital in most of the industrial sectors but still not as much of a reduction in productivity was assumed to occur in the service sectors. The effect of the non-linear absorptive capacity constraints was to somewhat reduce and also to smooth the consumption growth path as compared to solution S—1 and, in some respects as compared to solution S—2. It still retained some of the flip-flop characteristics of the S—1 solution as can be seen in Figure 5.4 in which the associated savings rates are plotted. They follow the general path of the unconstrained, all around linear solution S—1. The savings rates for solution S—4 do not, however, reach such high levels as in S—1. That indicates that the solution S—4 not only reflects the lower effective productivity of new capital but also, in such circumstances, there is a tendency within the solution not to allocate quite so many resources to investment.

Solution S—5 has distinctly lower levels specified for the productivity of new investment as described above. That productivity falls from 80 to 60 to 40 per cent in the successive tranches. Note, however, that the 'marginal productivity' of the new investment is not 40 per cent but is the weighted sum of 80, 60 and 40 per cent with the weights being the amount of investment which is undertaken in each range. A good deal of investment occurs at the higher 'marginal productivities': enough for 2 and 4 per cent rates of growth in the capital stock respectively. The effect of this new specification of the parameters of the absorptive capacity constraints is quite striking when solution S—5 is compared with the other solutions. The overall growth in consumption achieved in the six periods, amounting to eighteen years, is only about 32 per cent or 1·6 per cent per year on the average. That is not the result of a high time preference. The objective function is still the linear one used on the other solutions. The low growth is the result of the lower productivity of capital. It should be stressed, however, that the productivity of capital is lower only in the initial period in which it becomes available. There are, by assumption, long-run constant returns to scale and there is complete foresight and flexibility within the model. None the less the overall results are much lower.

In solution S—6 the productivity of new capital in successive tranches is not so low as in solution S—5 and the range over which the higher productivities prevail is larger. As a result higher levels of consumption are achieved in each period. Overall a growth of 59 per cent in consumption is achieved or an annual rate of about 2·9 per cent. This is much closer to the consumption growth rates actually achieved in the developing countries. So in this restricted sense the results are 'realistic'.

This is an important sense, however. The results show that even with long-run linearity or constant returns to scale in production and with linearity in the objective function, it is possible to simulate plausible-looking time paths for consumption. This is done by stipulating absorptive capacity – or maturation capacity – constraints which operate only in the short run on newly-available capital.

CONCLUSION

The argument of this paper has been tentative and illustrative rather than definitive. That is in part due to the nature of the economic phenomenon being discussed and, in part, due to the nature of the analytic tool which was used.

The existence of limitations to the productivity of new investment which are related to the rate of investment have been noted by Paul Rosenstein-Rodan and other development economists. The phenomenon appears to be so real that under the name of 'absorptive capacity' it is readily recognized. It has even been embodied in programming and optimal control models either in the form of a limit on the amount of new investment or as a permanent reduction in the productivity of new investment which depends on its rate. In spite of its apparent recognizability the sources of the absorptive capacity limits have not been investigated thoroughly and little, if any, empirical research has been conducted. In this paper an hypothesis has been developed and advanced which identifies the absorptive capacity phenomenon with the limited adaptability of labour and the processes of maturation of labour and capital which are inevitably associated with new investment. This capacity can be increased but its increase itself requires experience with new investment projects. For a variety of reasons the capacity can also be lost. According to the maturation hypothesis the higher the rate of investment the lower the level of productivity of the new investment. With time and with use, however, new investment projects can reach the level of productivity of seasoned projects. Thus, the limits are better described not as absorptive capacity limits but as maturation capacity constraints. They reflect the ability of the economy to bring new projects to the 'rated' levels of productivity which are expected of mature projects.

To return to anthropomorphic analogy as well as terminology: economists have conventionally assumed that bringing new investment projects into production was something like the birth and maturation of many insects and some mammals. The period of adolescence or maturation was so short as to warrant its being ignored for most purposes. On the other hand, birth and adolescence in humans are major features of the growth process. They must be taken into account not only to understand the behaviour of individuals but in order to project the potential for growth of an entire population. It is suggested here that the life history of investment projects has similar elements.

The absorptive capacity or maturation capacity constraints were embodied in a multi-sectoral inter-temporal programming model to illustrate their possible significance. The results show clearly that the constraints are capable of modulating the excessive flip-flop behaviour which characterizes the solutions of such models when not otherwise constrained.

The maturation capacity phenomenon which limits the productivity of new investment can also be considered as one type of adaptation or learning phenomenon. Analogous patterns have been recognized in other areas of economics. The 'infant industry' argument for tariffs, the recognition of the difficulties which firms have in penetrating new markets both in domestic and foreign trade, reflect similar processes in which the initial levels of performance are lower than the final levels which are expected to be achieved. The price adjustment processes in markets and the development of consumer choice are other areas in which learning and adaptation are important. These processes of adjustment are particularly significant for developing nations. It is important to understand the long-run growth prospects for such countries but it is also important to understand how the long-run growth is achieved through a series of short-run adjustments. The short-term features of production processes, as the analysis above has demonstrated, can have a determining influence on the long-run growth path which a country may follow.

CHAPTER 6

A Model of Growth of Capitalism in a Dual Agrarian Economy[1]

P. K. BARDHAN

I

The standard dual economy models in the development literature concentrate on the inter-relationships between an advanced industrial sector and a traditional agricultural sector and analyse the implications of essentially factor-market imperfections and institutional constraints for industrial growth. Far less common are models[2] that focus on the dual economy within the agricultural sector, although the problem has been extensively discussed in the descriptive literature on late nineteenth-century Russian and present-day Indian agriculture as well as in that on plantations in peasant agriculture of different countries in Asia, Africa and Latin America. The coexistence of peasant and capitalist agriculture is the starting-point of this paper and we have worked out a simple model of analysing growth of agrarian capitalism in such an economy.

There are many ways of defining the characteristics of a capitalist farm; some emphasize the extent of dependence on the market, some the pattern of investment, but in general we shall follow the Marxian criterion of distinguishing a capitalist from a pre-capitalist economy by a form of production organization in which labour-power is a commodity. In other words, a capitalist farm is primarily dependent on wage-labour whereas a family farm utilizes labour only of the

[1] Helpful comments from A. K. Sen and T. N. Srinivasan are gratefully acknowledged.

[2] See, however, A. K. Sen, 'Peasants and Dualism with or without Surplus Labour', *Journal of Political Economy*, vol. 74 (October 1966), no. 5; K. P. Anderson, *Peasant and Capitalist Agriculture in the Developing Country*, unpublished Ph.D. thesis at MIT (1968); D. Kumar, 'Technical Change and Dualism within Agriculture in India', *Journal of Development Studies*, vol. 6 (1970).

family members. It is often claimed that in many economies where both these types of farms coexist there is a substantial gap between the market wage rate at which the capitalist farm hires labour and the real cost of labour (that is, marginal product) on the family farm. In so far as this wage gap does not reflect any higher efficiency or any higher social cost of wage labour, it is a pure distortion in the labour market which works against the capitalist farm. Sometimes it is even suggested – Lewis-like – that the peasant leaving his family to work outside loses his average product on the family farm and the capitalist must pay him a wage rate that compensates for this.[3] On such grounds the family farm seems to have distinct advantages in the allocation of labour, as opposed to the capitalist farm.[4]

On the other hand, the family farm, typically operating a small-sized holding,[5] often faces a distorted credit market. For credit needs to buy production inputs, the small peasant has to go to the village money-lender who usually gives loans on the basis of the security of land. The smaller the size of land the borrower owns, the costlier are the terms of credit for him. The money-lender, of course, wants to reduce the risk of default, but even apart from risks he has a larger bargaining power with the small peasant to be able to dictate terms. This imperfection in the credit market thus tends to cancel the differential advantage of the family farm given to it by the labour-market imperfection. Report after report to the Government of India, Ministry of Food and Agriculture, has singled out credit as the major constraint on the small farmer's ability to buy the new inputs (like improved seeds, chemical fertilizers, pesticides, etc.) and to take part in the programme of technological breakthrough in agriculture.

Since capitalist farms have in general a higher propensity to save and invest, the impact of credit market imperfection tends to be larger and larger over time. Through higher savings the capitalist

[3] This, of course, assumes that the out-going peasant cannot rent out or sell his share in the land held by the joint family and also that the family refuses to subsidize him with remittances.

[4] As Sen, op. cit., points out, in such a world capitalist and family farms with different equilibrium labour costs coexist because of restrictions (in the form of protective tenancy and rent-regulating legislation in most countries) on the capitalist's tendency to rent his land out to the peasants with higher marginal productivity of land.

[5] In India the small farms are predominantly family-based. According to 1961 Census data in India, farms operating less than 1 acre use 93·84 per cent of the total agricultural workers from own family members, for farms operating between 1 to 2·49 acres it is 90·41 per cent and for farms operating between 2·5 to 4·9 acres it is 87·42 per cent.

farmer has an increasing ability to self-finance his purchase of modernizing inputs or through investment in land improvement or in buying additional land he raises the value of his collaterals and gets cheaper and cheaper credit compared to the small family farmer. The capitalist farm's differential advantage on this account is thus cumulative and it tends to dominate over time the purely static advantage the family farm has in its use of labour. As a consequence, capitalism grows and the relative income distribution tends to go against the small family farmers over time. This is the central point of the model in this paper. It is a fairly simple point, but still worth making, not merely because it is a matter of some practical significance in the development of land relations in many countries today but also because in the theoretical literature on development much is made of the static labour-market distortion and far less attention is given[6] to the dynamic impact of capital-market imperfections.

II

Suppose the family farm's production function is given by

$$(1) \qquad Q_1 = [B(N_1)A_1]^\alpha L_1^\beta$$

where Q_1 is agricultural output (a single homogenous commodity) on the family farm, L_1 is family labour devoted to the farm, N_1 is the amount of technological inputs (say, chemical fertilizers) used on the farm and A_1 is the amount of land-capital the farm has. In this model we do not distinguish between land and capital and one can invest in increasing the supply of both (in the case of land this means that one can invest in improving land with irrigation, drainage, etc., and thus increase its effective supply). It is assumed that inputs like fertilizers which add to the soil nutrients act as a kind of land-augmenting technical improvement factor.[7] The Cobb–Douglas form of the production function is taken as a simplifying device. We also assume the following restrictions on the production function:

$$(2) \qquad B'(N_1) > 0, \quad B''(N_1) < 0, \quad 1 \geqq \alpha + \beta.$$

[6] A major exception is Sen, op. cit., pp. 443–4, where he briefly notes the distorted capital market as a 'qualification' and that the allocational advantage of peasant farms 'is a purely static one related to the utilization of *given* resources'.

[7] Fertilizers are here described as a factor shifting the production function of traditional agriculture. Nothing is lost if we, instead, describe them as just a third factor of production. The special land-augmenting form in which fertilizers enter the production function is also not necessary for our subsequent results.

In other words, there are positive but diminishing returns to fertilizer use in the technical improvement function $B(N_1)$ and there are non-increasing returns to scale in the production function. We might briefly comment on the latter assumption. It has been argued that in agriculture, particularly in non-mechanical cultivation, technological economies of scale are not very substantial,[8] whereas diseconomies of scale with respect to supervision and co-ordination are supposed to set in fairly early (particularly in paddy cultivation, large farms are difficult to manage).[9] Since in our model big capitalist farms ultimately come to dominate the small family farms, let us at the moment stack the cards against the former and in our assumptions (2) we therefore do not rule out diminishing returns to scale.

The farm has to pay for the chemical fertilizers it uses. If fertilizers are bought with credit and if, as we mentioned earlier, credit is cheaper or dearer according to the size of land-capital the borrower has, one simple way of summarizing the whole situation would be to write the price per unit of fertilizer as:

$$P_n = p(A_1), \quad p'(A_1) < 0.$$

It is as if the larger the amount of land-capital one has the cheaper is the rate at which one can get fertilizers. In other words, the imperfection in the credit market is directly reflected in an imperfection in the fertilizer market since in this model fertilizer is the only commodity bought with credit.

So the net output of the family farm is

(4) $$q_1 = [B(N_1)A_1]^\alpha L_1^\beta - p(A_1)N_1.$$

Similarly, the net output of the capitalist farm is

(5) $$q_2 = [B(N_2)A_2]^\alpha L_2^\beta - p(A_2)N_2 - WL_2.$$

The subscript 2 refers to the capitalist farm, as subscript 1 refers to the family farm. We are assuming that both types of farms have identical production functions. L_2 is the amount of labour *hired* by

[8] See, for example, T. W. Schultz, *Transforming Traditional Agriculture* (1964).
[9] This is particularly serious for the new varieties of seeds. For example, a recent expert committee on Intensive Agricultural District Programme in a report to the government of India (Government of India, Ministry of Food and Agriculture, *Modernizing Indian Agriculture*, Report on the Intensive Agricultural District Programme (1960–8), vol. 1) observed: 'The high-yielding varieties of rice require so much close supervision that any farmer with more than roughly 7 hectares of land under these varieties is said to be under a handicap.'

the capitalist farm (for simplification, we assumed that nobody in the capitalist's family works) at the market wage rate W.

Let us suppose that labour hired on the capitalist farm comes only from the family farm (we are ignoring landless labourers in this model).[10] The family farm uses L_1 amount of labour on the farm and sends away L_2 amount of labour to work on the capitalist farm. If we ignore population growth[11] and if, without loss of generality, we take the total labour supply of family farmers as unity, we can write:

$$(6) \qquad L_1 + L_2 = 1.$$

On the allocation between L_1 and L_2 let us suppose, as we have mentioned before, that labour will be supplied to the capitalist farm only if the wage paid is equal to the *average* (net) product of labour on the family farm, that is,

$$(7) \qquad W = \frac{q_1}{L_1}.$$

III

We assume that capitalist farmers devote their savings to increase the supply of land-capital so that

$$(8) \qquad \dot{A}_2 = s\,Y_2.$$

where Y_2 is income of capitalist farmers (which is equal to their net output or profits, q_2) and s is the constant proportion of income saved.

For simplification, family farmers are assumed to consume all of their income (income from cultivation as well as wage income), so that A_1 is constant; without loss of generality, assume this constant to be unity. Define $p(A_1)$ as $p°$. Then (4) may be rewritten as:

$$(9) \qquad q_1 = [B(N_1)]^\alpha L_1^\beta - p° N_1.$$

The family farm uses fertilizers, N_1, to the extent that it maximizes q_1 such that

$$(10) \qquad \alpha[B(N_1)]^{\alpha-1} L_1^\beta [B'(N_1)] - p° = 0.$$

[10] According to National Sample Survey (19th Round) data in India, landless agricultural labour households constituted only 12·2 per cent of the total number of rural households in 1964–5.

[11] We have checked that our subsequent results are unaffected if we allow for population growing at a fixed percentage rate.

Similarly, the capitalist farm uses fertilizers, N_2, to the extent that it maximizes q_2 such that

(11) $$\alpha A_2^\alpha [B(N_2)]^{\alpha-1} (1-L_1)^\beta [B'(N_2)] - p(A_2) = 0.$$

In (11), $(1-L_1)$ is substituted for L_2 from (6). The capitalist farm also chooses how much labour to hire to maximize q_2 such that:

(12) $$\beta [A_2 B(N_2)]^\alpha (1-L_1)^{\beta-1} - W = 0.$$

Using (7) and (9), (12) may be rewritten as

(13) $$\beta [A_2 B(N_2)]^\alpha (1-L_1)^{\beta-1} L_1 - [B(N_1)]^\alpha L_1^\beta + p^\circ N_1 = 0.$$

(10), (11) and (13) give us three equations to determine the variables N_1, N_2 and L_1, given the stock of A_2.

Let us now analyse these three equations. The underlying 3×3 Jacobian matrix $[a_{ij}]$ is characterized by the following elements:

$$a_{11} = -\alpha [B(N_1)]^{\alpha-2} L_1^\beta \{(1-\alpha)[B'(N_1)]^2 - [B(N_1)][B''(N_1)]\}$$
$$a_{12} = 0 = a_{21} = a_{31}$$
$$a_{13} = \alpha\beta [B(N_1)]^{\alpha-1} [B'(N_1)] L_1^{\beta-1}$$
$$a_{22} = -\alpha A_2^\alpha [B(N_2)]^{\alpha-2} (1-L_1)^\beta \{(1-\alpha)[B'(N_2)]^2 - [B(N_2)] [B''(N_2)]\}$$
$$a_{23} = -\alpha\beta A_2^\alpha [B(N_2)]^{\alpha-1} [B'(N_2)] (1-L_1)^{\beta-1}$$
$$a_{32} = \alpha\beta A_2^\alpha [B(N_2)]^{\alpha-1} [B'(N_2)] (1-L_1)^{\beta-1} L_1$$
$$a_{33} = \beta A_2^\alpha [B(N_2)]^\alpha (1-L_1)^{\beta-2} (1-\beta L_1) - \beta [B(N_1)]^\alpha L_1^{\beta-1}.$$

Since $B'(N_i) > 0$ and $B''(N_i) < 0$, $i = 1,2$; $1 \geq \alpha+\beta$; and since from (6), $1 \geq L_i \geq 0$, it is easy to show with the help of (10) and (13) in evaluating a_{33}, that the Jacobian

(14) $$J = a_{11}(a_{22}a_{33} - a_{23} \cdot a_{32}) > 0$$

if the elasticity of the technical progress function $B(N_i)$ with respect to the use of fertilizers, N_i, is not greater than unity, that is,

$$\frac{B'(N_i)N_i}{B(N_i)} \leq 1.$$

We shall assume this condition to be satisfied.

Totally differentiating equations (10), (11) and (13) with respect to A_2, we can now write:

(15)
$$[a_{ij}] \begin{bmatrix} \dfrac{dN_1}{dA_2} \\[2mm] \dfrac{dN_2}{dA_2} \\[2mm] \dfrac{dL_1}{dA_2} \end{bmatrix} = [b_j]$$

where the elements in column vector $[b_j]$ are

$b_1 = 0$

$b_2 = -\alpha^2 A_2^{\alpha-1}[B(N_2)]^{\alpha-1}[B'(N_2)](1-L_1)^\beta + p'(A_2) < 0$
$\quad\quad\quad\quad\quad\quad$ since $p'(A_2) < 0$ by assumption.

$b_3 = -\alpha\beta A_2^{\alpha-1}[B(N_2)]^\alpha(1-L_1)^{\beta-1}L_1 < 0.$

Using Cramer's Rule we can now immediately solve for

(16) $$\frac{dL_1}{dA_2} = \frac{1}{J}[a_{11}(a_{22}b_3 - a_{32}b_2)] < 0$$

under our assumptions. This means that with savings and investment on the part of the capitalist farms as their land-capital A_2 grows, a larger and larger proportion of the labour supply available to the family farms is sucked into the capitalist system as wage-labour. Under the assumptions we have started with, capitalism inevitably erodes the domain of peasant agriculture. Essentially, in our model the two dynamic factors working in favour of capitalist farmers a) that capitalists invest in increasing the effective supply of land-capital whereas family farmers do not and b) that the former as a consequence get cheaper and cheaper credit relative to family farmers for buying inputs inducing technical progress – outweigh over time the two static factors working against capitalist farmers: a) the distortion in the labour market (caused by the market wage rate being equal to the average product of labour on family farms) and b) the possible case of diminishing returns to scale in large (and expanding) capitalist farms.

IV

What happens over time to income distribution between capitalists and peasants? We have seen that capitalist farms grow at the expense of family farms, but this may not immediately tell us that income distribution necessarily goes against the peasants. For, as capitalists prosper peasants may also share in that prosperity with an increasing fraction of them working as wage labourers on the capitalist farms and in the process raising the average product of labour on the family farms and hence the wage rate.

In order to reduce the amount of messy calculations in analysing this problem of income distribution, let us now adopt specific forms of two fairly general functions used in the earlier sections: we shall assume that

(17) $$B(N_i) = N_i^\theta, \ i = 1,2; \ 1 > \theta > 0$$

and

(18) $$p(A_i) = A_i^{-\varepsilon}, \ i = 1,2; \ \varepsilon > 0.$$

Both (17) and (18) satisfy all the restrictions imposed on the $B(N_i)$ and $p(A_i)$ functions in earlier sections. The special forms (17) and (18) only make them easier to handle.

We can now rewrite equations (10), (11) and (13) of the preceding section as

(19) $$\theta\alpha N_1^{\theta\alpha - 1} L_1^\beta = 1$$

(20) $$\theta\alpha A_2^{\varepsilon + \alpha} N_2^{\theta\alpha - 1} (1 - L_1)^\beta = 1$$

(21) $$\beta A_2^\alpha N_2^{\theta\alpha} (1 - L_1)^{\beta - 1} L_1 = L_1^\beta N_1^{\theta\alpha} - N_1.$$

The total income of peasants, Y_1, is equal to the net output on a family farm *plus* wage income of those hiring themselves out, so that

$$Y_1 = N_1^{\theta\alpha} L_1^{\beta - 1} - N_1 L_1^{-1}$$

(22)

$$= (1 - \theta\alpha)(\theta\alpha)^{\frac{\theta\alpha}{1 - \theta\alpha}} L_1^{\frac{-(1 - \theta\alpha - \beta)}{1 - \theta\alpha}}$$

where (19) has been used to evaluate N_1. Since we have seen in the preceding section that L_1 decreases over time as A_2 grows over time, it is easy to see from (22) that the absolute income of peasants *increases* over time.

But what happens to the peasants' income *relative* to that of capitalists? We have to look into the movement of Y_1/Y_2 over time.

Since $Y_2 = q_2$, we can now rewrite (5) with the help of (7), (9), (17), (18), (19), (20) and (21) so that after simplification

(23) $$Y_2 = \frac{(1 - \theta\alpha)}{\beta} (\theta\alpha)^{\frac{\theta\alpha}{1 - \theta\alpha}} (1 - \theta\alpha - \beta)(1 - L_1) L_1^{\frac{-(1 - \beta)}{1 - \theta\alpha}}.$$

It is not surprising that Y_2 is a decreasing function of L_1 and hence, by (16) an increasing function of A_2. Using (22) and (23),

$$(24) \qquad \frac{Y_1}{Y_2} = \frac{\beta}{(1-\theta\alpha-\beta)(1-L_1)}$$

Y_1/Y_2 is obviously an increasing function of L_1 and hence a decreasing function of A_2. So over time as capitalist farms accumulate land-capital, along with proletarianization of peasants, the *relative* income distribution shifts more and more *against* the peasants.

As we have mentioned before, what dominates in this model is the capitalists' superior investment behaviour and the imperfection in the capital or credit market (which is reflected in the market for inputs like fertilizers bought with credit). We have so far deliberately ignored another kind of imperfection that is very important in the real world, but if introduced in our model, it will only reinforce our conclusions. This is the imperfection in the market where agricultural output is sold. It is very common to observe in villages in countries like India that the price that the small family farmer receives for his output is significantly lower than that for the big capitalist farmer. The former has to sell his output in the immediate post-harvest period (when prices are at their lowest) out of liquidity needs or out of contractual obligation to the money-lender (quite often such sales to the money-lender-cum-trader are part of the debt contract) whereas the big farmer can wait and hold his output until prices are higher. As a matter of fact this is also ultimately due to the imperfection in the credit market that works against the small peasant.

We have also ignored in this model, by our assumption of a single homogenous agricultural commodity, the case of divergence of crop patterns between small family farms and big capitalist farms. The small family farmer, because of his precarious liquidity situation, is frequently obliged to diversify in crop pattern even when specialization would have been more profitable, whereas the capitalist farmer with access to cheaper credit can afford to reap the advantages of specialization. Once again this is evidently another way in which the credit market imperfection works against the small family farmer. Our conclusion about growth of capitalism and about income distribution will be reinforced if we take all these factors into account in our model.

CHAPTER 7

Short-Term Economic Policy[1]

J. CAUAS

INTRODUCTION

Modern planning has increasingly emphasized the design of short-term economic policy, in order to allow long-term goals to be achieved without destroying the stability of the system. Together with the use of economic indicators to decentralize the decision-making, this is a very recent development and the experience is rather scarce.

This paper describes the Chilean case from 1965–1969. Its purpose is to discuss the analytical procedures underlying the design of the economic policy, to analyse its content and goals and to compare them with the results achieved. The emphasis will be placed on the stabilization programme. Specifically, it will analyse the behaviour of cost pressures in the economy and will relate them to other aspects of the economic programme. Thus, this chapter is to be considered as the second part of a former paper of the author,[2] written when the policy began to be applied.

ANALYTICAL BACKGROUND

The analytical background for the stabilization policy was given by

[1] I am grateful for the insights I had through discussions with Professors Richard S. Eckaus, Arnold C. Harberger and Paul N. Rosenstein-Rodan. Moreover, I acknowledge the joint work in the design and implementation of policy with Ricardo Ffrench-Davis, Jorge Marshall, Carlos Massad Benjamín Mira, Sergio Molina and Cristián Ossa. I am specially grateful of the collaboration of Samuel Arancibia. Of course, the responsibility for the paper is mine.

[2] Jorge Cauas, 'Stabilization Policy – The Chilean Case', *Journal of Political Economy* (July–August 1970).

a model of the cost pressures on the economy.[3] This model allowed the study of the relationships between variations in prices of factors and increases in productivity with their impact on prices of products and their effects on the distribution of income.

The analysis of fiscal, monetary and foreign trade policy was based on the results of the model described. As inconsistencies did arise, the preliminary hypotheses were changed through successive stages, until the whole was consistent.

The costs model is based on an inter-industry analysis of prices. Taking into account the inter-relationship of all products, it led to the following equation:

$$(1) \qquad p = S(w - \beta)$$

where p: vector of variation of prices of products

w: vector of variation of prices of factors

β: vector of variation of productivity of factors

S: matrix of direct and indirect coefficients, with the property $Sl = l$ where l is a vector with unit components and proper dimension.

If a price index is defined:

$$(2) \qquad \bar{p} = \rho p$$

where: $\bar{p}$: weighted average of price variation

ρ: vector of weights with the property $\rho l = 1$

then

$$(3) \qquad \bar{p} = \mu w - \bar{\beta}$$

where $\bar{\beta}$: weighted average of the increases in productivity

μ: vector of weights with the property $\mu l = 1$.

If the analysis is done studying the effect of the variations in wages and salaries (L), payments to capital (K) and cost of imports (M), equation (3) can be written in scalar form:

$$(4) \qquad \bar{p} = \mu_L w_L + \mu_K w_K + \mu_M w_M - \beta.$$

Adopting for the purpose of the analysis the hypothesis that wage- and salary-earners tend to think in money terms, and capital-earners and the authorities responsible for the cost of imports think in real terms, the following relations are obtained.

[3] Cauas, op. cit.

(5)
$$w_K = p + \alpha_K$$

$$w_M = t$$

$$t = p + \alpha_M$$

where α_K: real variation of income of capital
t: variation of the rate of exchange
α_M: real variation of the rate of exchange.

These equations (5) assume that the variation in prices of capital goods is similar to the average of prices and that there are no other variations in the cost of imports such as international prices and tariff changes, but those derived from the rate of exchange. Both are approximate working assumptions, but do not weigh heavily on the results in the short run. Equation (4) then turns into

(6)
$$\bar{p} = w_L + \frac{\mu_K}{\mu_L}\alpha_K + \frac{\mu_M}{\mu_L}\alpha_M - \frac{1}{\mu_L}\beta.$$

The last equation relates the percentage variations in money wages, real income of capital, real rate of exchange and productivity and the percentage variation in the level of prices. This equation was used for programming policy. The aim was to obtain the minimum rate of variation in prices derived from cost pressures under the assumptions of behaviour:

$$w_L \geqslant w_L{}^*$$

$$\alpha_K \geqslant \alpha_K{}^*$$

(7)
$$\alpha_M = \alpha_M{}^*$$

$$\beta = \beta^*.$$

That is, the objective for wages is to obtain a minimum money wage variation, while real variation is the aim for changes in capital income and in the exchange rate, which is under control. Productivity variation is estimated by medium- and long-run forecasts.

Graphically this model can be used to determine the point P of minimum change in the level of prices and the area A of the probable outcome.

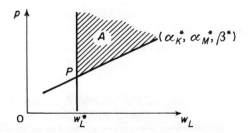

The analysis of the results can be obtained from an equation derived from equations (4) and (5), leaving the variation in the rate of exchange in nominal terms. This is done, because of the use of directly available information:

$$(8) \qquad \bar{p} = \frac{\mu_L}{1 - \mu_K} w_L + \frac{\mu_K}{1 - \mu_K} \alpha_K + \frac{\mu_M}{1 - \mu_K} t - \frac{1}{1 - \mu_K} \beta.$$

The analysis up to now has not discussed the effect of lags which are caused by delays in providing information, by erratic market behaviour, price fixing or other factors. These elements have not been considered because they make the model described—that is the analysis of certain main trends in the behaviour of the economy—unnecessarily complex.

The coefficients μ_L, μ_K and μ_M are derived from the same coefficients used in the former paper[4] for domestic products, that is 0·31, 0·44 and 0·25. Taking the weight for domestic products as 0·87 and for imports as 0·13, the coefficients become 0·27, 0·38 and 0·35. These values are assumed to be constant during the period of analysis. Even though this is not exact, it is not important to measure their change year by year, because they are average coefficients and their variation has only a small effect on the result.

Equation (6), used in programming the policy, can be written:

$$(9) \qquad p = w_L + 1·407\,\alpha_K + 1·296\,\alpha_M - 3·704\,\beta.$$

Equation (8), used for analysing the results, can be written:

$$(10) \qquad p = 0·435\,w_L + 0·613\,\alpha_K + 0·565\,t - 1·613\,\beta.$$

DEFINITION OF POLICY AND OUTCOME SITUATION

The policy defined in 1964 was based essentially on the concept of gradual stabilization to be obtained by means of increases in pro-

[4] Cauas, op. cit.

ductivity. It accepted the fact that money wages should be allowed to have variations equal to the variation in prices of the previous year. As a decreased rate of inflation was assumed, this policy led to an implicit increase in the purchasing power of wage-earners.

TABLE 7.1   *Programmed Variation in Prices for the Period*
(December to December)

Year	w_L	α_K	α_M	β	p programmed
1965	0·38[a]	0·02	−0·07	0·025	0·224
1966	0·25[b]	—	—	0·025	0·157
1967	0·16	—	—	0·025	0·067
1968	0·07	—	—	0·025	—[c]
1969	—	—	—	0·025	—[c]

[a] Consumer Price Index variation in 1964: 38·4 per cent.
[b] Higher than 0·224 to take into account a higher variation in the Consumer Price Index in 1965.
[c] Negative figures.

TABLE 7.2   *Expected Variation in Prices at the Beginning of Every*
Year (December to December)

Year	w_L[a]	α_K	α_M	β	p/pro-grammed	p/obtained consumer	whole-sale
1965	0·38	0·02	−0·07	0·025	0·224	0·259	0·245
1966	0·26	0·00	0·00	0·025	0·167	0·170	0·196
1967	0·17	0·02	0·02	0·025	0·131	0·219	0·197
1968	0·22	0·02	0·02	0·025	0·181	0·279	0·331
1969	0·28	0·02	0·02	0·025	0·241	0·293	0·394

[a] Variations in consumer prices in the previous year.

The programme for the period is given in Table 7.1. It is assumed that the real rate of exchange measured in local currency per dollar unit, deflated by the Consumer Price Index, would decline in 1965 in order to allow for increases in the other sectors, mainly the agricultural sector. The variations are measured from December to December.

The announced programme called for price increases of 25 per cent, 15 per cent and 10 per cent for 1965, 1966 and 1967 respectively in order to achieve stability.

Obviously, at the beginning of every year recalculations had to be made on the basis of the results of the previous year and of a study of the trends of the economy. These recalculations are given in Table 7.2.

Table 7.2 takes into account (starting with 1967) the resistance of the system to the continual redistribution of income implicit in the

TABLE 7.3 *Explained Variation in Prices* (*December to December*)

Year	$w_L{}^a$	$\alpha_K{}^b$	t^c	β^d	p/ex-plained	p/obtained con-sumer	whole-sale
1965	0·485	−0·017	0·146	0·038	0·222	0·259	0·245
1966	0·389	0·105	0·231	0·076	0·241	0·170	0·196
1967	0·282	−0·008	0·325	−0·011	0·320	0·219	0·197
1968	0·298	0·033	0·321	0·012	0·312	0·279	0·331
1969^e	0·390	0·030	0·302	0·016	0·333	0·293	0·394

[a] Variation in wages per worker. ODEPLAN, *Cuentas Nacionales 1960–8*.
[b] Real variation in payments to other factors. ODEPLAN, *Cuentas Nacionales 1960–8*.
[c] Variation in rate of exchange (*Bancario, futuro*). Central Bank of Chile.
[d] Increase in Gross Product per person. ODEPLAN, *Cuentas Nacionales 1960–8*.
[e] Estimates.

TABLE 7.4 *Explained Variation in Prices* (*annual averages*)$_a$

Year	w_L	α_K	t	β	p/ex-plained	p/obtained con-sumer	whole-sale
1965	0·485	−0·017	0·208	0·038	0·258	0·288	0·243
1966	0·389	0·105	0·208	0·076	0·228	0·229	0·229
1967	0·282	−0·008	0·258	−0·011	0·282	0·181	0·193
1968	0·298	0·033	0·349	0·012	0·328	0·266	0·305
1969	0·390	0·030	0·322	0·016	0·344	0·307	0·365

[a] Sources: as in Table 7.3.

initial programme, that is reflected in the assumption that capital income is assumed to gain 2 per cent per year in real terms. Finally, the situation resulting from actual data is analysed in Table 7.3, using values from December to December.

Since the use of December to December indexes tends to introduce distortions caused by irregular seasonal fluctuations, it is more convenient to analyse the situation using annual average indexes (see Table 7.4).

The short-term economic policy was designed to achieve simultaneously the goals of price stabilization, redistribution of income and economic growth. These objectives were conceived for an economy with secular inflation and with only very brief periods of relative relief; with important social sectors having no access to a market economy which coexist with a great urban concentration; and with a traditionally low rate of economic growth. More specifically, at the time of the design of the policy, inflation was increasing, real income of workers was diminishing, and the rate of growth was slackening.

Nevertheless, the policy was designed at a favourable time. A political group that favoured reforms was in power and it was felt that it might be a good time to conceive and apply measures requiring a high degree of consistency, and therefore a high degree of social acceptance. It was clear that any substantial disagreement over some of the proposed measures would seriously endanger the whole situation. Therefore, from the outset, the necessary steps to establish adequate communications and organization systems could not be and were not underestimated.

The basic elements considered were: a) choice of a policy of gradual deceleration of the inflationary process, based on an incomes policy which avoided undesirable effects on the programmed redistribution of income or the level of employment; b) promotion of access to markets of groups previously substantially excluded; to aim gradually towards a better distribution of income, through transfer to the workers of the increments of productivity, maintaining the real income of the other groups; and to correct some distortions in the economy, especially those in the agricultural sector whose situation had been systematically deteriorating in the past; c) movement towards a sustained high rate of growth, in the short run through the increased level of demand derived from the redistribution of income, demand that could be served by the unused capacity in industry; and in the long run through an increase in the level of savings and a gradual change in the structure of investment towards improvements in the social infrastructure of the country, that is, education and emphasis on productive activities such as agriculture, mining and industry. The basic strategy was to stress the improvement in the ability of the country to look towards higher external competitiveness and economic integration.[5]

Specific policies were designed taking into consideration the incomes policy required to obtain the above-mentioned goals. The growth hypothesis adopted was a rate of 5 per cent per year and 2·5 per cent for the productivity increase. The wages policy adopted was to give a readjustment equivalent to the variation in prices in the past year, a policy which would, with an appropriate slowdown in the rate of increase of prices in the current year, lead to an increase in the real income of workers that absorbed the whole increase of productivity. The only exception was in the first year when the programme considered an increase of income of the agricultural sector, both entrepreneurial and labour. The rate of inflation was to be decreased in such a way so as to reach negligible levels in three years.

Of course, the other policies were designed so as to be consistent with this analysis. Thus, the monetary and credit policy was built so as to finance the increases in production and programmed variation in prices, as well as shifts in demand due to changes in the structure of the economy. The fiscal expenditures policy assumed a financing that was compatible with the monetary programme so as to prevent pressures on the level of prices. The foreign trade policy was designed with the need for a progressive liberalization in mind. Measures were taken to normalize it and to avoid the danger of repeating the crises suffered in the past.

In particular, it is worth mentioning two policies. The first was to follow a consistent policy of real positive rate of interest; the second was to modify the exchange-rate, taking into consideration the changes in internal and external prices and the foreign exchange reserve situation. In both cases, even though in the short run some cost effects arise, in the medium and long run the measures are essential for an adequate stabilization policy.

At the beginning of every year the programme was revised, taking into account the actual outcome of the previous year and the changes in trend. These programme changes are given in Table 7.2. This shows that in 1967, there is a higher expected rate than was programmed in 1964. Nevertheless, the revised variation was largely

[5] This last point requires deeper discussion because it is the basis of the strategy of development. It will not be discussed here because it exceeds the aim of this paper, with the exception of the subjects that are essential for the understanding of specific statements.

surpassed and the following year the expected rate continued to grow and this fact was officially recognized.[6]

To analyse the situation, the information in Tables 7.3 and 7.4 can be used. These tables compare the changes explained by the model with the actual outcome. It is possible to observe a strong discontinuity of the trend in the model of analysis in 1967, discontinuity that showed itself in practice. As has been mentioned, no specific allowance for the effect of lags, price fixing and other factors was made but, nevertheless, the trend was identified.

The following characteristics of the period can be identified from the information shown in Table 7.4 which uses annual averages: a) The rate of variation in money wages exceeds substantially the variation in prices of the previous year; b) the income of non wage-earners shows a strong discontinuity in 1966; c) the real rate of exchange falls in 1965 and 1966 and recovers in real terms in 1967, 1968 and 1969; d) the growth of productivity was higher than the assumed rate in the programme in 1965 and 1966 but is smaller the following years; and e) only 1967 shows a strong difference between the explained and the actual rate of inflation measured in terms of the Wholesale Price Index.

Analyzing these results, it is obvious that the achievement of the programmed rates of inflation in 1965 and 1966 and its effects on redistribution of income were obtained in spite of a more rapid increase in wages. The explanation comes from the same analysis: the growth of productivity was much higher than expected. The main reason for this higher growth was the use of the excess capacity to serve the increases in demand derived from the redistribution of income and investment programmes; moreover, the high price of copper influenced this outcome through favourable conditions of foreign trade.

Nevertheless, it was clear from the beginning that the relief derived from these factors could not be taken permanently as the basis of the policy in future years. Moreover, warnings of difficulties to come were given in order to improve the situation.

At this stage it is important to analyse the monetary, fiscal and foreign trade situation. In Table 7.5 the most important indicators are given.

[6] Ricardo Ffrench-Davis, 'El Crédito Bancario y su Costo' and 'Dependencia, Subdesarrollo y Política Cambiaria', in *Estudios Monetarios II* (Banco Central de Chile, 1970); Arnold C. Harberger, 'Specific Problems in the Economic Development of Chile', in Zañartu and Kennedy (eds), *The Overall Development of Chile* (University of Notre Dame Press, 1969).

Table 7.5 shows that increases of the money supply in the hands of the private sector were very large during 1965 and 1966. Some of the increases were absorbed by changes in the demand for money derived from changes in expectations, the monetization of groups of the economy such as the agricultural workers, and the regulation of

TABLE 7.5   *Indicators of Monetary, Fiscal and Foreign Trade Situation*[a]

Year	Rate of Growth of Money in Hands of Private Sector (As to December of Each Year)	Credit in Escudos-Monetary System	Balance of Payments surplus (+) or Deficit (−) (Millions of Dollars	Net International Reserves of Central Bank (Millions of Dollars as of 31 December)
1964			−4·1	−164·5
1965	0·651	0·341	78·6	−124·4
1966	0·389	0·294	116·8	−48·0
1967	0·251	0·274	−4·3	−74·9
1968	0·383	0·353	133·8	41·6
1969	0·348	0·294	170·0[b]	211·4

Year	Rate of Growth of Public Expenditures	Public Expenditures as Proportion of Gross Product	Proportion of Public Investment over Expenditures	Proportion of Monetary Operations with the Government over Money Increases in the Private Sector
1964		0·357	0·281	
1965	0·573	0·399	0·282	0·98
1966	0·420	0·406	0·281	1·42
1967	0·324	0·410	0·283	1·41
1968	0·419	0·432	0·283	0·67
1969	0·393[b]	0·426[b]	0·290[b]	0·33

[a] *Sources*: Central Bank, Ministry of Finance and Planning Office.
[b] Estimates.

overdrafts in the banking system. But another part was due to monetary operations with the public sector and the favourable conditions of foreign trade.

The high financial requirements of the public sector are closely associated with the increases of current expenditures, that maintained its proportion of total expenditures, together with the high level of capital expenditures. The monetary effect of foreign trade is associated with a positive influence in the medium and long run: the recovery of the level of international reserves, indispensable for normal management of foreign trade. Obviously then, the monetary situation validated the pressures arising from the costs side.

Some important factors began to show up in 1967 which required that changes be introduced into the programme. Until 1966 it was possible to gain ground in spite of the negative factors, but it was predicted that unless some substantial corrections were introduced, the stabilization goal could not be achieved or if achieved, the price paid would be very high in terms of unemployment. These corrections were: a) The real redistribution of income could not continue by way of massive wage increases; b) the increases in public expenditures could not continue at the previous rate; and c) an increase in the rate of savings was needed to guarantee the future rate of growth and through an adequate structure of investment to guarantee the level of employment.[7]

In 1967, then, some substantial innovations were introduced. The savings need, even though clearly recognized from 1964 as being important but which was postponed because of the feeling that it was not yet crucial, was publicly discussed and a project of 'Popular Capitalization' was sent to Congress.[8] The project called for an increase in savings in all sectors of the population. The workers were asked to contribute with a part of their readjustment of wages. Unfortunately, and in spite of its attractive features from the social point of view, the project was not approved. Worse, its long discussion until mid-1968 caused serious problems in the working of the economic system, such as the delay in payment of the readjustment for public sector wages which led to problems in the level of demand. That fact, together with strong changes in the structure of the demand due to the introduction of electronic and automobile industries and the drought of 1967 and 1968, had strong negative effects on the level of activity without affecting the trend in prices (Table 7.4). It is interesting to note that in 1967 the cost model analysis showed an explained rate of inflation higher than the actual rate, whose turning-up point was delayed one year. This fact is related to the decreasing variation of monetary and fiscal variables as shown in Table 7.5.

In 1969 the rising trend of inflation continued but there was a

[7] Ministro de Hacienda, *Exposición sobre el Estado de la Hacienda Pública* (Chile, Dirección de Presupuestos, 1964, 1965, 1966 and 1967).

[8] As soon as the conditions of foreign trade were improved, the savings gap became the most important element of long-run economic policy, because the internal average savings rate was not sufficient. This subject will not be discussed here.

recovery in the rate of growth, explained by the effect of new industries and the higher activity in construction with their multiplier effect. 1970 has about the same characteristics.

In summary, the results of the period were closely related to two factors: the increases in wages and salaries (whose implicit aim was a larger than programmed transfer of real income from non-workers to the workers) and the trend to large transfers of real resources from the private to the public sector. Both are facts of a highly political nature.[9] Their resolution was tied to levels of growth which the system was not able to give with its limited capacity, which was, in turn, related to the preference of the community for present consumption. This last element and its implications became the core of the problem. But its solution, too, and perhaps more strongly than the problem of wages and public activities, is highly political.

SHORT-TERM ECONOMIC POLICY: ITS SENSE AND FACTIBILITY

What can be said of the described experience? The main points are: a) That it is possible to analyse and predict accurately and with reliability, even in countries with imperfect information, the probable trends of the economy; b) that in a democratic system there is a strong need to develop systems to make incomes policy possible; and c) that it is necessary to stress the importance of short-term economic policy for an efficient planning system.

Relative to the first point, it is clear that the system of analysis permitted knowledge at every moment of the trends and problems of the economy, even though it was very simple. In the specific case of Chile, the same simplicity was a virtue because it facilitated the communication of implicit economic ideas. Obviously, when it was necessary, the analysis was more sophisticated, introducing factors such as shorter time periods, more specific sectors, the influence of the financial setting and its changes, the influence of tax policy, etc.

Relative to the second point, it is convenient to draw attention to the importance that the understanding of incomes policy has for economics.[10] There are, of course, conceptual and practical difficulties, but few countries can go ahead without some steps in this direction. This comes from the very simple fact that the other means

[9] Ministro de Hacienda, *Exposición sobre el Estado de la Hacienda Pública* (Chile, Dirección de Presupuestos, 1967).

[10] Cauas, op. cit.

of controlling income distribution either result in a) a centralized system with its attendant loss of freedom, or b) a high political price in trying to obtain a normal working of the economy by purely monetary or fiscal means. Obviously the institutional system must be very efficient in obtaining solidarity when there is no desire to use force. This requires a high personal involvement of the people and a very clear process of communications. Even though there are great developments in those fields, the social process is demanding more and the answer now is becoming more difficult. This is one of the most challenging questions of the world today, especially for the developing countries.[11]

In relation to the last point there is an observation that seems important. Planning is a process which can hardly be ignored in modern economies. But planning is not only the elaboration of targets. In developing countries, because of their dimension, the relative dimension of their components, and their vulnerability, economic policy should be built around basic rules to lead the economy which should be permanently studied to admit the corrections coming from the changes induced in the system. This means that the most adequate procedure seems to be the establishment of policy mechanisms and definitions of strategy that show the broad goals to every unit of the economy. There are two examples worth mentioning in the specific case under analysis: the exchange rate and the rate of interest. In Chile both have already helped improve the working of foreign trade and credit, and for that reason, create the possibility of basing future stabilization policies on solid ground. They are not easy to apply, mainly when solidarity is needed in other less institutionally independent decisions in order to make the whole consistent. But it is the only wise approach.

[11] Paul N. Rosenstein-Rodan, 'The Role of Income Distribution in Development Programmes', *Rivista Internazionali di Scienze Economiche e Commerciali* (May 1965).

III

INCOME DISTRIBUTION AND
REGIONAL DEVELOPMENT

CHAPTER 8

Income Distribution and Agricultural Development

L. LEFEBER[1]

INTRODUCTION

It is a generally accepted contention of development economics that at least in the initial stages of development an adverse or skewed income distribution may be favourable to the attainment of a rapid rate of economic growth. The argument is based on the assumption that the marginal savings rate is greater in the higher than in the lower income groups and that the larger savings realized from an unequal income distribution will lead to a high rate of investment. This would be the case if Say's Law prevailed and if the economy behaved like a purely competitive general equilibrium system in which at any moment of time the demand for the different goods and services is exactly what is needed to motivate and absorb the desired rates of production. In fact, these are properties of neo-classical growth models in which, however, the sustainable growth rate is independent of the savings rate. There the savings rate determines the competitive choice of techniques and, hence, the functional distribution of income, but the latter does not affect the long-run growth rate which is uniquely determined by the growth of the labour force. A conflict between income distribution and growth arises only if the neo-classical framework is altered, for instance, by assuming that labour is in excess supply and that employed labour consumes its entire

[1] This paper makes use of the material in chapters 4 and 5 of a report to the United Nations Research Institute for Social Development (L. Lefeber and M. Datta Chaudhuri, *Regional Planning in South and South-East Asia* (Geneva, UNRISD, 1969; The Hague, Mouton, 1971)) jointly prepared with Mrinal Datta Chaudhuri of the Delhi School of Economics whose contribution I gratefully acknowledge.

(subsistence) wages so that all savings come from profits.[2] In any case, the growth paths derived from all such models are sustained by purely competitive temporal and inter-temporal general equilibrium relationships which, however, may or may not have real life counterparts. If they do not, as is the case if for reasons to be discussed the welfare optimal rate of employment is not attained and, hence, the demand for consumer goods and induced investment in the consumer goods sector is less than optimal, the relevance of these models and the validity of the conclusions with respect to the relationship between income distribution and growth has to be reconsidered.

It is, of course, well known that each and every output combination is a function of the structure of demand which, in turn, depends on the income distribution. If, for example, development requires the growth or modernization of a large industry the primary market of which depends on domestic mass consumption, the purchasing power of the lower income groups has to increase for the desired output to be absorbed.[3] I shall argue that such an increase cannot be taken for granted in the case of agricultural development in surplus labour economies which have large agricultural sectors and whose populations are predominantly rural. The primary example is India whose recent experience provides the basis for the argument of this paper, but the case for continuous improvement in income distribution as a necessary concomitant of a widely dispersed agricultural transformation can be generalized to other labour surplus countries or regions which have proportionately large agricultural sectors and rural populations.

In the discussion that follows all references to improvements in income distribution – unless otherwise specified – will signify changes brought about through increasing the demand for labour and employment rather than redistribution through direct transfers of income and wealth. Apart from land reform – a one-shot measure,

[2] For detailed analyses of such models see A. K. Sen, *Choice of Techniques*, 2nd edn (Oxford, 1968); S. A. Marglin, *The Political Economy of Surplus Labour* (October 1969), preliminary mimeographed; L. Lefeber, 'Planning In a Surplus Labour Economy', *American Economical Review*, vol. 53 (June 1968), pp. 343–73; L. Lefeber, 'Trade and Minimum Wages', in J. Bhagwati (ed.), *Trade, Balance of Payments and Development*, Essays in honour of Charles Kindleberger (Amsterdam, North Holland, 1971); S. Chakravarty, *Capital and Development* (Cambridge, MIT Press, 1969).

[3] Alternatively, direct purchasing by government followed by storage and/or rationed distribution is also a possibility. In what follows I dismiss this, however, as a non-feasible alternative, since it requires a larger organization and capital investment than most underdeveloped countries are capable of.

albeit a very important one – direct transfers cannot be expected to result in more than marginal changes in the income distribution of overpopulated, low income countries. The institutional and organizational requirements are not available for effecting the transfer; but even if they were, the transferable margin is small relative to the size of the low income population. On the other hand, as long as underemployment exists, improvements in income distribution can be obtained by creating new employment opportunities faster than the free market and by improving the conditions of self-employment which, particularly in the case of small holders and tenant farmers, can be a close substitute for increasing the demand for labour. Then, if the marginal productivity of labour is positive, the income distribution is changed in favour of the low income groups by an approach which makes use of the production obtained from the increase in employment; hence, the adverse savings effect of the redistribution is less than would be the case with direct income transfers.[4]

Finally, before entering into the argument of this paper, it is to be

[4] Though this point is evident, it can be readily illustrated with the well-known Sen diagram (see Sen, op. cit.). Given that Q denotes output, E is employment and w is the wage rate, the profit maximizing employment is shown at E_1, where

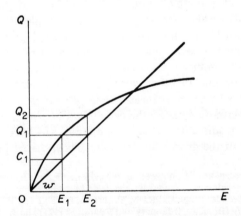

C_1 represents wage consumption and $Q_1 - C_1$ is surplus. If consumption redistribution is desired so as to attain a higher rate of consumption such as Q_1, it can be effected through direct redistribution of the surplus or by expanding employment to E_2. In the latter case, the higher employment brings about an increment in the output which is the surplus corresponding to E_2. Under these conditions direct transfer comes entirely from surplus while redistribution by means of employment is covered by an increment in output accompanied by only a partial reduction in surplus.

emphasized that the evidence in its support is limited by its availability.[5] Such evidence as does exist has to be interpreted in the context of a very imperfect world which does not conform to purely competitive models and about which the statistical information is, in general, slim. In any case, the market evidence indicating changes in wage rates and prices could not be rigorously interpreted without solving a formidable identification problem. Hence, as in most cases involving development policy, the analysis is based on assumptions which may be different from and, perhaps, more restrictive than those taken for granted in industrialized economies and which can frequently be supported only in terms of the observer's judgement of what is relevant or plausible.

THE GENERAL ARGUMENT

The argument of this paper is outlined as follows. The only potentially significant advances in agricultural technology are confined, at least in India, to the production of food grains. Since these do not have export markets, the profitability of adopting the new technology and, hence, the development of the agricultural sector depends on the adequate growth of domestic demand for food grains. This, in turn, depends on the income growth of the people in the lower income groups who are the primary users of food grains and who, given their income levels and corresponding nutritional standards, would spend a significant part of any additional income on more food grain consumption. In other words, the income elasticity for food is very high whether it is measured in *per capita* or total income terms. Furthermore, because the *per capita* elasticity is high, it is the growth of income rather than population which is the primary determinant of the growth of demand.[6] Thus, the frequently heard

[5] Two very recent articles, however, quote evidence that the income distribution in India has deteriorated over the last decade and thereby reinforce the argument of this paper. See Dandekar and Rath, 'Poverty in India', I and II, *Economic and Political Weekly* (Bombay, 2 January and 9 January 1971) and K. Bardhan, 'On the Incidence of Poverty in Rural India of the 1960s', Discussion Paper No. 55 (Indian Statistical Institute, January 1971), mimeographed. Also see a report on the 1971 census in the *Overseas Hindustan Times*, 'Ranks of Landless Labour Swelling' (New Delhi, 23 October 1971), according to which the numbers of landless labour are swelling, particularly in the wheat-growing areas of India.

[6] This can be shown as follows. e^* and n represent the *per capita* income elasticity of demand and the population growth rate, respectively; g_d and g_y are

argument that population growth automatically translates itself into a corresponding growth in the demand for food is, at best, an incomplete proposition. What is important is that there should exist an adequate market mechanism or other means for translating into actual consumption the potential demand for additional food, whether it is due to population growth or other causes.

If agricultural development depends primarily on adequate demand by low income consumers, the growth in the rate of employment may be the best indicator of the change in the purchasing power of the lower income groups. In this respect the effect of the new agricultural technology on the incomes of agricultural labour, tenants and small holders is of no small interest. The form in which the new technology is adopted and, particularly, its consequences for the demand for labour and the conditions of self-employment will determine to a large degree whether adequate additional income and, hence, demand can be generated to absorb the increased grain output made possible by the new technology. This is so, because in labour surplus economies, such as India, the overwhelming part of the population is still in agriculture, a condition which can be expected to change only slowly even if the rate of industrialization significantly accelerates.[7]

The current Indian evidence concerning the rate of growth of income in the lowest income groups in agriculture and other sectors is

---

the percentage growth rates of total demand and total income while g_d^* and g_y^* are the percentage growth rates of *per capita* demand and *per capita* income. Then, by definition,

$$g_d^* = g_d - n = e^* g_y^* = e^*(g_y - n),$$

so that

$$g_d = e^* g_y + (1 - e^*)n.$$

It follows that the larger e^*, the smaller must be the multiplier of n and, hence, its contribution to g_d. Incidentally, for any given g_y and n, the higher the total elasticity of demand (e) the higher the *per capita* elasticity (e^*) and vice versa. This is evident from the tautological relationship, $e^* = (eg_y - n)/g_y^*$. When $e^* = 1$ then $e = 1$.

[7] In fact, given that in India the amount of labour employed in the organized manufacturing and service sectors does not exceed, say, 5 per cent of the entire labour force (20 per cent being employed in traditional service and cottage-type industries), even a small adverse change in the growth of agricultural demand for labour could generate an intolerable burden on the organized sector's capacity to absorb the unemployed. At the same time, the capacity for growth in the traditional service and cottage industrial sectors is limited and closely dependent on the prosperity of agriculture itself. Hence, for a long time to come, the primary source of employment and income creation would have to be in the agricultural sector.

not favourable. Hence, it is doubtful that the domestic market demand for grains will be increasing at a rate commensurate to what would be needed to sustain a rapid growth in grain production.[8] The indication is that particularly in those areas where the new technology has been introduced, the conditions for self-employment for small holders and tenant farmers have deteriorated and that, at the same time, the hoped for increases in the demand for labour may not have come about, at least not at an adequate rate. Instead, income in the agriculturally developing areas has been redistributed in favour of larger farmers who have a tendency to substitute capital for labour and to terminate tenancy in favour of owner cultivation. Thus, the form in which the new agricultural technology is adopted may lead in the direction of increased income inequality and could cause not only a relative but also an absolute deterioration in the income position of the rural poor.[9] As a consequence, the needed demand for sustaining a continued growth in the production of those grains which are subject to rapid productivity gains may not be forthcoming either. In other words, the form in which the new technology is adopted may, through its consequences for income

[8] Wheat prices in India are down at the support level and the government is considering the lowering of support levels in order to encourage market clearing. See *Overseas Hindustan Times*, 'Green Revolution Problems' (New Delhi, 27 March 1971) and *Overseas Hindustan Times*, 'Glut of Wheat in Haryana' (New Delhi, 29 May 1971). It is well known that the type of wheat which is successfully adopted in India (Mexican Dwarf) is not particularly favoured by the North Indian consumer. None the less, the weakening of the wheat market is not only an indication of an increase in supply relative to the demand by those who are already wheat consumers, but also of the fact that the incomes of the people in the lowest income groups, who do have a potential demand for additional food grains and who would prefer even red wheat to other inferior grains, have not developed *pari passu* with productivity increases. Lowering the support levels would, of course, result in lower market prices and thereby contribute to some increase in wheat consumption both on account of substitution of wheat for other grains and the effect on real incomes. But lowering the price would do little to increase the demand for wheat by the unemployed or the marginal self-employed. Furthermore, because of its adverse effect on the relationship between profit and risk, it would also slow down the rate at which the new agrarian technology is adopted, particularly by owners of small and medium-sized farms. For this reason, lowering wheat prices is not a substitute for a vigorous employment policy.

[9] As mentioned earlier, the most recent evidence about income distribution in India and, particularly, the increase in the proportion of population with incomes not greater than Rs 15 per month (in 1961 prices) is consistent with such an outcome. However, to what degree the shift in distribution is due to the adverse effects of the new agricultural technology, is not possible to evaluate on the basis of the existing data. See Dandekar and Rath, op. cit., Bardhan, op. cit., and the news report on the 1971 census, op. cit.

distribution, destroy the economic basis for the continued spreading and growth of agricultural development.

THE DEMAND FOR THE MARKETABLE SURPLUS

The production of food grains in India represents the most important agricultural activity in terms of value produced and land utilized.[10] At the same time – as mentioned above – the significant advances in technology are also confined to food grain production.[11] Hence, it is reasonable to assume that if there is going to be an agricultural revolution, it will have to be based – at least in the foreseeable future – primarily on the production of food grains. This is all the more significant, since expenditure on cereals represents by far the largest share of the consumer food budget.[12] Furthermore, the demand for grain is entirely domestic and it is likely to remain so; hence, the profitability of adopting the new technology depends primarily on domestic income growth and income distribution.[13]

[10] In 1964–5 food grain production made up 55 per cent of the total value of crops and used about 80 per cent of the total cultivated land.

[11] The exception is cotton which shows important productivity gain; however, it represents only an insignificant fraction of the total agricultural output and land utilization. The gains in food grain production, on the other hand, are not only significant but fairly widespread, even if unevenly distributed. The greatest strides in productivity have been registered in wheat production, particularly in the north-west of India, and there has been an important increase in the share of wheat in total grain production. The gains in rice productivity (excepting the case of Tanjore and West Godawari districts) have been more moderate. This, combined with the fact that in North India considerable acreage has been shifted from rice to wheat, explains that after the recovery from the consecutive failures of the monsoon, rice production regained its 1964 level only in 1969. For the pattern of productivity gains see Government of India, *Modernizing Indian Agriculture: Report on the IADP (1960–8)* (Ministry of Food and Agriculture, Expert Committee on Assessment and Evaluation, 1969).

[12] According to Dandekar and Rath, op. cit., the median rural household in 1960–1 spent about 75 per cent of its entire consumer budget on food, two-thirds of which (or 50 per cent of the budget) was spent on food grains. These figures exclude the cost of cooking fuel. In the lowest income groups as much as 65 per cent of the total budget was spent on food grains alone.

[13] The development of export markets for grains is unlikely. Surpluses are again accumulating in the traditional surplus areas and the exporting countries, many of which accumulate exportable surpluses to solve domestic political problems with respect to their own farm sectors, are unlikely to change their current behaviour. See W. P. Falcon, 'The Green Revolution: Generations of Problems', Economic Development Report No. 154 (Harvard University, Development Advisory Service, August 1970). Of course, the traditional export products of India, that is, tea and jute, form an important part of the total

It is, of course, well known that the new technology relies to a much greater degree on manufactured inputs (for example, chemical fertilizers, pesticides and equipment) than is the case in traditional methods of production. Hence, the farmer has to be assured that he will be able to produce a marketable surplus and that he will be able to sell it at prices which will permit him to obtain the manufactured and other necessary inputs as well as the minimum profit margin required for undertaking the investments needed for the new technology. Thus, the problem is the determination of the relationship between a desired or projected rate of growth of agricultural production and the generation and absorption of that marketable surplus which is needed to sustain the projected rate of growth of production.

The problem can be illustrated by the following hypothetical computation which is, however, based on numbers not unlike those from the Indian experience. Suppose that agricultural production is to grow at an annual rate of 5 per cent and that this can be translated into a corresponding growth of agricultural incomes. Assume further that the *per capita* income elasticity for the consumption of staples is 0·6 in the farm sector. Then, if population growth is 2·25 per cent, the rate of growth of *total* food consumption in the farm sector would be 3·9 per cent.[14] Since total farm production is assumed to grow at 5 per cent and food consumption on the farm

agricultural output, but their production is not affected by technological change and in any case the rate of growth of demand is independent of domestic policies. Other crops, such as sugar, oil seeds, fruits and vegetables should become increasingly important and more effort is needed to encourage increases in productivity and acreage. However, their cultivation is not yet significantly affected by technological change, and rapid production increases – at least on a broad scale – will still have to overcome a variety of technical and other obstacles. On the demand side, fruits and vegetables are high income consumption items with limited domestic markets. On the other hand, the domestic demand for sugar and vegetable oils is a function of domestic income growth in the low and middle income groups and those changes in the income distribution which adversely affect the spreading of the green revolution in grains, would have similar effects on the demand for these products.

[14] For simplicity it is assumed that all staples, that is, fibres as well as grains are included here. Note that the assumption of 5 per cent growth in farm productivity and farm incomes may be optimistic but certainly not excessive for purposes of analysing the requirements of an agricultural revolution. In fact, Indian planners assume a 5·5 per cent increase in production and implicitly assume that it can be translated into a corresponding income growth. Furthermore, though the hypothetical computation of this paper assumes the same rate of growth for the entire farm sector, separating staple production from slower growing outputs would show that the marketable food grain surplus would have to grow even

grows at a rate of only 3·9 per cent, it follows that the corresponding marketable surplus must be growing faster than production. On the assumption that in the initial period half of the farm output is consumed by the farm population and by extrapolating output and farm consumption over an arbitrary fifty-year period, the implied annual rate of growth of the marketable surplus over this fifty-year time period turns out to be approximately 5·8 per cent. The question is then whether this rapidly growing surplus could be absorbed by the rest of the economy and, if so, how or by whom.

Since the marketable surplus represents partly direct consumption of staples and partly inputs into processed consumer goods, its absorption depends on the relative strength of the demand for its alternative uses in the non-agricultural sectors. In this instance, however, so as to stay within the limited framework of the hypothetical computation, it will be assumed that the *per capita* income elasticity of the non-agricultural direct and derived demand for staples in all their uses is 0·45. Then, in order to absorb the marketable surplus growing at a rate of 5·8 per cent, *per capita* incomes would have to grow in excess of 7 per cent in the non-agricultural sectors.[15]

The attainment of such a growth rate does indeed represent a difficult, if not impossible, target, particularly if one considers that not all non-agricultural sectors are capable of rapid development. Rapid growth is more likely to be feasible in the organized service and manufacturing sectors which, though significant in terms of value produced, represent only a fraction of the total non-farm employment and, hence, market for food and staples. The bulk of the surplus would have to be absorbed by an amorphous group of traditional service and cottage industries the growth of which re-

faster than implied by the above numerical example. Finally, the computation assumes a constant *per capita* income elasticity of demand for food in the farm sector. This being an average over all income classes, the implicit assumption is that the distribution of income will remain unaffected by the process of agricultural development. If the distribution of income deteriorates, the extrapolation of the absorption of the output in the agricultural sector and elsewhere will represent an overstatement and the problem of disposing of the marketable surplus will be correspondingly larger.

[15] If *per capita* income elasticity is 0·45, the surplus is growing at 5·8 per cent and population growth is 0·025, *per capita* income growth

$$g_y^* = (0·058 - 0·025)/0·45 = 0·073,$$

and total income growth

$$g_y = g_y^* + n = 0·098 \text{ that is } 9·8 \text{ per cent.}$$

Note that in this computation the assumptions concerning the size of the income elasticity and population growth are indicative of prevailing conditions.

quires much greater organizational and investment effort than it currently receives.[16]

Let us now return to the problems relating to the growth of income and consumption in the agricultural sector itself. Specifically (in contrast to the assumption of a constant overall income elasticity in the above hypothetical computation), primary consideration will have to be given to the potential changes in income distribution. This is so, because the largest source of demand for the type of outputs which need to be absorbed consists first and foremost of the needs of the lower income groups in rural areas. As pointed out earlier, the income distributional changes would be determined to a large extent by a) the choice of techniques, that is, the employment effects of the specific form in which the new technology is adopted and b) the consequences of modernization for the conditions of self-employment, that is, the welfare of tenant farmers and small holders.

EMPLOYMENT EFFECTS

The new agricultural technology is expected to increase the demand for labour on two counts. First, an increased output per unit of land may require a greater labour input during the growing season and for harvesting. Secondly, if the new technology leads to double cropping, it increases the frequency of the peak demand for labour from one to two harvest periods.[17] Accordingly, if the induced increase in the demand for labour is sufficiently strong relative to its supply, a measure of the developing scarcity would be registered in the form of an upward trend in rural wages. No such trend is discernible in India.

This is, of course, partly because the so-called green revolution has taken hold selectively in a few areas only and its spread does not even encompass all the districts of the Indian government's Intensive

---

[16] Incidentally, it must be remembered that the output of the organized sectors provides indispensable inputs for the traditional cottage and small-scale industries. However, the growth of the former is only a necessary but not sufficient condition for the growth of the latter. Since the markets of the cottage and small-scale industries are primarily in rural areas, their rate of growth also depends on agriculture and, particularly, on the spreading of broad-based and geographically widespread rural prosperity.

[17] In India multiple cropping has not gone beyond two harvests. This is, however, not necessarily the limit. In Taiwan, for instance, through a restructuring of the subsoil so as to perfect the means of water control, four and even five annual crops can be grown. Thus, agriculture is turned into a nearly continuous operation in which the demand for labour is evenly distributed around the year.

Agricultural District Programme (IADP) especially established for the introduction and propagation of the new technology.[18] But even in those areas where the new technology has taken hold, there seems to have been no significant wage response, not even where developing seasonal labour shortages have not been relieved by migration from surplus into deficit regions. In the case of the district of Ludhiana in the Punjab, the star performer of the IADP in wheat production, the labour supply for *continuous* year-round employment has remained infinitely elastic at a wage rate which in terms of the changes in the Consumer Price Index does not seem to indicate any significant improvement in the real wage rate over the last decade.[19] This is so in spite of the fact that there has been no significant immigration into the district of Ludhiana from labour surplus areas and that additional sources of labour demand due to sustained industrialization and growth in the services ancillary to industry and agriculture have also been developing.

Careful empirical investigations would be needed to throw more light on the state of the labour markets; but in the absence of such studies one can conclude only that if the wage response in the most vigorous district of India is as weak as seems to be the case in Ludhiana, in areas of slower growth the hoped for increase in the demand for labour may not be materializing at all. For instance, in the Kosi region of Bihar where progress in wheat production is taking place in response to increasing irrigation facilities, the wage scales seem to remain at the level of lowest subsistence.[20] Similarly, in West Godawari, a successful IADP rice-growing district, wages do not seem to be affected by the increased rate of agricultural production.

The fact that the supply for *continuous* employment is infinitely elastic at relatively low wage rates does not preclude the possibility of seasonal labour shortages developing at harvest times. In the Punjab and other prosperous agricultural regions, the wages of seasonal workers may jump to five or six times the regular daily rate in the peak-demand periods and the effort to hold down such seasonal wage fluctuations by bringing migrant labour to the deficit areas

---

[18] See *Modernizing Indian Agriculture*, op. cit. In most IADP districts the rate of growth of output is not noticeably greater (and is in some instances smaller) than in other, non-programme districts.

[19] W. Ladejinsky, 'Green Revolution in the Punjab', *Economic and Political Weekly* (Bombay, June 1969).

[20] W. Ladejinsky, 'Green Revolution in Bihar', *Economic and Political Weekly* (Bombay, September 1969).

resulted in the much discussed case of violent confrontation between landowners and landless labour in Tanjore district.[21] These seasonal labour shortages do indicate that the increase in productivity does, in the first round, lead to increases in the demand for labour which in the absence of perfect labour markets, that is, immigration from labour surplus areas, are signalled by increased seasonal wage movements. The latter taken together with the insecurity of an adequate labour supply during the harvest period and the potential for conflict between owner and worker powerfully contributes to the desire to substitute capital for labour which, in turn, threatens to offset the beneficial effects of the new technology on the demand for labour.[22] And, in fact, there are increasing indications of substitution of capital for labour beyond what may be needed for satisfying the minimum capital requirements of the new technology. In the Punjab the move towards mechanized farming is well on its way and there is little reason to believe that the trend will be interrupted or reversed.[23]

There are several additional reasons why continued substitution of capital for labour may take place beyond what is warranted by technology and relative resource endowments in the economy. First, the distortions in the price system favour the use of capital. This is so because the overvaluation of domestic currency and preferential loan rates at which capital is made available subsidize the use of capital. At the same time, there are no subsidies for the use of labour. The net result may well be a bias in the direction of relatively more capital intensive techniques than correspond to relative scarcities. Secondly, limited alternative opportunities for the uses of profits and savings in the farm sector may also lead to increased farm capitalization. A shortage of manufactured consumer goods contributes to increased savings or hoardings. At the same time, interest bearing accounts or papers may not be appealing during periods of price

[21] See A. Beteille, 'Agrarian Unrest in Tanjore', *Times of India* (20 September 1969) and A. Thapar, 'Warning from Tanjore', *Times of India* (20 January 1969).

[22] The argument could be made that the government should ensure a smoothly functioning labour market by encouraging the flow of surplus labour to deficit areas. However, the government would also have to solve, at the same time, some very difficult welfare problems. Resistance to seasonal immigration by landless labour residing in the deficit areas can naturally be expected, since it is during the harvest period when a sufficient income to provide also for seasonal unemployment periods has to be earned. Thus, the smoothing out of the wage fluctuations would have to be accompanied by measures for creating employment opportunities between harvest periods; in fact, it is reasonable to assert that without such measures the problem cannot be solved.

[23] See Ladejinsky, op. cit. (June 1969).

increases. The purchase of monetary gold for hoarding is not only illegal but increasingly costly. Other outlets for savings are not well established and as yet rare.[24] Thus, from the point of view of the landowner, additional farm investment is not an unreasonable use of savings. Thirdly, there are also some sociological factors leading to the substitution of capital for labour. These may consist in part of a fear of violent confrontation between owners and labour, such as took place at Tanjore, or of traditional reasons such as a reluctance to deal with landless labour on a commercial basis.

In summary, the existing evidence indicates that the new technology has had an impact on the demand for labour. However, particularly in the wheat-growing regions, there seems to be a trend towards substituting capital for labour which, if it continues in the face of evident and perhaps growing unemployment, will lead to further deterioration in the distribution of income.

CHANGES IN THE CONDITIONS OF SELF-EMPLOYMENT

The distributional effects of the new technology are also notable in terms of the changes in the income position of farmers and tenants. As in the case of employment, the evidence is not conclusive but what is known does not appear to be favourable either. This is the case even though, according to a recent study based on the experiences in five districts under the IADP, it seems that with the exception of small holders and tenant farmers, those cultivators who introduced modern methods of agriculture did, in general, experience some improvement in income and yields.[25] At the same time, it also appears that the distribution of the gains from the new technology have been very uneven. According to the study, in the above-mentioned district of Ludhiana the farmers with less than 10 acres experienced a significant setback in their *relative* income position. In Ludhiana, farmers cultivating less than 10 acres represent less than 20 per cent of all farmers but in other wheat areas, such as in Bihar and Uttar Pradesh, farmers operating less than 8 acres make up over 80 per

[24] Though investment in a fertilizer plant was recently undertaken and financed by certain Punjabi farmers, this does not represent a trend.

[25] See F. Frankel, 'Agricultural Modernization and Social Changes', *Mainstream* (New Delhi, November 1969). The districts of the study were located, one each, in the Punjab, Andhra, Tamil Nadu, Kerala and West Bengal. The conclusion is more representative of the wheat-growing regions where improved varieties could be adopted on a broad scale, but it also holds, even though to a lesser degree, in rice-growing areas where the adoption of high yielding varieties met only with limited success.

cent of all farms. Based on this information the study makes the not unreasonable assumption that the majority of the farmers in these areas lost out on their relative income position, even though the farmers owning between 5 and 10 acres did seem to have registered at least some absolute gains. In contrast, the small owner who supplements his income as tenant (or labourer) and the pure tenants experienced an *absolute* deterioration in their economic conditions.

It seems that farmers with at least 20 acres managed to obtain the greatest absolute and relative gains and farmers who started out with 10 acres or more could proceed to land consolidation by using their profits to buy more land. The reason is that owner-farmers who own 10 or more acres, that is, a small minority of cultivators, have ready facilities for obtaining the capital needed for investment. In contrast, farmers of smaller landholdings could not benefit to the same degree from the new technology because they could not raise enough capital. And the small owner-tenant or pure tenant farmers were adversely affected because there was a steep increase in land rents and because there also seems to be an increasing tendency towards personal cultivation of the land.[26]

In the rice areas the qualitative outcome seems to be essentially similar. The majority of the farmers may have lost in their relative income position and the small owners experienced an absolute deterioration. Where high-yielding varieties were adopted the high fixed and circulating capital costs led towards an increasing gap between larger farmers and the majority of small owners and tenants.

Much of the outcome is due to the very nature of the Intensive Agricultural District Programme which favours the larger and more efficient cultivators and does not provide adequate assistance to small farmers. According to the cited study, the scale of the programmes for the benefit of small cultivators is such as to suggest that 'the small farmer is still being treated as if he belonged to a residual or marginal category. Unfortunately the opposite is true. . . .' As far as the IADP and other programmes are concerned 'they have not only

---

[26] The trend towards personal cultivation is caused by a) a desire to avoid confrontations with tenants and share croppers about rent or owners' share when output per acre is increasing in response to the new technology and b) the fear of vigorously enforced land reform in which tenants and share-croppers may have primary claim on the land of non-cultivating owners. Whatever the case, this trend may heavily contribute to increasing inequality, because the income potential of dispossessed tenants joining the ranks of landless labour naturally diminishes.

intensified the process of economic polarization in the rural areas, but they have also contributed to an increasing estrangement between landlords and tenants and landowners and labourers.'[27]

POLICY IMPLICATIONS

It does seem, then, that the new agricultural technology has failed to contribute to the improvement of the income distribution and, in fact, the way it is being introduced, it may do the opposite. In any case, such an outcome is not inconsistent with the earlier cited studies indicating not only relative but also absolute deterioration in the income position of a significant portion of the lower income groups.[28] Furthermore, it may lend substance to the argument that in spite of continued poverty and inadequate nutritional standards an increasing wheat surplus may be developing which could lead to a crash in wheat prices and discourage the spreading of the agricultural revolution.[29] Clearly the problem can be solved only by adequate policy intervention.

But what kind of intervention would be adequate? In the long run, of course, industrialization will have to absorb an ever increasing proportion of the labour force and in order to accelerate the transfer of labour from agriculture an increased rate of industrial growth will be required. But the period of transition will take a very long time even under conditions of rapid industrialization. Given that the current rate of unemployment is already significant, the population growth is rapid and the size of the organized sectors is proportionately small, full employment through the transfer of labour into industrial occupations will not be obtained within any visible time horizon. Thus, in addition to accelerating the rate of industrialization, other intermediate policies are also required.

These policies must be aimed at raising productivity in agriculture

[27] F. Frankel, op. cit. Incidentally, the evident rural tension growing out of the conditions analysed by this study was noted and further discussed in an unpublished report by the Research and Policy Division of the Ministry of Home Affairs, GOI, entitled 'The Causes and Nature of Current Agrarian Tensions' (1969).

[28] Dandekar and Rath, op. cit., Bardhan, op. cit., and *Overseas Hindustan Times*, op. cit. (October 1971).

[29] See, for example, *Overseas Hindustan Times*, op. cit. (March 1971) and op. cit. (May 1971). It is to be assumed that the subsequent increase in the demand for food grains due to the influx of refugees from East Bengal was a short-run phenomenon and did not represent a trend. Hence, in the long run the problem remains.

and simultaneously improving the distribution of income. To accomplish such a dual purpose, the current agricultural strategy will have to be a) altered so as to obtain an increase in the labour intensity of production and b) supplemented by programmes for labour-intensive forms of rural capital formation. It is not within the scope of this paper to analyse such policies in detail but it may be useful to provide at least an outline of what could be feasible.

Strategy of agricultural development. Reference was made above to the Indian government's Intensive Agricultural District Programme which is based on the principle of concentrating the governmental effort and organizational capacity in the most promising agricultural areas. In these, technical progress and productivity were to be accelerated by means of a 'package programme' consisting of the provision of a broad range of technical, financial and other services and manufactured inputs. However, because of its selective impact which was not broad-based but confined to larger and more enterprising farmers in a few chosen districts, the IADP itself contributed to increasing income and wealth inequalities as, in fact, had to be the case with an effort designed to support only the best.[30]

A different strategy aimed at providing support to and raising the productivity of the *average* farmer would have very different income distributional consequences. At the same time, in view of the limited success of the IADP the overall productivity effects of such an alternative strategy need not be inferior. Furthermore, while the IADP is uniquely concerned with the introduction of the new technology for grain production, there is an evident need to broaden the effort to include other crops such as oil-bearing seeds and sugar beets.

[30] From the IADP districts the new technology was expected to spread to slower-growing regions. It seems, however, that in this respect the IADP programme failed and its success can be questioned even in the original fourteen programme districts. See evidence of performance in *Modernizing Indian Agriculture*, op. cit. Since much of the private farm investment was undertaken at a time when, due to failure of the monsoon, grain prices were abnormally high and the acceleration in production took place after the return of normal monsoon conditions (underlining the importance of water as the dominant factor), the causal factors underlying increased production cannot be unequivocally identified. Furthermore, apart from two spectacularly successful districts (Ludhiana and West Godawari), none of the other districts showed more rapid productivity increases than the neighbouring ones and some showed even less. Interestingly, Tanjore district originally was not part of the programme and its initial success (based entirely on traditional techniques) was clearly motivated by the extraordinary rice prices and the lucky circumstance that Tanjore did have water when the failure of the monsoon made cultivation impossible in less fortunate districts.

Labour intensity. More attention will have to be paid to the employment effects of agricultural development. Specifically, the labour–land and the labour–capital ratios will have to be influenced in the direction of higher labour intensities. As far as the capital intensity is concerned, it was pointed out above that government pricing and loan policies result in subsidizing the use of capital without, at the same time, providing any premium for the additional use of labour. The argument is not against the use of capital; but farmers will have to be encouraged to explore the relatively labour-intensive portions of the new production function. Adequate pricing and loan policies can help to assure that excessive mechanization does not take place. In this connection it is useful to point out that it is the larger farms which can be expected to use excessively capital intensive techniques because of their capacity to raise capital due to their greater credit worthiness. This is reinforced by the IADP bias which favours larger producers. Perhaps credit rationing which facilitates the provision of the required capital to smaller farms and limits the excessive use of capital on larger farms may be useful.

As to employment in relationship to size of farm, several recent papers argue that labour and/or other inputs per hectare decrease inversely with farm size.[31] None of the papers provide definitive empirical evidence; nonetheless, there may be sufficient *a priori* and empirical grounds for believing that employment and output per acre would not diminish – and perhaps, increase – by a suitably conceived land redistribution.[32] In any case, this would go a long way towards improving the rural income distribution particularly if agricultural strategy were reoriented to help the average cultivator.

Employment programmes. Given the current population growth and the corresponding increase in the labour force on top of the already sizeable unemployment or underemployment, the revamping of the agricultural strategy, even if it is combined with land redistribution, may not be sufficient to solve the problem of unemployment. To bridge over the time period needed for the transfer of a sizeable

---

[31] The most recent argument is by T. N. Srinivasan, 'Farm Size and Productivity', Discussion Paper No. 53 (Indian Statistical Institute, January 1971), based on the implications of choice under uncertainty. See also Sen, op. cit., J. Bhagwati and S. Chakravarty, 'Contributions to Indian Economic Analysis: A Survey', *American Economic Review*, part 2 supplement, vol. 59 (September 1969) and others whose discussions are referred to or reviewed by Srinivasan.

[32] Redistribution would have to be accompanied by a rationalization or consolidation of fragmented small holdings.

part of the population from agriculture into industry and organized services, large-scale employment programmes will have to be undertaken to supplement the market economy's capacity to absorb labour. These programmes would have to be so organized as to increase the productive capacity of both agriculture and industry; thus, since most of the real wage counterpart consists of grain and other staples, the programmes themselves would contribute both to the production and to the absorption of the marketable surplus.

This latter point is of the utmost importance. Employment programmes which are of the make-work type are not essentially different from personal income transfers which, as argued earlier, the Indian economy cannot afford beyond insignificant levels. On the other hand, suitably selected forms of rural capital formation (for example, water control and irrigation, transport improvement, etc.) which directly contribute to production and productive capacity, reduce the real cost of the income transfer in terms of savings and investment.[33]

The major problem of large-scale employment programmes is that the institutions required for their organization and maintenance are not available. Short of making use of the army organization (an approach not favoured in India either by the civil authority or the army) there is currently no bureaucratic and technical organization which can launch and sustain an effort of adequate size. In addition, local, regional and national institutions for the speedy resolution of a whole range of problems relating to or concerned with labour markets, land surveys, ownership, eminent domain, compensation, distribution of burdens and benefits, etc. would have to be newly created or rebuilt from inadequate existing ones before major and minor earthworks, drainage and irrigation projects could be effectively carried out on a broad scale.

In fact, it may well be the case that the solution to the joint problems of improving the distribution of income and agricultural pro-

[33] Since there is frequently a correlation between unemployment, low agricultural productivity and regional retardation, there are exceptional opportunities in India to combine effort in the pursuit of several goals which otherwise might conflict with each other. For instance, a determined move towards rapid development and termination of the Rajasthan Canal would a) relieve the considerable regional unemployment, b) increase agricultural productivity, and c) contribute to the easing of the balance of payments by creating capacity for long-fibre cotton production (currently imported). Other unemployment and underprivileged regions such as Eastern Uttar Pradesh, Bihar, West Bengal and Telengana, could also rapidly benefit from rural capital formation in the form of improved water control.

ductivity hinges as much on the capacity for introducing and implementing adequate and, perhaps, drastic institutional changes as on the understanding of the relevent economic and technical relationships. At the same time, the creation of the new institutions will have to be undertaken in a manner which is consistent with and mindful of the latter.

Of this there is increasing recognition in India. The strategy of planning, in a state of flux since the termination of the Third Five Year Plan, is once again under reconsideration. If the income distributional problem is to be solved, the plan will have to be restructured so as to explicitly account for the material and organizational requirements of a high-employment-oriented development path. This, in turn, implies that rural and urban employment programmes – hitherto always relegated to a residual category – will have to be organically built into the plan. But when all is said and done, the problem will not be resolved by changing planning strategy alone. Ultimately, the question is whether the Indian democracy can accommodate itself to those social and institutional changes which will be necessary if a more egalitarian plan is to be implemented.

CHAPTER 9

Trade-Off Curves and Regional Gaps

B. HIGGINS[1]

I INTRODUCTION

Perhaps the outstanding characteristic of Paul Rosenstein-Rodan is his uncanny ability to see sooner than his colleagues the importance of some new concept, some new field for investigation. The 'North–South Problem', or the problem of regional disparities, is no exception. At a time when most economists were still thinking of 'regional economics' as a somewhat curious speciality, removed from the mainstream of theory and policy, Rosenstein-Rodan was already deeply immersed in the plan for the reconstruction of the Italian South. He is, indeed, known as one of the chief architects of the plans for development of Italy's retarded region. Perhaps even more important, he was one of the first to appreciate the significance of the overlap of sectors and regions, and thus of 'technological dualism' and of 'regional dualism'. In developing countries obviously, and in advanced countries less obviously but just as surely, the 'rich region' is the one where the modern sector is concentrated, the 'poor region' the one where the traditional sector predominates. Now, of course, regional economics and its close relative, urban economics, are at the forefront of the interest of the profession. The development plans of most less developed countries (LDCs) include some target for reduction of regional gaps. Advanced countries (ACs) also are becoming increasingly concerned with regional disparities: Canada, with the sweeping powers accorded to its recently-created Ministry

[1] This paper is a substantial revision of my Harris and Partners Lecture entitled 'Regional Disparities and National Welfare', delivered at York University on 5 March 1970. The revision has benefited from discussions with Raphael Rubio de Urquia, who was writing a dissertation of the subject under my direction at the time.

152

of Regional Expansion, has perhaps gone farthest in terms of legislation to deal with them.[2]

Despite the growing interest, however, many professional economists and more politicians still think of 'poor regions' as an aspect of the more general problem of 'the poor', a problem demanding attention in terms of social justice and political stability, rather than as an integral part of the general problem of generating higher rates of growth and reducing unemployment without aggravating inflation, a problem that now plagues LDCs and ACs alike. Elsewhere, the present writer has presented historical evidence to support the thesis that high rates of growth in national economies, and so ultimately high levels of development, are associated in the long run with regional convergence.[3] Here we shall be concerned with only one aspect of this broader thesis: the relationship between the position of a country's 'trade-off curve', relating rates of price increase to levels of unemployment, and the magnitude of the regional gaps within the country. Virtually all governments are inhibited in their efforts to accelerate growth and reduce unemployment by their reluctance to face the higher rates of price increase that such efforts will bring. The argument to be supported in this chapter is that reducing unemployment, and thus accelerating growth, without unacceptable increases in rate of inflation, is easier the more regionally integrated the national economy, and more difficult the wider are the regional gaps.

The starting-point for the argument, naturally enough, is the simple observation that countries with low indices of regional gaps tend to have trade-off curves close to the axes, and countries with high indices of regional gaps tend to have trade-off curves that are high and to the right. This relationship is illustrated in Figure 9.1. Without theoretical support or more exacting empirical proof, however, the thesis is hardly likely to be accepted as a 'law'. In the next section we shall present some analytical reasons for expecting a relationship to exist between the position of a country's trade-off curve and the size of its regional gaps, whether measured (as in Figure 9.1) by an index of regional dispersion or by a simpler (and

[2] For a discussion of Canadian regional development policy, see Benjamin Higgins, 'Issues in Canadian Regional Development Policy', in J. R. Lasuen (ed.), *Growth Poles: Hypotheses and Policies* (The Hague, Mouton, 1972); and 'Growth Pole Policy in Canada', in Niles Hansen (ed.), *Growth Centres and Regional Development* (Glencoe, Illinois, 1971).

[3] Benjamin Higgins, 'Regional Interactions, the Frontier and Economic Growth', in O. J. Firestone (ed.), *Economic Growth Reassessed* (Ottawa, 1972).

often more revealing) figure showing the percentage gap between the richest and the poorest region.[4] In the following section we shall discuss some of the problems of providing more rigorous empirical proof of the thesis. In Section IV we present some pertinent facts, mainly from Canadian experience. Finally, we discuss policy implications.

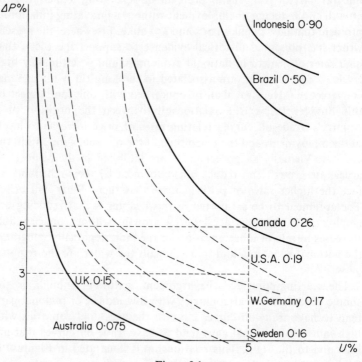

Figure 9.1

The empirical basis of Figure 9.1, and of the three following diagrams, is discussed in Section III below. Econometrically derived Phillips or trade-off curves are available for Canada, France, Sweden, the United Kingdom, the United States and West Germany. Curves for other countries are illustrative representations of the great variety of experience with price increases and unemployment since the Second World War. (For example, in Brazil price increases of 130 per cent per year left unemployment plus underemployment at

---

[4] In Section III reasons are given for preferring the gap between richest and poorest regions to an index of dispersion as a measure of regional gaps.

very high levels, and in Indonesia price increases of 1,500 per cent per year left unemployment plus underemployment at high levels.) The regional trade-off curves for Canada, presented in Figure 9.3, are based on the work of Ronald Bodkin *et al.* on trade-off curves, referred to in Section III. The indices of regional dispersion in Figure 9.1 come partly from Chernick and partly from Williamson (Section III). The indices of sub-regional dispersion in Figure 9.4 come from Chernick. However, as explained in Section III, both the trade-off curves and the indices of dispersion should be regarded as illustrative rather than quantitatively precise. Only the relative position of the trade-off curves and the rank-order of dispersion indices are important for the argument of this paper.

II SOME THEORETICAL CONSIDERATIONS

It can hardly be maintained that the body of theory relating to regional gaps, or the theory relating to trade-off curves (relating rates of price increase to unemployment) and the underlying concept of the 'Phillips curve' (relating rates of wage increase to unemployment) is in satisfactory condition. It is therefore not easy to evolve a satisfactory theory relating the concepts. We shall, however, offer some observations to suggest why it is reasonable to expect that they are in fact related.

Regional Gaps

Let us imagine a country consisting of an undifferentiated flat plain, with natural resources distributed evenly throughout its surface. Let us also assume that there are no inherited differences in education, skills, or technology from one part of the country to the other. We can then divide the country into arbitrary 'regions' as we like, and occupational structures, productivity, and incomes will be identical in all regions.

Now let us assume that the 'North' has minerals and the 'South' has good agricultural soils, but that there is complete mobility of all factors of production, perfect knowledge of all market conditions, and pure competition throughout. The occupational structures will differ between North and South, but marginal productivities and incomes will be equalized by factor movements. No regional gaps will appear.

Next let us impose restrictions on factor movements but retain the other assumptions, and in particular the assumption that production functions (technology) are the same in both regions. These are the conditions of the neo-classical theory of international and inter-regional trade, which lead to equalization of factor prices. Again we have no regional gaps.

Thus we are left with the somewhat trite conclusion that regional gaps must be due to one or more of the following factors:

1. Incomplete knowledge of market conditions
2. Incomplete mobility of factors of production
3. Imperfect competition (and in particular differing degrees of monopoly by sector, and thus by region, where resource endowment and occupational structure differ from one region to another)
4. Imperfect diffusion of technology, and thus differences in production functions, including differences in levels and patterns of education.[5]

The question is, then, what have any of these factors to do with trade-off curves?

Trade-Off Curves

The status of trade-off curves in the economist's tool kit is uncertain. Even the facts are still subject to discussion, and reconciliation of the concept with either macro – or micro – theory is still far from complete. Even more vagaries surround the Phillips curve. Part of the trouble is that the original relationships were cast in terms of experience in the United Kingdom, and thus far analyses for equally long periods have not been forthcoming for other countries (or if they have, they have escaped the present writer's attention). Even for the period since the Second World War attempts at construction of Phillips or trade-off curves are available only for a few countries. We cannot accept empirical observations of so narrow a range of phenomena as evidence of a 'law' unless the same results emerge clearly from received theoretical doctrine. We are not yet in that situation.

We cannot enter here into the entire controversy regarding Phillips and trade-off curves. We shall confine ourselves to a few observations

---

[5] A mathematical model of these inter-relationships is presented in Chapter 5 of *Les Orientations du développement économique régional du Québec*, by Benjamin Higgins, Fernand Martin and André Raynauld (Ottawa, 1970); and in Benjamin Higgins, 'Pôles de crôissance et poles de développement comme concepts opérationnels', *Cahiers Vilfredo Pareto*, no. 24 (April 1971).

regarding this controversy which seem to us particularly germane to the relationship between trade-off curves and regional gaps.

In his fundamental review of the empirical and theoretical aspects of Phillips curves, Richard G. Lipsey writes: 'Until more is known about the causal links between $\dot{W}$ (rate of increase in wage rates) and $\dot{P}$ (rate of increase in prices) it is very dangerous to argue as if either of these variables were independent of the other.'[6] He adds that Phillips regarded the high correlation between $\dot{W}$ and U (the level of unemployment) as evidence in favour of a demand-pull as against a cost-push theory of inflation, but that his own analysis, relating $\dot{W}$ to excess demand for or supply of labour, makes the correlation consistent with 'some versions' of the cost-push theory.

Let us begin with Lipsey's efforts to find a theoretical model to explain the facts as he saw them.[7] He postulates that the rate of change in wages is a function of excess demand for or supply of labour, and introduces the equation $\dot{w} = f[(d-s)/s]$. He establishes the relationship between $\dot{W}$ and U indirectly, by first establishing a relationship between each of them and $(d-s)/s$. He found his model to be consistent with the facts. Later, Gerald Marion found a way of measuring excess demand directly, and obtained results that also seemed to confirm Lipsey's model.[8]

More important for our present purposes than the general conclusion that the rate of change in wages (or prices) is related to excess demand for labour, and excess demand for labour related in turn to the level of unemployment, is a corollary of Lipsey's 'theory': when $d = s$ and excess demand is zero it does not mean that unemployment is zero, but only that unemployment is limited to frictional or structural unemployment. Thus the actual position of a trade-off curve will depend on the amount of frictional and structural unemployment in the economy. In Lipsey's words, the amount of such unemployment will be related to 'the amount of movement and the time taken to move'.[9] He suggests an 'adjustment function' to measure the speed of adjustment of disequilibrium, but adds that

[6] Richard G. Lipsey, 'The Relation between Unemployment and the Rate of Change of Money Wage Rates in the United Kingdom', *Economica* (February 1960), p. 31.

[7] It must be said that Lipsey's 'theory' is not very 'theoretical'. That is, his 'theory' is not deduced from accepted principles of economic behaviour; it is designed rather to isolate other *facts* which might explain the trade-off curves.

[8] Gerald Marion, 'La Demande Excédentaire de Travail et la Variation des Salaires dans L'Industrie Manufacturière au Canada', *Canadian Economic Review* (August 1968), pp. 519–39.

[9] Lipsey, op. cit., p. 14.

knowledge of the shape of this function does not enable us to distinguish the causes of the disequilibrium.

Still more significant for our analysis is Lipsey's finding that the macro-adjustment curve for the economy as a whole will lie above the individual market adjustment curves, and that the more unequal is the distribution of unemployment among various markets (he speaks of two) the higher will be the trade-off or Phillips curve.[10]

The 'real-world implications' Lipsey draws from these conclusions are that to predict the rate of change in money wage rates (or prices) we must know not only the level of unemployment but its distribution among markets, and that the Phillips or trade-off curve for the economy as a whole can be shifted by a policy that reduces the degree of inequality among individual markets.

Finally, Lipsey makes some observations regarding cyclical behaviour that will prove to be important in relation to patterns of regional cycles. Phillips found evidence of 'loops' in the course of economic fluctuations: the rate of change in wage rates (prices) is more than 'expected' when unemployment is falling and less than 'expected' when unemployment is rising. Lipsey concludes that these 'loops' can be explained by the different rates of recovery in different 'markets': 'sectoral' inequality is greater in the early upswing than in the early downswing.

Corry and Laidler also attempt to make sense of the trade-off curve by introducing frictional and structural unemployment.[11] Equilibrium with a positive level of unemployment then becomes possible. They suggest that as the labour market tightens two offsetting factors will alter the amount of frictional or structural unemployment: average time between jobs should fall, but labour participation rates may rise. There is no basis in pure theory to say which will predominate. Their general conclusion is that it is not possible 'to show a relationship between the rate of change in money wages and the level of unemployment' of the kind depicted by the Phillips curve. The empirical evidence of the existence of such a curve such as it is may reflect changes in the level of structural unemployment and frictional unemployment through time, or it may depend on variables other than excess demand for labour, such as the 'geographical distribution' of job vacancies. They do not, however, follow up this pregnant suggestion, contenting themselves

[10] Ibid., pp. 18–19.
[11] Bernard Corry and David Laidler, 'The Phillips Relation: a Theoretical Explanation', *Economica* (May 1967), pp. 189–97.

with the final observation that 'the root of the problem seems to lie in the determination of the level of frictional unemployment'.[12]

III   THE NATURE OF TRADE-OFF CURVES

What these attempts to find a theoretical explanation for trade-off and Phillips curves seem to show is that neither has meaning when

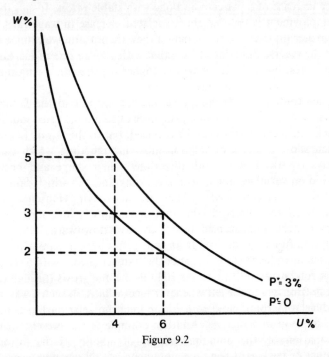

Figure 9.2

divorced from movements through time. That is to say, they do not themselves express basic causal relationships, but merely record the net result of the interplay of a number of variables, some of which are not expressed in the usual diagrams at all. A demand curve, a supply curve, an indifference map, a consumption function - these apply to a point of time and are presumably valid throughout a period of time. They express in themselves fundamental functional relationships which are consistent with observed individual be-haviour, and which can under specific conditions be aggregated to provide meaningful relationships for the economy as a whole. For

[12] Ibid., p. 196.

whatever period they are relevant, we can move all over the diagram in any direction and the relationships still hold. Trade-off and Phillips curves, on the other hand, have precise meaning only when events take place in a given sequence; the relationships are not always reversible. Figure 9.2, for example, is based on one of the diagrams in the study by Ronald G. Bodkin *et al.*[13] It shows two Phillips curves, econometrically derived, one with an assumed rate of price increase of 3 per cent and one with stable prices. It says that if unemployment is reduced the associated increase in wage rates will be greater if prices are rising than if they are not. But we cannot read it in the reverse direction; to say that with a given rate of increase in wage rates, unemployment will be higher if prices are rising than if prices are stable, is obvious nonsense.

Thus trade-off and Phillips curves belong, not to the family of curves depicting fundamental principles of economic behaviour from which other conclusions can be deduced, but to the family of curves which show a series of relationships through time which cannot always be travelled in both directions. Their shape and position depend on variables not shown in the diagram, and which cannot be relegated to *ceteris paribus*. They are like Alvin Hansen's reconciliation of the observed facts that consumption functions derived from budget data seemed to be concave downwards while consumption functions derived from time series were apparently linear: Hansen introduced the concept of the 'ratchet effect', with a series of short-run curves shifting to the right as income grows through time, and shifting less to the left whenever income falls, in such a way as to produce something close to a linear long-run relationship between consumption and income. Another example is the present writer's explanation of 'the unlimited supply of labour' as the historical product of backward bending supply curves and demand curves for labour which both shift to the right through time, with population growth and with technological progress, so as to produce a long-run supply curve approximating a horizontal straight line.[14]

In the same fashion, empirical trade-off curves cannot be derived from general theory alone, either micro or macro. They can be explained only in terms of a specific sequence of economic events within a particular institutional framework, including government

[13] Ronald G. Bodkin, Elisabeth P. Bond, Grant L. Reuber and T. Russell Robinson, *Price Stability and High Employment* (Ottawa, Economic Council of Canada, 1966).

[14] Benjamin Higgins, *Economic Development: Problems, Principles and Policies* (New York, 1968), pp. 237–8.

policy, in particular countries at particular times. This conclusion does not, of course, mean that they are unimportant; far from it. But it does mean that changes in the institutional framework, or in the structure of the economy, or in government policy, can shift the curves, without any changes in *basic* economic behaviour on the part of individuals or groups.

To illustrate this point let us construct a micro-theory directly relating $\dot{W}$ to U. To do so it is necessary to assume a specific institutional framework as well as specific patterns of economic behaviour. Let us suppose, then, that wage rates in each industrial sector are set periodically through a process of bargaining between trade unions and employers. We shall assume also that the labour force is growing through time and that the government, with high growth rates and high levels of employment in mind, pursues a monetary and fiscal policy designed to assure an expanding money supply. Finally, we shall assume that trade-union leaders and employers are economically sophisticated and think in macro-economic terms. Employers are aware of the link between wages and consumer spending, expect other industries to follow similar patterns of wage adjustment, and expect the government to continue a policy of maintaining high rates of growth and high levels of employment. They are therefore prepared to grant periodic wage increases, because they expect to be able to pass on all or part of the wage increases by raising prices. The unions are reconciled to the continuing existence of a certain amount of unemployment, particularly if it is confined mainly to new entrants to the labour force who are not yet union members.

At low levels of employment the employers offer little resistance to wage increases, expecting them to be offset by price increases with no drop in sales, and would in fact accept wage increases higher than those on which the unions would insist. This relationship is shown by the 'employers-actual' curve in Figure 9.3. For bargaining purposes, however, they pursue a lower curve, shown by 'employers-bargaining' in the diagram. As actual unemployment increases, the employers, fearing that the government may fail to expand the money flow enough to prevent a recession, resist wage increases more strongly. The unions, similarly, pursue a 'bargaining curve' higher than their 'actual curve', as shown in the diagram. As unemployment increases, cutting into the trade-union membership, the union leaders are prepared to accept smaller and smaller periodic wage increases. Thus the bargaining process determines both the wage increase and the level of employment and unemployment for each industrial sector.

Aggregating, we obtain the wage increase and level of unemployment for the economy as a whole.

So far we have only one point on a potential Phillips curve, the equilibrium point, W_e. As time passes, however, and both the labour force and the money supply increase, the curves will shift. Unfortunately, the purely behavioural assumptions underlying this micro-theory cannot tell us how they will shift; the movement of the curves through time depends both on the relative increases in labour force

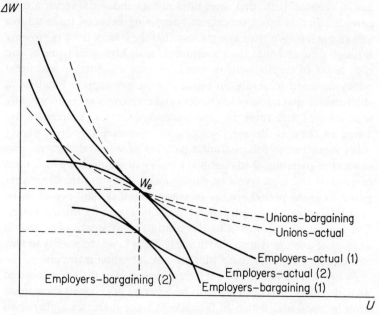

Figure 9.3

and money flow and on the reactions of employers and union leaders to these changes. This micro-theory conforms well enough to actual conditions in a number of advanced countries since the Second World War. It gives us a 'Phillips curve' of a sort. That is, it will give us a scatter diagram to which some sort of curve could be fitted, more or less well. But we have no way of knowing from the theoretical model by itself what the shape and position of such a curve might be. For each country the 'Phillips curve' that emerges is a species of historical accident.

More important, within the limits of this theoretical model there is no way of improving the situation unless the unions become 'more reasonable and more responsible'. The government can shift the employers' curve downwards by threatening the 'classical medicine' for price increases – checking the monetary expansion – as shown by the curves Emp-actual(2) and Emp-bargaining(2) in the diagram. But unless the unions' curves shift downwards in the same fashion there will be no equilibrium position, no solution to the bargaining process, and strikes or lockouts will ensue.

Thus even if we attempt to explain Phillips curves by assuming that demand and supply in the labour market are governed by wage increases rather than by the level of wages as assumed in neo-classical theory, we still have no micro-theoretical explanation of Phillips curves of a particular shape and position. We must resort to further specific institutional and behavioural assumptions. Each Phillips curve is a historical record, and we cannot move back along it. The explanation of Phillips and trade-off curves in terms of imperfectly integrated markets, as outlined above, is a good deal more satisfactory in pure theory, and offers more hope for a policy solution.

The importance of this conclusion for the present analysis should be clear. In order to reduce unemployment without accelerating inflation, we do not need to change basic economic behaviour. We do not even need to operate directly on the variables shown in the trade-off or Phillips curves themselves – and we might do better not to try to do so. Instead we can operate on the structural elements of the economy which determine the position of a country's trade-off curves – notably regional gaps.

IV   THE RELATIONSHIP BETWEEN TRADE-OFF CURVES AND
REGIONAL GAPS

By now the relationship between trade-off curves and regional gaps should have emerged. In the first place, with complete, instantaneous and costless movement of all factors of production, plus perfect knowledge, we would have neither regional gaps nor trade-off curves in their present form. The system would of course produce some relationship between changes in the level of unemployment and increases in wages and prices; but the policy trade-off which plagues us today would not exist. Price increases reflect excess demand somewhere in the economy, and under the conditions assumed the flow of unemployed labour and other resources to that 'somewhere' would tend to check any increase in wages and prices, not accelerate it.

There could still be underemployment equilibrium of the Keynesian variety, due to the 'liquidity trap', but this equilibrium would not be inflationary at the same time.

Once the conditions for existence of regional gaps are introduced, the conditions for existence of trade-off curves are also introduced. It is obvious that imperfect knowledge, or imperfect mobility due to other causes, will bring both regional gaps and the structural and frictional unemployment on which the existence of trade-off curves rests. Differences in production functions (imperfect diffusion of knowledge, or differences in factor endowments, or both) can produce regional gaps, particularly if the isoquants are 'well-behaved' in one region and approximate fixed technical coefficients in the other. These are the classical conditions for 'technological dualism', and in many countries, especially the developing ones, regional dualism is scarcely distinguishable from technological dualism. But it is enough that the isoquants be 'badly behaved' and different in both regions, as Richard Eckaus showed years ago. Under such conditions mobility is limited; the unemployed in one region cannot flow quickly and easily to markets with an excess demand, because production techniques are not adapted to the excess supply. Once again we have frictional and structural unemployment – hence trade-off curves. Imperfect competition, by limiting freedom of entry, can also slow down transfers of manpower, thus contributing both to regional disparities and to structural and frictional unemployment, and so to the presence of trade-off curves.

Indeed, in the 'theories' of Lipsey and of Corry and Laidler briefly summarized above, one need only substitute 'regions' for 'sectors' or 'different markets' to deduce the principle: 'The amount of frictional and structural unemployment, and hence the position of the trade-off curve of any country, depends on the degree of regional disintegration of the economy, as indicated by the magnitude of the regional disparities.' We also have here a simple clue to the tendency for the trade-off curves of developing countries to be more troublesome (higher and further to the right) than those of advanced countries. Almost by definition, the developing countries are those that are least integrated regionally, and where the overlap of regions with 'sectors' or 'markets' is most complete. In Indonesia, for example, the 'rich region' (Sumatra and to a lesser extent Kalimantan) in which the modern export sector is concentrated sells virtually nothing to the poor region (essentially Java) where traditional agriculture is concentrated, and buys very little from it – and vice versa. Few countries are so regionally disintegrated, and few have such disadvantageous trade-off curves. In our list, Brazil comes next in terms of regional disintegration and in terms of troublesome trade-off curves. Canada is less integrated regionally than the United States or Australia, and has a significantly worse trade-off curve. By now it should be clear why these relationships exist.

In short, trade-off curves appear when inflationary pressures are generated in one sector (market) while unemployment is concentrated in another sector (market) and there are obstacles to quick and costless movement of labour from one market to the other. Trade-off curves are in more awkward positions in regionally disintegrated economies precisely because in such economies the obstacles to rapid and complete movement are particularly formidable: frictional and structural unemployment is a high proportion of the total. The problem becomes particularly intractable when economic disparities are compounded by socio-cultural differences, as in the case of Java, the Brazilian North-East, the Italian or Mexican South, or the Canadian province of Quebec. In such cases the cultural as well as the geographical differences between the places where unemployment is concentrated and the places where the jobs are (and where the inflationary pressure is generated) may be very great indeed. Neither the speed nor the volume of movement between jobs is sufficient to prevent unemployment from remaining, or even increasing, in the lagging regions (Quebec, the Atlantic Provinces) despite levels of investment in the leading region (Ontario) being sufficiently high, when added to public and private investment taking place elsewhere in the economy, to create overall inflationary pressure. Price increases are diffused throughout a single economy quickly enough; employment is not, when the economy consists of a collection of more or less loosely-related regions. The whole process is aided and abetted by monopolistic practices on the part of trade unions and employers alike, and by the reluctance of governments committed to high rates of growth and low levels of unemployment to apply the 'classical medicine' for excessive wage-price demands.

Under the conditions analysed above, there will be a strong tendency, once marked regional gaps and troublesome trade-off curve set in, for the situation to get progressively worse. Entrepreneurs will be attracted by the dynamic urban centres (development poles) of the leading region and the agglomerative tendencies will be strong. Moreover, once the population of the leading region attains a level that is a high proportion of the total population (Ontario in Canada) a high rate of growth of the labour force, reflecting past high rates of fertility, accompanied by technological progress of a labour-saving type, can keep the process going, continuing to generate a high level of investment in the leading region, without creating job opportunities much in excess of the growth of the labour force within the leading region itself. This worsening situation will tend to reduce mobility further by increasing the risk to the job seeker who is willing to

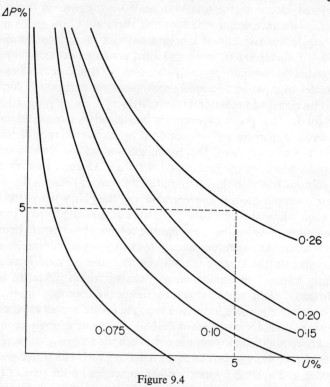

Figure 9.4

move. Structural unemployment becomes higher and the trade-off curve moves further to the right. Moreover, once regional discrepancies become so marked that there are significant differences in the socio-cultural ambience from one region to another, and particularly as between the urban centres of leading and lagging regions, another 'feedback' mechanism sets in. The pattern of migration will tend to dilute the quality of the population in the lagging region. It will be the best trained, most progressive, most ambitious men and women – those with the highest level of 'need-achievement' – who will move.

Those who remain behind will be those least wanted in the leading regions, those for whom effective mobility is least. Thus immobility tends to be aggravated, frictional and structural unemployment increased – and trade-off curves more bothersome than ever.

Diagrammatically, the conclusions of this section may be expressed by a reinterpretation of Figure 9.1 as shown in Figure 9.4. We may think of the diagram as showing a 'family' of trade-off curves, all applicable to a single country – Canada, for example. The diagram then indicates the reductions in regional disparities that are needed to push the trade-off curves downward to the left. I do not wish to suggest that I am in a position at the present time to put precise numbers on these curves; at the time of writing they remain conjectural, and only the relative positions have real meaning. We shall deal with some of the statistical problems in the next section; let me simply note here that apart from the general problem of distinguishing movements along trade-off curves from shifts in the curves, in the case of Canada the statistical problem is complicated by the fact that there have been no sharp shifts in the index of regional dispersion.

V REGIONAL TRADE-OFF CURVES

There is a third way in which the family of trade-off curves can be interpreted: each curve might apply to one major region in a particular country; for example, the diagram might depict the five major regions of Canada (Figure 9.5). Figures for prices, unemployment and sub-regional disparities are available for Canadian regions, and these curves can be regarded as essentially empirical. In recent years, the lowest curve would apply to the Prairie Provinces, using official figures of registered unemployment, with Ontario just above it. However, if allowance were made for seasonal unemployment and disguised unemployment not reported in official figures in the more highly agricultural prairies, it is likely that the Ontario curve would be lowest. British Columbia would be represented by the intermediate position, with Quebec higher and further to the right and the Atlantic Provinces in the upper right hand quadrant. The national trade-off curve is the result of aggregating these regional curves.

This same relationship shows up in the regional patterns of economic fluctuations. As may be seen from Table 9.1, the timing of upturns and downturns is much the same in all five regions: at least there are no consistent leads and lags. There are, however, significant differences in amplitude. Since price movements are similar in all regions, these differences in amplitude refer mainly to differences in amplitude of fluctuations in employment and unemployment. In other words, employment and unemployment are more responsive to fluctuations in national income in some regions than in others. Thus in recent years (1963–7) each 1 per cent change in Gross

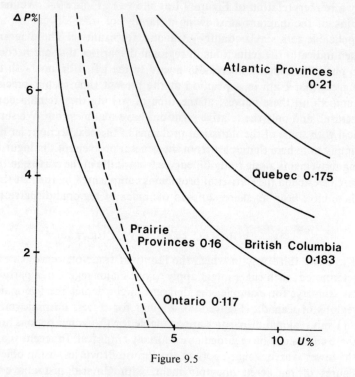

Figure 9.5

National Product brought a 0·32 per cent change in the level of unemployment in Quebec, compared to 0·26 per cent in Ontario, 0·21 per cent in British Columbia, and 19 per cent in the Prairie Provinces. The relationship of changes in unemployment to changes in Gross National Product is less systematic in the Atlantic Provinces. The problems of that region are more purely structural than those of Quebec; a purely 'Keynesian' policy of raising national effective demand would go far towards elimination of unemployment in Quebec, although if no attack were made on Quebec's structural problems at the same time the rate of price increase might become uncomfortably high. In the Atlantic Provinces there is some tendency for the difference in unemployment rates in the region and in

Ontario to fall, as Ontario approaches full employment, but the gap remains large and the movements are a bit erratic. It is clear that an attempt to eliminate unemployment in the Atlantic Provinces by a simple, Keynesian aggregate policy of increasing aggregative effective demand, without a frontal attack on the structural problems of the region itself, would produce intolerable rates of inflation in the national economy.

Thus it is mainly on the side of employment that the regional disintegration of the Canadian economy appears. Regional price differentials on transportable goods which are in excess of transportation costs cannot prevail for very long. Inflationary pressures are diffused throughout the economy rapidly enough. But employment is not. Capital does not, generally speaking, move to 'reserves' of labour; areas of high unemployment are usually unattractive to new investment for other reasons (including relative poverty and limited markets) and labour mobility is not high enough to eliminate the marked differences in rates of unemployment. It may be observed that the relatively short periods of regional convergence have been periods in which unemployment fell more sharply than prices rose. Unemployment is concentrated in the two poorer regions, and periods of falling unemployment since 1926 (when statistics of *per capita* incomes by Province start) have not been periods of violently rising prices.

Finally, there is some evidence, which we are examining more carefully, that the position of each regional trade-off curve is related to the magnitude of sub-regional gaps within each region. There is also evidence that regional gaps are related in part to differences in labour force participation rates; the rates are higher in the rich regions than in the poor regions. The cyclical behaviour of labour force participation rates for each region needs further study, but at first blush there are grounds to suspect that one reason for the recalcitrance of Canada's trade-off curve is that participation rates tend to rise during the upswing, particularly in the more prosperous regions. Consequently generally rising prices cannot be counted upon to reduce unemployment, even in Ontario where most of the inflationary pressure is generated, below about 4 per cent.

VI   EMPIRICAL TESTING

Clearly, my thesis would be more convincing if buttressed by direct econometric tests of the relationship between measures of regional

TABLE 9.1   Index of Employment by Province

	Prince Edward Island	Nova Scotia	New Brunswick	Quebec	Ontario	Manitoba	Saskatchewan	Alberta	British Columbia
1926				53·1	49·9				52·0
1927				55·6	52·9				52·5
1928				57·9	56·9				55·2
1929				60·6	61·7				57·9
1930				58·9	57·4				56·0
1931				53·9	50·7				49·6
1932				45·7	44·4				41·7
1933				43·8	42·2				40·5
1934				49·0	50·8				46·9
1935				51·0	51·8				50·7
1936				53·8	53·5				52·5
1937		68·1		61·7	59·2				55·4
1938	59·9	66·0	62·4	62·5	57·1	58·4	70·2	52·0	54·1
1939	64·1	66·8	59·6	64·6	57·3	59·7	71·4	55·1	55·8
1940	67·2	71·4	67·4	67·4	64·2	63·4	70·1	57·4	58·0
1941	75·7	90·0	82·1	80·3	77·9	74·1	76·1	65·5	67·9
1942	70·8	103·3	89·8	94·1	87·0	80·0	78·1	70·9	82·2
1943	74·7	106·8	95·0	100·9	90·0	83·1	81·5	74·3	94·5
1944	85·9	105·0	98·4	99·1	89·5	85·8	85·5	77·6	92·5
1945	81·9	101·5	98·6	92·8	86·7	85·3	86·4	76·3	87·5
1946	87·2	95·4	98·1	90·4	86·8	89·6	92·2	82·6	83·6
1947	93·3	92·1	104·3	97·8	94·7	93·6	97·2	88·1	97·1
1948	102·6	99·6	105·2	101·2	98·9	97·2	99·5	93·7	101·3
1949	100·0	100·0	100·0	100·0	100·0	100·0	100·0	100·0	100·0
1950	110·3	95·6	102·6	100·5	102·7	100·8	100·8	104·5	100·8

1951	112·6	100·3	109·0	109·2	110·4	103·9	106·0	112·4	106·1
1952	123·2	104·0	109·5	113·4	112·0	106·0	111·4	120·8	106·7
1953	115·5	101·0	100·8	112·4	114·5	107·0	116·2	128·5	108·4
1954	109·9	97·6	98·0	104·3	110·6	104·7	118·0	128·0	106·2
1955	114·2	97·1	103·5	112·5	113·5	105·2	117·0	133·0	111·9
1956	117·4	101·7	110·1	120·1	121·4	108·6	121·1	148·5	121·5
1957	115·2	100·2	103·8	121·5	124·3	110·9	125·3	152·2	123·9
1958	114·9	95·5	98·0	117·0	119·6	108·7	126·6	150·5	114·7
1959	126·3	96·3	101·7	118·5	121·3	112·2	130·0	155·0	115·1
1960	128·5	95·5	103·4	118·6	119·2	111·0	126·0	153·3	114·7
1961	130·7	94·0	103·9	118·3	118·7	110·0	123·1	154·2	112·3
1962	135·8	94·4	103·8	121·6	123·0	111·1	124·6	158·1	115·7
1963	132·1	95·3	104·9	124·4	126·9	112·9	127·9	160·3	119·9
1964	136·1	98·0	109·7	130·2	133·1	116·2	132·3	167·4	125·4
1965	157·0	102·7	115·0	136·6	140·8	119·1	138·9	177·6	135·5
1966	159·8	106·9	120·8	143·0	149·0	124·9	146·6	190·1	144·6
1967	160·4	107·2	122·2	144·6	151·2	129·2	150·4	199·1	147·5

Source: BFS, *Revue statistique du Canada: Sommaire Chronologique* (1963).

gaps and the position of trade-off curves. The diagrams presented above are not econometrically derived in the strict sense of that term. They do reflect the available econometric studies and the pertinent statistics that have been published; they also reflect modifications, based on theory and judgement – 'informed hunch' if the reader prefers – to take care of the more obvious limitations of these studies and statistics. A truly rigorous empirical proof of my hypothesis regarding the relationship between measures of regional disparities and price increase-unemployment trade-off curves would require a major research project, and even under the best of conditions would encounter formidable obstacles, some of which might prove insurmountable.

There are very few studies of either regional disparities or trade-off curves which cover enough countries to provide statistically signi-ficant results and permit meaningful international comparisons. The number of countries for which both measures of regional disparities and trade-off or Phillips curves are currently available is very small indeed; few people have been thinking in these terms.

Regional Disparities
Sydney Chernick's study of regional gaps provides indices of regional disparities for Canada, Australia and the United States for the years 1926–64.[15] These tend to support the hypothesis: the 'rank correla-tion' between indices of dispersions and the position of trade-off curves is perfect. Obviously, however, three countries are far from sufficient for empirical proof. The most extensive study of regional gaps known to the present writer is that of Jeffrey G. Williamson, covering twenty-four countries for periods ranging from one to more than one hundred years.[16] This study has two major limita-tions:

1. Regional disparities are measured by the dispersion of regional *per capita* incomes around the national mean, either unweighted or weighted by regional populations. However, particularly when the number of regions is large, this measure may tell us little about the seriousness of regional gaps or about changes in total gap. It would be possible for Williamson's dispersion index to fall while the gap between richest and poorest region increased, through

[15] S. E. Chernick, *Inter-regional Disparities in Income* (Ottawa, Economic Council of Canada, 1966).
[16] Jeffrey G. Williamson, 'Regional Inequality and the Process of National Development', *Economic Development and Cultural Change* (July 1965).

movement of several regions towards the national mean while the richest and poorest regions moved further apart. From a national welfare viewpoint, in Canada it is the gap between Ontario and Quebec or the Atlantic Provinces that counts, not the average dispersion around the mean.

2. Much more serious is the fact that such international comparisons, in order to include enough countries to be significant, must use 'regional' figures for whatever political and geographic subdivisions have figures of *per capita* income. These may be anything from vast States in Australia to tiny *municipios* in Puerto Rico. Thus we end up with six regions (States) for Australia, eleven regions (Provinces and Territories) for Canada, and nine regions for the United States (groupings of States). But for Brazil, which is comparable in total area, we have twenty-one regions (States) and for India, which is substantially smaller but still large, we have eighteen. These might be regarded as roughly comparable 'regions' – with some reservations. But then for middle-sized countries we have more regions, not less: fifteen for the United Kingdom, nineteen for Italy, forty-six for Japan, fifty for Spain, and twenty-five for Sweden. Some of the smaller countries have more 'regions', and some many more regions, than Australia or Canada: eleven for the Netherlands, twenty-six for Ireland, twenty for Norway, twenty-three for Finland, and seventy-six for Puerto Rico. Obviously, these are not 'regions' in the same economic sense as Australian States or the five regions of Canada. Indices of dispersion tend to increase as the size of the unit is reduced; Chernick's figures for Canada, for example, suggest an increase in his dispersion index (unweighted) from 19·1 to 27·2 when the number of regions is increased from ten (Provinces) to 238 (economic regions and countries). If countries were used throughout Canada, instead of economic regions in Ontario and Quebec, the dispersion would increase even more, and it is obviously Canadian counties that are most comparable to some of the regional units in small countries.

Chernick's choice of 'economic regions' for Ontario and Quebec, and counties for the other Provinces also creates problems in the use of his figures as measures of gaps among sub-regions in Figure 9.4, showing trade-off curves for major regions of Canada. This approach provides Ontario and Quebec with ten regions each, British Columbia also with ten, but the Prairie Provinces with fifty-three and the Atlantic Provinces with forty-six. For this reason it seems desirable to increase the measures of dispersion for the

Prairie Provinces and Atlantic Provinces somewhat in making comparisons of their trade-off curves, but at the time of writing I have no accurate means of deciding *how much*. Chernick's figures for Canada with ten or with 238 regions provide only a very rough guide.

Trade-Off Curves

The most thorough effort at international comparisons of Phillips curves or trade-off curves to have come the author's way is the study made for the Economic Council of Canada by Ronald G. Bodkin, Elizabeth P. Bond, Grant L. Reuber and T. Russel Robinson.[17] Here comparisons are made for Canada, the United States, France, West Germany, Sweden and the United Kingdom under a variety of assumptions. This study has a number of limitations for the purposes of the present paper, apart from the small number of countries included. Some of these are inherent in any attempt to determine statistical Phillips or trade-off curves, some arise from the design of this particular study.

1. As already stated, conceptually a Phillips or trade-off curve applies to a point of time, and is presumably stable through some period of time. But Phillips or trade-off curves – like statistical demand and supply curves – must be derived from time series. Accordingly we are confronted with our old bugbear: how to distinguish movements along the curve from shifts of the whole curve? There can be little doubt that the curves do shift. The present writer has little doubt that one of the reasons why the authors had particular difficulty with the curves for West Germany (which indeed seem to bear little relationship to a simple comparison of price movements and unemployment in the country in recent years) is that the curves shifted downward to the left as the reconstruction period ended and steady and rapid growth began. This downward shift of the entire curve may also explain the statistical importance of the 'dummy' variable (zero from the first quarter of 1949 to the last quarter of 1957, one from the first quarter of 1958 to the last quarter of 1965) which was introduced by the authors to 'permit the secular rate of growth in productivity to take on a different value in each sub-period'. The Williamson study shows a decline in the index of regional dispersion in West Germany in the same period – which fits my hypothesis, but can hardly be convincing as a single case.

2. Definitions of unemployment vary from country to country,

[17] R. Bodkin *et al.*, op. cit.

making international comparisons of trade-off curves difficult. Even when formal definitions are the same, they may need different interpretation. Thus the trade-off curve for the Prairie Provinces seems low in comparison to the index of sub-regional dispersion provided by Chernick. This aberration may be due primarily to the fact that Chernick has so many more regions for the Prairies than for any other major region, but it may be due also to the fact that the seasonal unemployment and underemployment typical of agricultural societies does not get reported as registered unemployment. For both these reasons it would seem appropriate to place the trade-off curve for the Prairies further from the origin than the available statistics would indicate.

3. The Bodkin *et al.* study is not directed towards weighing the importance of regional disparities in the explanation of the shape and position of trade-off curves, and regional gaps are not included in their equations. On the other hand, a number of other variables in which the authors were interested, such as the effect of increases in the United States price level, were included. Some of these (including the American price level) have significant effects on the position and slopes of the curves. Among the other variables tested were past changes in wages, the ratio of corporate profits to manufacturing output, and the 'dummy variable' already mentioned. The result is a variety of equations which may still be over-simple for a complete explanation of changes in wages, prices, and unemployment, but which are none the less too complicated for a test of the hypothesis outlined above. That requires a test of the relationship of regional disparities to the shape and position of trade-off curves *whatever* the other forces acting on the trade-off curves, although a multiple regression analysis should be used to measure the relative importance of regional disparities and other factors. As it is, the Bodkin *et al.* curves are disturbingly different according to the equations chosen, and none seems close to the results of a simple, common-sensical inspection of relations between annual increases in prices and rates of unemployment in recent years.

For example, the study presents curves for 'non-inflationary' conditions where United States prices are (hypothetically) stable, 'inflationary' conditions where they are hypothetically equal to 2 per cent per year, and 'moderately inflationary' conditions where the increase is hypothetically in-between. The curves shift too much according to the assumption chosen to allow me to be comfortable in choosing any one of them for testing my own hypothesis, for which the impact of changes in the United States prices is not of primary importance. The marked difference in Phillips curves (wage increase-unemployment) and trade-off curves (price increase-unemployment) is hard to explain in terms of any accepted theoretical model. For example, under 'non-inflationary conditions', the study suggests that Britain might achieve stable wage rates with around 5 per cent unemployment, and Sweden with perhaps 8 per cent unemployment, while none of the other countries can achieve wage stability at any level of unemployment. Yet in the past price stability has been achieved in the United States at about 4 per cent unemployment and in Canada at about 5 per cent, while the other countries cannot achieve price stability at any level of unemployment. Surely such marked differences in wage movements and price movements are difficult to explain.

Again, it is difficult to accept the conclusion that the United States 'trade-off curve' is below that of West Germany and the United Kingdom (for price increases below about 2 per cent per year, for either 'non-inflationary' or 'moderately inflationary' conditions) when one looks at actual figures of price increase and unemployment in the period since 1958. During the period 1958–65 unemployment in the United Kingdom ranged between 1·5 per cent and 2·4 per cent, while in 1965 the Price Index, with 1958 = 100 was 107. In Germany the corresponding figures are 0·6 per cent to 1·2 per cent unemployment, and 104.

4. The curves derived from the Bodkin *et al.* study cross each other, even on the 'moderately inflationary' hypothesis which is on the whole most realistic. The question thus arises as to which parts of the curves are more relevant for comparison with measures of regional disparity. Some of the intersections take place outside the range of normal experience, others seem to be related to the peculiarities of the curves and their underlying equations. For example, with 'moderate inflation' the United States curve cuts the West Germany and United Kingdom trade-off curves when the rate of price increase is below 2·2 per cent; this intersection reflects the same aspects of the curves as those discussed in the previous paragraph.

On the whole, it would seem desirable to return to the original data, and conduct a tailor-made test of the empirical relations between measures of regional disparity and the position and shape of trade-off curves.[18]

[18] Raphael Rubio de Urquia is testing shifts in the Canadian Phillips and trade-off curves in relation to changes in regional gaps measured by: (average

Policy Implications

The policy implications of my hypothesis, if substantiated by further empirical testing, are enormous. Measures to reduce regional gaps, far from being a 'luxury' to be afforded when things are otherwise going well in the country, are the essence of a policy to accelerate growth, reduce unemployment, and maintain price stability. For developing countries, where efforts to accelerate growth are inhibited by fear of aggravating inflation, reduction of regional disparities may well be the *sine qua non* of a successful development policy. Even for advanced countries, where regional integration is imperfect, the achievement of tolerable combinations of growth, unemployment, price increases and balance of payments position will require a frontal attack on the problem of regional gaps. The obverse of this conclusion also holds: where regional disintegration is serious, no unified, aggregative monetary and fiscal policy applied uniformly throughout the country can deal effectively with the problem of co-existence of unemployment and inflation, compounded in some cases by slow growth and in others by balance of payments problems as well. What is needed instead is a regionally differentiated policy, including a consciously differentiated monetary and fiscal policy for each region.

per capita incomes in Ontario and British Columbia) minus (average *per capita* incomes in Quebec and the Atlantic Provinces) over (average incomes in Quebec and the Atlantic Provinces). The early results look promising and seem to confirm the thesis.

CHAPTER 10

Tendencies and Determinants of Income Distribution in Western Countries – A Note

J. TINBERGEN

I INTRODUCTION

During the last decade or so a number of partly antiquated forms of critical analysis of Western societies have gained popularity especially with some youth groups. One cannot help thinking sometimes that part of the explanation is the age of the adherents which implies their not having known Western societies of, say, half a century ago. It would, of course, be silly to forget about more valid grounds for criticism.

One illustration of the critical attitude is the use of the word 'capitalism' to characterize today's society, an expression introduced by Karl Marx to characterize Western societies almost a century ago. Another example is the word 'exploitation', used to indicate some types of human relationship. What is really important is, among other things, income distribution rather than the question of whether one individual is employed by another, namely a private manager. The emotional appeal of strong contrasts and words plays a role in the recent revival of this type of critical analysis. It helps to further a phenomenon much more dangerous to everybody now than a century or even half a century ago: polarization. Whatever one's position or preferences, however, a study of facts and figures is useful to anybody involved. As a first instalment of a more thorough analysis, I take the liberty of offering a few figures on income distribution which are not generally known.

II SOME CONCEPTS

It is useful to remind the reader of a number of concepts relevant to the subject, before giving some figures on it. The list of concepts

178

will not be complete, but will be restricted to the aspects on which this note concentrates.

Since the most penetrating studies on income distribution in developed market economies have been based on income-tax data, a first concept of relevance to the subject is the extent of *tax evasion*. After having attempted to correct for evasion, we can study income distribution according to a) *factor shares*, that is, the share of labour income and of capital income, where capital includes land; and b) *income size*. Since inequalities in income result for about 75 to 80 per cent from inequalities in labour income, and this category includes managing directors of corporations as well as workers, the size distribution is the most interesting part of the problem.

Here a distinction should be made between:

i. income before tax; usually including benefits in money from public authorities' activities;
ii. income after tax;
iii. income after tax and benefits in kind from public authorities' activities;
iv. income after complete redistribution, including the one resulting from social insurance schemes, not run by public authorities.

All these concepts still refer to income *earners*, however, and not to 'income *users*', that is, the individuals living in the families of income earners. I submit that the best measure of income distribution therefore is the distribution of:

v. income per family member after complete redistribution.

III INCOME DISTRIBUTION TRENDS IN THE PAST

From a considerable number of sources I collected the following figures about the changes in income distribution over the last half century or the last few decades.

An idea of the *reduction in evasion* (mostly due to improved organization of tax collection) can be obtained from a comparison between national income based on production and national income based on tax returns. For Great Britain, Feinstein[1] found the difference to be 7·3 per cent for 1870/9 as against 0·3 per cent for

[1] C. H. Feinstein, 'National Income and Expenditure, 1870–1963', Reprint Series No. 225 (Cambridge, Dept of Applied Economics, 1964).

1953/62. For the Netherlands, Oomens[2] found 8·4 per cent in 1952 as against 1·1 per cent in 1964.[3]

Factor shares. Income from capital in Great Britain was estimated at 36 per cent for 1910/14, falling to 18 per cent[4] for 1960/3. For the Netherlands the same share fell from 33 per cent in 1930 to 21 per cent in 1968.[5]

Income distribution according to size. This may be illustrated by the percentage of national income drawn by the 5 per cent richest income earners in the United Kingdom; in 1880 this amounted to 48 per cent; in 1957 to 18 per cent.[6] Inequality is sometimes measured by the Gini coefficient of concentration, which is 0 for complete equality of all incomes and 1 for complete concentration of all national income with one single income earner. For the USA this coefficient fell from 0·52 in 1939 to 0·37 in 1959.[7] For the Netherlands, another measure, the average percentage deviation of incomes from their average, fell from 0·72 in 1921–30 to 0·61 in the last 15 years (1950–64).[8] All this refers to *income before taxes* have been paid.

For *income after tax* the figures are less unequal because of the progressive taxes which have increased considerably over the last decades. The situation is illustrated by the income share of the richest 1 per cent in the United Kingdom:

	1938	1957
Before tax	16%	8%
After tax	12%	5%

Source: H. Lydall, 'The Long-Term Trend in the Size Distribution of Income', *Journal of the Royal Stat. Soc.*, A 122 (1959), p. 1.

[2] C. A. Oomens and T. Palthe, 'The Distribution of Income Between Socio-Economic Groups' (Tel Aviv, Internat. Ass. for Research in Income and Wealth, 11th General Conference, 1969).

[3] It is not certain, however, whether this decline can be mainly attributed to decreased evasion, an information for which I want to express my thanks to Dr J. B. D. Derksen.

[4] See Feinstein, op. cit.

[5] *Memo on Income Distribution* (*Nota over de inkomensverdeling*, Annex 15 to Budget Proposals 1970: Netherlands Government, 1969).

[6] S. Kuznets, *Modern Economic Growth* (New Haven and London, 1966), p. 208.

[7] H. Lydall, *The Structure of Earnings* (Oxford, 1968), p. 178.

[8] Central Bureau of Statistics, the Netherlands, *Statistische en Econometrische Onderzoekingen* (1960: 2nd quarter), p. 57. Supplemented by Dr J. B. D. Derksen in private correspondence.

Similarly the inequality in the Netherlands falls, in 1962 from 0·61 before tax (already mentioned) to 0·57 after tax.[9]

After *complete redistribution* by public authorities the Gini coefficient, being 0·32 in 1959 for the United Kingdom[10] before taxes, falls to 0·251. A comparable figure for 1937 taken from Barna[11] amounts to 0·265. Put in another way, the complete redistribution through public finance transfers 6 per cent of total national income from the incomes of the rich to those of the poor, in the Netherlands in 1935/6;[12] a figure which had risen to 9 per cent for 1962.[13]

A study for Denmark[14] states that in 1963, 13 to 18 per cent was transferred, if *social insurances* were also included. The same figure for 1938/9 and for 1955 was about 6 per cent.

So far the figures have referred to income earners. If we now pass from earners to users of income, it appears that inequality has declined still further. This phenomenon is due to the fact that for several Western countries the average family size was relatively large for poor families (in comparison to richer families) in the past, whereas this size has decreased more quickly for poor families than for rich families. The phenomenon is more pronounced in the Netherlands: around 1925 poor families showed twice the size of rich families (taking the groups distinguished by budget statistics); in 1962 the richest 10 per cent families had a size double that of the poorest 10 per cent.[15] This implies that the income distribution for users has improved four times as much as for income earners. For other, more important, countries the phenomenon is much less pronounced. Taking richest and poorest 20 per cent groups I found for the United States between 1903[16] and 1959[17] an improvement

---

[9] Ibid.

[10] J. L. Nicholson, 'Redistribution of Income in the United Kingdom in 1959, 1957, 1953', Income and Wealth Series No. 10 (London 1964), pp. 147, 165.

[11] T. Barna, as quoted in Nicholson, op. cit.

[12] H. Vos, *Enige kwantitatieve onderzoekingen over de betrekking tussen overheidsfinanciën en volkshuishouding* (Quantitative Investigations on the Relations between Public Finance and the National Economy: Haarlem, 1946).

[13] *Memo on Income Distribution*, op. cit.

[14] C. Iversen (Chairman of Det Økonomiske Råd), *Den personlige indkomstfordeling og indkomstudjaevningen over de offentlige finanser* (Copenhagen, 1967).

[15] *Memo on Income Distribution*, op. cit.

[16] Commissioner of Labour, *Cost of Living and Retail Prices of Food*, Eighteenth Report (Washington, 1904), part 1, pp. 582–3.

[17] Selma Goldsmith, 'Impact of the Income-Tax on Socio-Economic Groups of Families in the United States', Income and Wealth Series No. 10 (London, 1964), p. 247.

in this phenomenon in the ratio of 1·08. For the United Kingdom I found similar results, using Prais and Houthakker[18] and Nicholson;[19] here the improvement due to this factor between 1937/9 and 1957, using deciles, amounts to 1·73; for (Western) Germany between 1927/8 and 1965 it amounts to 1·95, derived from family budget statistics,[20] also using deciles.[21]

The evidence shown proves that the developed market economies have experienced a considerable reduction in inequality in income per user.

IV DETERMINANTS OF INCOME DISTRIBUTION

Even so, further reduction in inequalities is desired by the majority of citizens. The question arises then as to what instruments are available for such a further reduction. To answer the question we must know the determinants of income distribution. In the preceding sections we have come across several already, such as taxes, social insurance and several types of other activities of the public authorities. Among them the provision of education is very important. Most modern analysts of the problem of income distribution have emphasized the impact of differences in productive capabilities on income distribution. While these differences are partly innate, they can be considerably influenced by various types of education. In this train of thought authors such as Lydall and Mincer[22] suggest that income distribution (before tax) is largely determined by education distribution. Wealth distribution constitutes another determinant, but a minor one, since only 20 to 25 per cent of income differences are due to differences in capital income, and a large part of this difference is eliminated by taxes.

The suggestion implied in Lydall's work is that incomes could become equal only if education (and hence capabilities) can be made equal for all. This is impossible, as a result of the existence of

---

[18] S. J. Prais and H. S. Houthakker, *The Analysis of Family Budgets* (Cambridge 1955).

[19] Nicholson, op. cit.

[20] 'Die Lebenshaltung von 2000 Arbeiter-, Angestellten- und Beamtenhaushaltungen' (Berlin, 1932), Teil, I, p. 14; *Wirtschaft und Statistik* (1969), p. 397.

[21] More exact comparisons, using both deciles and quintiles, will be shown in a forthcoming study.

[22] See Lydall, op. cit. (1968); and Mincer, 'The Distribution of Labour Incomes: A Survey', *Journal of Economic Literature* (1970), p. 1.

innate differences in capabilities. I submit, however, that the determinant of income distribution is not education distribution alone, but the 'tension' (difference) between *the education distribution demanded by society* (as a reflection of its production, education and other activities) and *the education distribution supplied by the population*. I have made a start now with the verification of this theory, already formulated in 1956 by (Tinbergen).[23] One illustration is that, while in the USA education has been spread considerably over the last decades,[24] income distribution before tax has remained unchanged. In my opinion this means that education has not been spread sufficiently to meet the increased demand (from modern production and other activities) for more schooling. For the Netherlands there is a moderate improvement in this 'competition' or 'race' between supply of and demand for more educated people.

V FUTURE POLICIES

Future policies should be directed at narrowing the gap between the two distributions: the demand for education by the organizers of production, in the broadest sense and the supply of educated people. Such policies should be based on more refined research in various directions, part of which is already under way. This type of research should be part and parcel of any improved system of long-term planning.

In the field of taxes further measures are conceivable as well, though to a different degree in different countries. In many developed market economies higher taxes on material wealth than those prevailing today are possible and, in the opinion of many citizens, desirable. This is particularly true for inheritance taxes in a number of Western countries.

Social security systems too are far from complete in a number of these countries; in other cases their financing could be changed so as to produce more income redistribution. Without suggesting that the extremes of social security present in some countries (different for different elements of the systems) are necessarily the best ones, a comparative study would reveal a range of possibilities for some more backward developed countries.

[23] J. Tinbergen, 'A Positive and a Normative Theory of Income Distribution', *The Review of Income and Wealth* (1970), series 16.
[24] Lydall, op. cit. (1968).

What I wanted to illustrate in this chapter is that 'gradualism' has been successful in the past in introducing a considerable degree of equalization; furthermore, there is no reason to believe that the process has already been completed.

CHAPTER 11

The Process of Industrialization of an Overpopulated Agricultural Area – The Italian Experience

P. SARACENO

I ECONOMIC BACKWARDNESS IN SOUTHERN ITALY

The Italian development policy for the Southern overpopulated agricultural regions – the so-called Mezzogiorno – began in 1950, with the decision taken in that year to create a special institution, the *Cassa per il Mezzogiorno* (Fund for the South), with the task of implementing a development programme which, following a succession of considerable increases both of the responsibilities devolved on it and of the resources placed at its disposal, is now to continue its activities until 1980.

Thus nearly twenty years[1] have passed since the time when Italian policy was committed to long-term action with the objective of industrializing a huge part of the country which exhibited the typical features of an underdeveloped region. At the time, as much as 55 per cent of the region's labour force was dependent on agriculture; of the remaining 45 per cent only a small part was employed in production units of truly industrial character. Moreover, these industrial units, for the most part, belonged to firms with headquarters located in the northern part of the country. They therefore made a relatively limited contribution towards the creation in the

---

[1] One of the factors determining the institution of the *Cassa*, whose role can certainly be defined as being of historical significance in the process of developing Italian society, was the prospect of a World Bank loan to be used for the very purpose of implementing (naturally together with a considerable contribution by Italy itself) an organic investment programme. The preparation of the project and its actual application owes much to Paul Rosenstein-Rodan. Rosenstein-Rodan has contributed (and still contributes today) to the study of the Mezzogiorno problem through his participation in SVIMEZ, which is a private association set up in 1946 to study and promote activities in favour of Italy's Mezzogiorno.

south of a modern homogeneous society such as was growing up in the rest of the country.

Italy's Mezzogiorno accounted at the time for a little over 17 million inhabitants. Its population was therefore greater than that of many countries committed today to national development policies. The experience obtained in Italy's Mezzogiorno could therefore be usefully studied with reference to the policies being applied in those countries. However, the Mezzogiorno is part of a far larger national unit which then involved 47 million inhabitants and had reached, in other regions, a significant degree of industrialization. The experience of the Mezzogiorno, in which 37 per cent of the Italian population was living, could also be considered as an example of another type of phenomenon: that of backward areas. It may be said that this problem exists in all industrialized countries seeing that those areas not industrialized in the past together with the rest of the country, or where leading industries had been struck by some crisis, were not capable, without specific public action, of launching an independent development process and of reaching income levels close to those of other regions.

If all these points are borne in mind, the Mezzogiorno appears, all the same, to be a case apart. On the one hand, because of its size and population, it experiences problems typical of under-developed countries; but, on the other hand, it is included in a partially industrialized country. This, however, does not seem sufficient to class it entirely alongside backward areas, given the importance of its size in relation to the country as a whole. On the latter score, it has to be remembered that the Mezzogiorno, with 37 per cent of the Italian population, supplies, because of its higher birth-rate in the various regions, 65–70 per cent, and in some years even more, of the natural increase in the country's labour force. It has therefore played and continues to play, through emigration, an essential role in the economic growth of other regions of Italy, without enjoying, as we shall see later, corresponding weight in determining the economic and social structure of Italian society.

II   CRITERIA FOR ASSESSING MEZZOGIORNO DEVELOPMENT
POLICY

The results of the action taken in the Mezzogiorno over two decades can be assessed under two different headings: a) the economic improvement that has taken place in the area in absolute terms and

b) the change in the economic gap, as it existed at the start of intervention between the north and the south.

As to the first of these headings: there is no doubt that the progress achieved has been immense; the real *per capita* income of the whole region rose from about $400 in 1950 to about $1,000 in 1969, an average increase of 5·1 per cent a year. The labour force engaged in non-agricultural activities increased from 2·5 million in 1950 to 4·1 million in 1969. It has to be added that the number of jobs created in non-agricultural activities was even greater than the increase in employment, given that during the period many artisan and trading activities ceased which had had very low earning power and had occupied an unknown, but certainly very considerable, labour force. Lastly, it should be remembered that the agricultural labour force, which in 1950 was, as has already been said, 55 per cent of the total force, in 1969 accounted for only 33 per cent.

The improvement was, therefore, very great indeed and certainly greater, from the point of view just considered, than the most optimistic forecasts which could have been formulated when intervention started. But similar improvement is not to be found in the reduction of the income gap that exists between the Mezzogiorno and the rest of the country. The *per capita* income in the Mezzogiorno in 1950 was in the order of 50 per cent of that in the rest of the country; today it is reckoned to be 56–8 per cent. Account also has to be taken of the part played by emigration in the improvement in income and employment levels in the Mezzogiorno. The migration outflow can be reckoned at about 2 million workers, equal to about 35 per cent of the initial labour force. It is not inaccurate to say that if there had been no emigration, the gap would not have been narrowed but would rather have widened.

Emigration certainly has its advantages in an economy whose labour force is underutilized. However, the disadvantages outweigh the advantages when emigration involves such a large part of the available labour force. Not only does it subtract from the underdeveloped region (because of its selective character) a larger part of the human resources required for its development and increases the load of the inactive population bearing on those in employment, but it also provokes in the urbanized regions subject to immigration serious environmental imbalances and perhaps even more serious social tensions.

Two opposing judgements, therefore, can be passed on Mezzogiorno development policy: favourable, if the assessment takes into consideration the improvements that have occurred in the area's economic conditions; unfavourable, if instead it is considered that the gap persists to a large extent and if account is taken of the fact that the gap would have been even greater if there had not been such an intense outflow of migrants.

There seems to be no doubt that among the various factors available on which to base an opinion and which permit such contrasting assessments, only those which measure the progress made towards the objective which development policy seeks to achieve should be utilized. So what was this objective? Numerous declarations made on a variety of occasions and under varying circumstances leave us in no doubt on this score; the objective is the elimination of the gap existing between the Mezzogiorno and the rest of the country. It is worth adding that when one talks of a gap, one does not just mean the economic gap measured by the differences between *per capita* income in the two groups of regions or by other economic indices. The fact that the industrialization process could not extend itself over a group of regions inhabited by one-third of the Italian population and, on average, providing two-thirds of the increase in the total labour force, has consequences far beyond the economic sphere.

The advent of industry, as is well known, makes for the evolution of social structures and of ways of life, and above all creates and continually reinforces new centres of power. Lack of industry and emigration of good human resources therefore gives rise not only to the income gap, but also to divergencies in the cultural field, in social patterns and especially in political strength. Industrialization must therefore be seen as a means not only of reducing deformities in existing living conditions, but also of making a given community more homogeneous, more united. In the Italian instance, the industrialization of the Mezzogiorno is the means employed to attain that moral and social unity which has not yet been accomplished after a century of political unification.[2] Naturally enough, the elimination of divergencies presupposes an improvement in the living conditions of an underdeveloped area; yet such improvement is to be considered as an obvious result of action, not its objective.

If the objective of development action is to render Italian society more homogeneous, to distribute centres of power more equitably

---

[2] It should be remembered that the Italian State was created between 1859 and 1870 by the unification of six formerly independent States and a region — Lombardy and Veneto — previously part of Austria.

round the country, then it must be said that this objective has not yet been achieved. Indeed, the political tension that exists in Italy today is confirmation of the fact that the greatest need is the economic and social unification of the country (and not simply the economic improvement of the poorer part of it), and that this need has not been satisfied.

However, the judgement cannot be concluded with this statement. It would be unreasonable to expect that within twenty years a largely agricultural area would reach the degree of industrialization existing in the technically more advanced parts of the modern world, such as those industrialized parts of Western Europe, among which must now be included the northern and central regions of Italy.

In order to pass judgement on the policy applied, it still must be asked whether, from the positions reached today, the Mezzogiorno can, within a reasonable period, acquire a structure which will be, if not equal to, at least homogeneous with that of the rest of the country. To assess this, it must first of all be remembered that according to studies made by SVIMEZ, the Italian economy will reach a state of full employment around 1985. This forecast is based on the intensity of development underway in Western Europe and on the fact that the labour supply in the Mezzogiorno in the period 1970–85 will not, according to SVIMEZ calculations, be very large: 2·6 million persons. To appreciate the significance of this figure, it is enough to point out that, by SVIMEZ estimates, the progress of the Italian economy alone could bring about a state of full employment of the Italian labour force, without any need for emigration abroad. In fact, if the demand for labour for non-agricultural activities increases in Italy at an average annual rate of 1·7 per cent, the whole Italian labour force will find employment by around 1985. Such a rate of growth seems entirely plausible considering that from 1950 to 1969 the non-agricultural labour force increased in Italy at a rate of about 2·3 per cent a year.

None the less this prospect, albeit favourable in many respects, is not sufficient for it to be claimed that Mezzogiorno development policy has been successful. In the first place, if full employment of the southern labour force were to be achieved mainly through emigration, such a serious state of abandonment would result in the Mezzogiorno that there would be grounds for maintaining that elimination of the gap could never be achieved. It would persist not only in the strictly economic sense, given that the north and centre would contain the greater part of high earning level activities and of investment income;

but also there would be stagnation in the way of life, culture and political strength, just because of the weakness of the economic structure which, on such a hypothesis, would result in the Mezzogiorno. In other words, it would no longer be possible to achieve the objective of development action which, as has been said above, is the country's social unification.

There is another very interesting aspect of Italian experience which is worth underlining; even allowing for the favourable hypothesis that the greater part of the southern labour force finds employment in that same area, this would be a consequence of the intensity of development of the north-central economy, development which, at a certain point in its history, after using up its own labour force, has found it advantageous to utilize the labour force of the overpopulated agricultural areas. This means that overcoming the dualistic situation is possible only in the final phase of the industrialization of a country and not during such a process. The gravity of this conclusion is shown by the following consideration: if the development of the north and centre of Italy had been less intense in the past or were to be less intense in the future, and the state of full employment were only attainable, let us say, in the year 2000, the elimination of the gap – and the cessation of the serious social tensions which the gap causes – would be delayed until that time.

III REGIONAL IMBALANCES AS A CONSEQUENCE OF THE INDUSTRIALIZATION PROCESS

From the Italian case, therefore, stems the general consideration that, if regional imbalances arise in economic development, they cannot be corrected, not even through the type of action undertaken in Italy. The development of the backward area of a country is, in other terms, a by-product of the development of its wealthy area; this area continues to expand through its own mechanisms – mechanisms which cannot be modified in the interest of the national community as a whole.

This consideration is the more serious in that the development of the Mezzogiorno has taken place under exceptionally favourable conditions, which probably would not be found in other countries.

Above all, the volume of capital transferred to the Mezzogiorno from the rest of the country must be stressed, and especially the scale and quality of intervention carried out by the *Cassa*. According to reliable reckoning, all capital accumulation in the area during the period has been financed by savings made outside it; the income produced within the area in the period was, in fact, about equal to consumption in the area itself. Moreover, the capital supplied to the area was provided in the form of grants and not loans. It cannot thus be seen how other underdeveloped areas, similar in size and population to the Mezzogiorno, could count upon such a large-scale injection of capital on such terms as these over such a long period. Regarding the action of the *Cassa per il Mezzogiorno*, what has to be underlined is not so much the scale, great as it may be, of the capital invested, as the fact that the *Cassa* was a technical instrument whereby public action was able to expand rapidly and widely in an extensive territory, which was for the most part poorly endowed with technical personnel and infrastructures.

Another distinguishing element of the Mezzogiorno experience appears to be the utilization outside the area of a large share of the labour force available in that area; this utilization has been made possible by the fact that the Mezzogiorno, besides being part of an industrialized country, has found itself, since 1957, within the still greater area of the European Common Market and in the neighbourhood of other countries of Western Europe (for example, Sweden, Switzerland, etc.) in which there were marked labour shortages. The negative aspects of a very large migratory outflow have already been mentioned; there is no doubt, however, that intervention is facilitated, in the initial stage, by the fact that part of the available labour force may emigrate and thus benefit from the capital accumulation taking place in other areas – it does not have to remain idle, waiting for the necessary capital to accumulate in its own area. As has already been said, the southern labour force, which in 1950 amounted to 5·6 million, has since lost 2 million persons through emigration to the rest of the country and abroad. Such a utilization is quite inconceivable in an underdeveloped area that is not part of a larger industrialized one.

A third factor that distinguishes the Mezzogiorno experience is the fact that since it is part of an industrialized country the Mezzogiorno is endowed with institutions that suit the needs of the more advanced part of the country and that facilitate development action to no little extent.

What unforeseeable difficulties and what errors of judgement have prevented the action carried out so far from bringing about a significant reduction in the gap? To give a brief answer to this question, it seems useful in this chapter, addressed as it is to readers for the most part not conversant with the country, to consider not only the two decades following the inception of the *Cassa*, but also the whole cycle Italy has passed through – from being an agricultural country practically devoid of industry, to becoming an industrialized country endowed with capital sufficient to raise the productivity of its labour force to levels comparable with those of Western Europe.

This cycle began around 1890, and since SVIMEZ forecast that full employment would be reached by about 1985, it will last for about one century. It is true that at the beginning of this century-long cycle there were differences in economic and social development between the northern and southern provinces, and it was because of these differences that, initially, the northern location of industry appeared more convenient. The result was that a productive structure of a dualistic type arose in Italy, that was to weigh heavily on the whole of subsequent Italian history.

That a dualistic situation is created or, if it already exists, is accentuated by the launching of an industrialization process is certainly inevitable if the industrial districts, as happened in Italy, are concentrated initially in only one part of the country. This is an obvious consequence of the fact that the average wage of a non-agricultural worker is higher than the average income of the mass of the population which, in the rest of the country, continues to live on agriculture. That this state of affairs cannot be avoided is shown by the fact that when industrialization started in southern Italy the dualist phenomenon occurred inside that area. It is enough to mention that the *per capita* income of the southern provinces with the lowest rate of income does not reach 50 per cent of the income of the provinces in which the industrialization phenomenon has acquired some importance. This is in spite of the fact that investment in public works, intervention in agriculture and, generally, the whole of public action, has been spread fairly uniformly throughout the whole area, and that the poorest provinces have contributed the most to emigration flows.

Limiting the industrialization process to just one part of a territory has the effect of creating imbalances which in most cases continue to worsen, given that productivity of non-agricultural work increases at a faster rate generally than agricultural income, even when, as has happened in the Mezzogiorno, there are substantial migratory outflows. In Italy, in fact, this tendency will begin to slacken only in the last phase of the industrialization process and will eventually disappear when the country reaches a state of full employment.

This is on the condition that, at least in the final phase, emigration is greatly reduced and possibly ceases altogether. This is probably unavoidable in the course of an industrialization process. Italy's case, however, shows that social tensions due to imbalances are very much more serious today than they were in the past in countries which are now fully industrialized. This can be attributed to two circumstances: first, because more advanced technology is being applied and therefore the divergence between industrial productivity and the *per capita* income of the agricultural labour force is greater than it was during the last century when the first steps towards industrialization were taken; secondly, the development of communications and the speed with which higher cultural standards are attained in those societies where industrialization is already underway make differences between regions less acceptable.

Dualism has caused more problems in Italy than it has in other countries in the past. This is due to the nature of urbanization problems that have arisen. Because the development of such phenomena has been so rapid and because the labour reaching metropolitan areas from the countryside often exceeds the demand for workers, urbanization processes are more haphazard. Consequently, problems arise which often absorb the benefits produced by industrialization.

But perhaps the most serious consequence of dualism is the change it causes in the balance of the country's political forces. The industrialized part inevitably becomes the politically stronger section of the country; consequently, the interests of that part alone are stated – in the name of economic progress – to be the interests of the country as a whole. Balanced economic and social development will not be the fundamental objective of public action; it will become *de facto*, if not openly, one of many problems to be faced, but only within those limits permitted by the laws of development of the more wealthy regions. It is not too much to say that, with the protraction of a dualistic situation, a relationship grows up between the wealthy and the poor areas which can be defined as being of colonial type. The miserable though homogeneous society that existed before the industrialization process commenced, is now prelaced by a two-tier society; the dominant one, located in the industrialized regions, and the dominated one, lying in the non-industrialized regions.

Italian experience shows quite clearly, therefore, that the development programme for an overpopulated agricultural country must even in the initial stages resist any dualistic tendency. If the tendency is not immediately repressed, a mechanism will be started which, on both political and economic planes, will work in the direction of accentuating rather than attenuating imbalances. Very serious tensions will thus be produced which will end only in the distant future when, as has been said, development of the wealthy part of the country will make it advantageous to offer employment to the whole labour force living in the poor area and, at least in the final phase, when industrial investments in the poor area reach such a volume that the advantage of emigration is reduced and eventually ended.

IV HOW CAN REGIONAL IMBALANCES CAUSED BY THE INDUSTRIALIZATION PROCESS BE AVOIDED?

An industrialization process then causes serious and growing regional imbalances for two reasons: a) industrial investment tends to be concentrated initially in a few places; and b) earnings of the non-agricultural labour force are considerably higher and increase more rapidly than earnings of the agricultural labour force.

The Italian case shows that the correcting action undertaken about a century ago – from the very beginning of the industrialization process – and intensified through the *Cassa* in the last twenty years, has made it possible to avoid an increase in divergencies. But it has not been able to bring about their gradual reduction, which is especially serious considering the overall progress made by the country during the period.

Since dualism is born and consolidated as an effect of the gap existing between non-agricultural incomes and agricultural incomes, one of the first steps to be taken could be the introduction of an incomes policy that seeks to establish a certain link between earning rates current in these two occupational areas. More precisely, it would be a question, if not of breaking, of at least attenuating the link which, under trade-union pressure, tends to be formed between the productivity of non-agricultural work and the rates of remuneration for such work. The resources thus obtainable could then be directed to the improvement of the situation in areas not touched by the industrialization process.

Such a course, however, cannot in practice be followed. The non-agricultural labour force, organized by their trade unions, cannot be persuaded to renounce all the benefits accruing to them from productivity increases; and this attitude does not change even when they are dealing with public enterprise, that is to say with firms *vis-à-vis* which it is certainly not possible to raise the objection that to forego an increase in remuneration is to increase profits and not to increase the resources available for use in the public sphere.

On the point of distribution of income, a phenomenon occurs which is in a certain sense the opposite of that described above; experience shows that in all industrialized countries, rates of pay generally increase faster than productivity. This tendency produces two unfavourable effects for the poor regions; it makes it more advantageous to aim at more capital-intensive investment rather than at more labour-intensive investment. Secondly, inflation reduces the real value of resources available to the public for intervention in favour of the poorer regions of the country.

Appreciable modifications in the tendency towards dualism cannot be awaited, from what Italian experience teaches us, not even drawing on the line of reasoning, so dear in the past to economic thought, that a country with an abundance of labour must prefer labour-intensive investment.

The argument is obvious, but tested against hard facts, it is shown to be rather superficial. Preference for labour-intensive investment can refer in the first place to the choice to be made between different kinds of production, (for example, electronics or steel-making). Our experience tells us that in making this choice the availability of a labour force is only one of the many factors at play (the existence of a favourable domestic market, availability of raw materials, opportunities for professional training, type of production in which it is easy to promote initiatives from national and foreign groups, and so on). Labour is a factor whose importance is declining with technical progress. So steel works are built, or cement works, refineries, textile mills or others in relation to laws of technical and economic development of the entire system, laws of development which do not differ very greatly whether there is an abundant labour supply or not.

Then again, the term 'labour intensive' may be used in the sense that, in undertaking a given industrial investment, from among the various techniques available, the one to adopt must be that in which the contribution by labour is higher relative to the capital invested. But in this sense, too, the possibilities for making a choice are not many; firms producing industrial machinery do not in practice offer such a range of equipment that considerable differentiation in the combinations of capital and labour is permitted. A plant producing cement will be almost the same whether it has to be utilized in a highly industrialized region where there are high wage levels, or in an underdeveloped region where there is a huge labour supply.

In conclusion, Italian experience surely indicates that neither income policies nor the adoption of special guidance in the industrial sectors to be developed and, within each sector, the techniques to be applied, can impede the formation of substantial differences in incomes between regions of a country undergoing industrialization. Taking into consideration as well the greater political strength acquired by the industrialized regions, it no longer seems possible to correct a dualistic situation once it has arisen. As Italian experience shows, the most that can be done is to prevent it from becoming acute.

If it is recognized that a dualistic situation creates a permanent state of serious tension, fomenter of no less serious problems than those of underdevelopment, and if at the same time it is admitted that this situation, where it arises, cannot be corrected, there remains no other line of action but that of preventing its formation – imposing, from the very start of the industrialization policy, a decisive plan for the decentralization of investments.

In Italy this standpoint has been the subject of considerable controversy, the terms of which are of great interest to the matter under discussion here. Among its instruments for industrialization policy, Italy has the so-called development *pole* which is, as is well known, an area to be endowed with the infrastructures and institutions needed for economic industrial operations. Now, on this subject, it was thought that it was advantageous to prepare a limited number of development poles so as to minimize, given equal industrial investment, the burden falling to public action in the creation of such poles. The belief that the concentration of industrial plant in a single place creates important external economies for such plant also leads to such a view. This policy of concentration, had, however, to be moderated in Italy when it came to its application, on political grounds, which suggested the advisability of permitting a larger number of development poles than these criteria would have justified. It was felt, however, that this represented a deviation from the one criterion – that of concentration – alone recognized to be the rational one.

This concept should certainly be reviewed; politicians, obtaining the attenuation of the concentration principle, today appear as the bearers, albeit unwittingly, of a more rational principle. The concentration criterion ends as discrimination in favour of only part of the underdeveloped area; it is only in that place that jobs are available, public institutions and services are offered, agriculture is given special support by the additional outlets offered for its produce, and farmers are enabled to benefit from services and institutions which do not exist in the rest of the country.

It is obvious that to carry out all this in fifty localities, not very close to one another, instead of in five localities, entails a considerably higher cost; however, this does not represent a waste, but rather an expression of a development policy extended across the whole area, though clearly a more costly policy than that based on the criterion of concentrating effort in a few zones. The benefits to be expected from such a choice are, however, only apparent. They derive from a short-term evaluation of a liberalist nature which does not take into consideration, on the economic plane, those liabilities which will be created by future tensions and the costs of urban concentration in cities devoid of social services; on the political plane, its weight cannot be ignored: the destruction of values and the suffering caused by considerable population movements. Actually, applying the concentration criterion, the same relationship is created within the underdeveloped area as existed on a world scale between the industrialized countries and the Third World.

Moreover, the concentration criterion overestimates the value of external economies determined by the contiguity of a large number of industries. Many things have changed since the time, now long ago, when the idea of external economies first grew up. Some spread of industrial assets across the territory is economically feasible under the new operating conditions created in modern industry by modern transport techniques. It is a question of identifying the constraints within which the spread must be contained, while at the same time being prepared to accept some burdens in those cases where these constraints have to be relaxed in order to avoid still greater burdens arising in the future from the alteration in the relationship between population and territory.

To sum up, Italy's case, an experience which can be seen as a cycle that will reach its conclusion after a period of about one century, puts into relief the necessity of impeding, in the initial stage, the concentration of industry in only one part of the country. It must, then, be a fundamental criterion behind the industrialization process that industrial assets be distributed over the territory in such a way that they reflect, as far as possible, the territorial distribution of the population. This will be the only way to disseminate social and economic progress equitably throughout the community, and to impede the formation of political as well as economic imbalances which, as Italy's case shows, cannot be corrected. It is not intended to say by this that every tiny community must be endowed with industrial plant; even adopting the above criterion, population movements cannot be avoided. Their consequences, however, will be less serious because they will be more limited and in any case will take place within restricted areas. It is necessary, in any case, to prevent the formation, in the early stages, of a dualistic situation between a compact industrial area and a stagnant agricultural area and, in a subsequent phase, the inevitable, migratory outflows from the latter area to the former – flows destined to overturn the structures of both societies.

Again, the Italian experience seems to indicate that the additional burdens caused by decentralization will certainly be compensated by the possibility of avoiding the burdens determined by dualism and by the cost of the social tensions it causes.

IV

DEVELOPMENT AND INTERNATIONAL TRADE

CHAPTER 12

Restrictions on Direct Investment in Host Countries

C. P. KINDLEBERGER

Economic history and a number of specialized fields of Economics, such as agriculture, are filled with debate between those who claim that man is economically irrational in many respects (or possibly consciously maximizing a non-economic variable), and those who believe that economic sense can be made of actual choices, if only on a Darwinian basis. This paper explores restrictions on direct investment by host countries to see whether these can be rationalized in economic terms. That such restrictions abound is taken as needing no demonstration. Various countries maintain prohibitions against whole classes of investment: in natural resources, transport, communication, banking, retail distribution, newspapers, etc.; and within allowed fields, most countries require *ad hoc* application to the foreign-exchange or fair-trading authorities who may decline a given proposal on one ground or another. The question is whether such prohibitions and rejections are in the true economic interest of the host country, or whether they are non-economic responses reflecting the peasant, mercantilist, populist, nationalist, xenophobic instincts which most people start life with, or the irrationality which indulges in the fallacy of misplaced concreteness, or wants to have its cake and eat it too.

The contribution of direct investment is capital, technology, management, access to markets and other similar advantages needed to make direct investment possible. These are sought after by the host country. What is resisted is foreign ownership and especially control, or decision-making. We exclude two possible bases of restriction unconnected with foreign control: a) the monopsonistic argument that a country might limit capital inflows in order to obtain capital more cheaply; and b) the income-distribution

201

argument which would limit (or accelerate) capital inflows in an effort to prevent a reduction in the return to capital in the host country (or a rise in the marginal product of labour). The first is often given as a reason for restricting capital outflow in an effort to prevent the fall in the average return on foreign investment. It is an optimum-investment argument, comparable to the optimum tariff, and can be inverted to restrict inflows, as well as outflows. The second is analogous to the Stolper-Samuelson theorem about tariffs and income distribution. We exclude these arguments for restriction on the grounds that the optimum tariff is unrealistic in policy terms: tariffs do improve the terms of trade, but historically are imposed for different purposes, typically for protectionism or to change income distribution; and because while restrictions on foreign investment could be imposed for reasons of income distribution, there is no evidence that they are being so used. Most restriction sought by disaggregated interests is industry-specific, not factor-oriented. Pressure for restriction on direct-investment outflows has been expected on the part of, say, labour in the United States. It arises only in limited groups, like the United Automobile Workers.

Reference to the optimum tariff and the Stolper-Samuelson theorem suggests the line of argument: restriction on inflows of direct investment can be justified on the same grounds as a tariff: for national defence, infant industry, and second best, plus one more argument not found in tariffs, anti-monopoly.

The national-defence argument goes back at least to Adam Smith and to 'Defence is greater than opulence'. It is used to exclude domestic dependence on foreign military supplies, or on foreign sources for critical survival items such as food and fuel. In every case, however, the economic cost of greater self-sufficiency must be calculated, and the cost of alternative sources of supply which can be turned to in timely fashion in the event that a foreign economical supply is interrupted. Self-sufficiency is a matter of degrees, and some degrees are so expensive that they are abandoned. Thus most less developed countries and many developed ones import sizeable proportions of their military supplies, and Britain depends on imported oil coming through two deep-draft ports highly vulnerable to nuclear attack, because dependence on local coal and North Sea gas for its fuel requirements would be too expensive.

The national defence argument in direct investment goes beyond weapons, food and fuel in several dimensions. In the first place, the production of food, fuel and weapons inside the geographical boundaries but under the business control of foreign nationals poses a defence problem of uncertain dimensions. The foreign owners might destroy plant needed for defence, or sabotage its output. It is hardly very likely. Bausch and Lomb and General Analine and Film, German owned, and operating in the United States, were taken over very early from foreign control. By the same token, the International Telephone and Telegraph Company minority interest in the Folke-Wulf airplane company in Germany presumably had no impact on German military capabilities.

An extension of the national-defence argument leads into transport and communications, industries which are excluded from foreign ownership in the United States and Canada on the ground of their vital importance in the maintenance of the national existence. Still further extended to prohibit cabotage, the use of foreign vessels in transporting freight from one United States port to another, or permitting foreign aircraft going to more than one airport of the United States to carry passengers between them, smacks of protection, not national defence. National defence, like patriotism, may be the last refuge of a scoundrel who is seeking selfish protection but willing to wrap the flag around his interests; this is true both in tariffs and in prohibitions against foreign direct investment in particular fields.

A wider extension of the national-defence argument leads to national independence, including cultural independence, and pure nationalism. Albert Breton has called nationalism a collective consumption good which the electorate may choose to buy and which should presumably be included in national income on some opportunity-cost basis.[1] The Canadian Watkins Report on the Structure of Canadian Industry emphasized 'national independence' as a goal of policy, mentioned in four of five paragraphs listing separate goals.[2] This raises the question of how much foreign ownership and control of separate industries, broad sectors, or beyond a percentage or range of the total economy (or the more dynamic portions of it) compromise independence. Brecher and Reisman asserted that foreign ownership of a Canadian firm would make no difference to its behaviour because if both foreign and Canadian

[1] Albert Breton, 'The Economics of Nationalism', *Journal of Political Economy*, vol. 72 (August 1964), no. 4, pp. 376–86.
[2] Task Force on the Structure of Canadian Industry, *Foreign Ownership and the Structure of Canadian Industry* (Ottawa, Queen's Printer, January 1968).

owners maximized in the same fashion, they would behave identically.[3] This statement was unacceptable in so far as it was implied that the Canadian firm was a local one and the American firm international. Operating in a different spatial horizon, and possibly within a different temporal one, facing different pressures overall, both firms might maximize and behave differently. But assuming that the Canadian and American firms were of equal size and extent, would their behaviour differ in either Canada or the United States because of nationality? The answer is probably yes. In such matters as trade with Cuba and mainland China, anti-trust or remittance of profits to the United States for balance of payments reasons, the United States government could direct the behaviour of the American subsidiary in Canada, through the US head office, but not of the Canadian head office in Canada through its subsidiary in the United States. If the Canadian people objected to this intrusion of United States policy into the Canadian body politic, they could prohibit or limit direct investment, at a cost in investment, technology and management for domestic industry from the United States. Or they might find cheaper and easier ways of accomplishing the same end: insisting that foreign subsidiaries in Canada follow Canadian rather than United States policy in these matters, or negotiating directly with the United States on the extra-territorial extension of United States policies via corporate subsidiaries.

Opinions will surely differ as to the importance of the extension of the policy of one country to the policy of another via foreign subsidiaries, the extent to which foreign control of national firms compromises national independence, and how much national independence is worth. The economist has nothing to contribute to these issues beyond urging that various degrees of national defence, national independence, cultural independence or simply nationalism should be costed in terms of the economic growth and efficiency they would sacrifice, and that alternative means of achieving the same ends be similarly priced. If a country wants to pay for something and has found the cheapest way to get it, the economist has nothing more to say, since, on the basis of revealed preference, the national defence bought is worth the amount of opulence which the society will give for it.

A number of countries worry about foreign ownership of key industries, especially banking and communication, 'the commanding

[3] I. Brecher and S. S. Reisman, *Canadian-American Economic Relations* (Ottawa, The Queen's Printer, 1957), chapter 8.

heights of the economy'. There may be something to the point about newspapers, radio, television, telephone, telegraph, where unfriendly foreign ownership may distort information, intercept significant government and private messages or, *in extremis*, yield the control over communication to outsiders at critical times. It seems unlikely. Prohibition of foreign ownership of banking facilities seems based more on populist fears, or protection from foreign competition, than on reasonable measures for national protection.

The infant-industry argument for tariffs also goes back as far as Adam Smith. Today economists regard the tariff solution as a poor one, and prefer a combination of taxes and subsidies which aim directly at the distortion between social and market value which limit the efficiency of market choices. Adding direct investment to the analysis raises the question of whether by infant industry we mean the existence of the industry within the national boundaries or the existence of the industry run by citizens of the host country. A tariff by itself may encourage foreign interests to come and start the industry. If what is sought is industrialization by domestic rather than foreign factors, the infant-industry tariff should be accompanied by an infant-industry prohibition of direct investment.

Again, of course, it is important to be clear about the benefit, the cost, alternative ways of achieving the same objective, and the use of the argument by those who are basically protectionists not entitled to claim the privileges of infants. With respect to the benefit, the question of foreign control arises again. Does it make a difference whether the industry located within the borders is foreign- or domestically-controlled? If foreign entry into retail trade is prohibited, for example, is this because of the industry's fear of competition or because there is a serious training effect to be gained by schooling in the commercial arts native citizens, long excluded perhaps by Chinese domination of trade? Where the population is homogeneous, the infant-industry argument may be valid for a tariff, but the investment prohibition may degenerate into an instinctual xenophobic attack on foreign control.

As far as costs are concerned, the interest on the lost income of the community while the infant is growing to manhood must not be neglected. The relative costs to be compared are the present discounted values of the income to the country of foreign investment in the industry and of domestic industry, each presumably with a different time profile. If the prohibition of foreign and reliance on domestic industry involves a long wait and substantial outlays until the capital is amassed, the difference in costs includes interest on the additional costs and the income foregone in the near term.

The infant-industry argument presents itself especially in connection with natural resources. These deposits, let us say, are our resources, God-given, and in the domain over which our sovereignty has been traditional. These arguments are the instinctive reaction of the peasant, or the fallacy of misplaced concreteness which thinks that natural resources are different from other capital assets. If the present discounted value of the deposits are worth more to the country through sale to a foreign interest, or through a concession valued at the present value of the stream of future taxes than would be the case if it were exploited by domestic interests, it is better to sell or concede the deposits to the foreigner. The value of domestic use includes all external effects of training, etc., which are incremental to those from foreign exploitation. But the slower time profile of returns from domestic use imposes a substantial cost, if a proper shadow rate of interest is used in the calculation, which is seriously limiting to the applicability of the infant-industry's defence of prohibitions, valid though it be.

From time to time foreign investment has been prohibited in non-essential industry, such as coffee-bars, soft drinks, simple products such as ink, or for balance of payments reasons. These can be justified only on the basis of the second-best reasoning. There must be failure of the market to reflect social values, and the better way to correct the discrepancy must be unavailable.

In non-essential industries, the typical pattern is to prohibit foreign investment in, say, coffee-bars, but to permit domestic resources to be used in competitive enterprises. This is surely mistaken. If consumer sovereignty is rejected as failing to follow social priorities, and interference with the market is called for as a second-best policy, prohibition of foreign investment in coffee-bars should be accompanied by similar prohibitions for domestic investors. Better would be excise taxes which produced the socially-correct market prices.

The notion that foreign investment should be excluded from the production of simple goods, such as textiles and ink, or simple activities such as retail trade, and limited to complex, modern industries is normally another example of the fallacy of misplaced concreteness. A second-best argument can sometimes be made for it on the ground that foreign investors use capital-intensive factor proportions whereas the shadow price of labour is very low and domestic labour-intensive methods are needed to give employment. Where foreign investors would use the same technology as domestic entrepreneurs, their willingness to invest in retailing, textiles or ink suggests that profits are unduly high in these fields. To prohibit external investment is to preserve domestic monopoly.

A last example of a second-best argument may be drawn from the balance of payments. Here foreign investment is sometimes prohibited on the ground that it is 'expensive', or it may be restricted to export- or import-saving industry to ensure that transfer of profits to the foreign owner will not put undue burdens on the balance of payments. An Indian statement suggested that in considering applications for foreign investment, the authorities would balance the contribution of the enterprise to productivity against its burden on the balance of payments. This last statement is virtually meaningless (apart from monopoly considerations), since the more productive an enterprise, the higher will be its burden on the balance of payments. A balance between the two suggests two intersecting curves. When the functions are highly correlated, the two must be balanced against an external standard.

The statement that foreign investment is expensive presumably means it is profitable, and this, again apart from monopoly aspects, means efficient. With free entry, high profits are transitional, calling attention to what the society wants or can produce more cheaply than it has been doing. The second-best argument for prohibiting foreign entry where domestic monopoly exists is discussed below. A better course of action on the face of it, however, is to encourage entry by lower tariffs, action against retail price maintenance, or government competitive enterprise.

The second-best argument that the economy cannot remit profits on foreign investment and had therefore best prohibit investment in the domestic as contrasted with the foreign-trade sector, is lamentably true in some circumstances. It reflects a failure of the economy to capture enough of the productivity of the investment to meet service (rarely) or failure to expand exports or reduce imports in lines other than that of the investment sufficiently to effect transfer. This may be the result of an inflationary expansion of purchasing power, associated with the investment, which obviates the necessity for its purchasers to contract expenditure or increase output and income in other directions. A micro-economic solution (prohibiting investment) for a macro-economic problem (the balance of payments) is always inefficient. There can be little doubt, however, that balance of payments problems of many developing countries which have gone a long distance in expanding exports to the point of inelastic demands, or in contracting imports to the point where imports of consumers' goods are at low levels and only imports of capital equipment, raw materials and foodstuffs are left to cut on any scale, are obdurate.

Finally, monopoly. It is increasingly recognized, with Hymer, that direct investment belongs more to the theory of industrial organization than to that of international capital movements. The direct investor operates at a disadvantage in a foreign market, using foreign factors of production, and at a long distance from his decision-centre. To overcome these disadvantages, he must have a substantial advantage of some kind. (In a limited number of cases, direct investment takes the form of policing of each other's markets by oligopolistic competitors, or defensive investment by erstwhile monopolists who are just about to be pushed out of a market.) The advantage may lie in technology, management, access to markets, the huge amounts of capital needed for entry into the industry, and so on. If the direct investor can take over a competitor, perhaps the only competitor in a national market, he can establish a monopoly which may prove costly for the economy.

But the monopoly features of direct investment are complex. Many of its features reflect bilateral monopoly, that is, a monopoly firm, bargaining with a monopoly government. The outcome of such bargaining, as is well known, is indeterminate. A given investment may introduce a monopoly advantage but destroy an old monopoly, a large foreign firm competing with and putting out of business small but non-competitive enterprises, settled into a rut of low volume and high mark-ups. Or sustained high profits in the oil industry may be in process of decline because of widespread entry when governments of the oil-producing States move in to try to take over and maintain the monopoly.

Monopoly is thus no basis for rule-of-thumb exclusion of foreign investment. As a rule, the competitive effects of direct investment in breaking down old monopoly are likely to be more significant than the spread of monopoly, and the cry of exclusion is not on the side of the angels who favour competition. Nor is the rule of thumb allowing new production but not takeovers a sure guarantee of preventing the spread of monopoly and ensuring competition, though the addition of another firm in the industry is *prima facie* a move towards more workable competition. The added new firm may join the domestic cartel, or the old firm, taken over by new management with new technology, may become a vigorous competitor.

The monopoly argument requires that decisions about direct investment be made on a case-by-case basis, going against the grain of those who want government by law, and not by men. If Company A merges with Company Alpha abroad, competition may be reduced, whereas if Company B is the partner, competition may be increased. Decision must be made on the basis of the facts, and in particular on the potential gain or loss from increased entry and competition in crowded, inefficient, and high-mark-up industry now, as compared with an industry with limited numbers of deliberate rather than enthusiastic competitors later.

But prohibition is in any case a second-best remedy. Tax and subsidy are presumptively superior in any case. Where there are balance of payments problems, the remedies are macro-economic. Where competition is stodgy, a more effective approach than discouraging foreign entry of firms may be to enlarge competition by reducing tariffs and encouraging imports, and possibly to render monopolistic practices illegal.

Bodies politic want to have their cake and eat it too. So do governments. In the bilateral bargain between company and host country, the latter frequently signs up for extended periods of tariff protection for a new entrant and then complains when the company makes large profits. Or Australia is tolerant of retail price maintenance and then irritated when foreign investors find the resultant monopoly profits attractive. Monopoly for us and competition for them is a beguiling fantasy but it is not the way of the world.

In summary, there are valid arguments for restriction on direct investment: national defence, including cultural independence, infant-industry, second-best reasoning more generally, and anti-monopoly. Each must be applied in particular situations with extraordinary care, taking into account the particular circumstances, the costs as well as benefits of the action, and the alternative costs and benefits of other approaches. When so weighed, it will probably be found that there is a presumption in favour of *laissez faire*, perhaps even a stronger presumption than in tariffs where the 'effective rate of a tariff' discussion makes clear that tariff reductions in particular cases may lead to increased rates of protection.

CHAPTER 13

Adjustment Under the Bretton Woods Code
with Special Reference to the Less
Developed Countries [1]

A. KAFKA

This paper deals primarily with the development, up to the present,[2] of the process of balance of payments adjustment under the Bretton Woods Code.[3] It pays special attention to the manner in which the Code has affected the adjustment process of the less developed countries (LDCs), both by influencing their own policies and by influencing the situation in which they find themselves through the Code's effect on the policies of the developed countries (DCs). But it also discusses the complex problems which may be posed for LDCs by changes in the Code which are now under discussion in the IMF and elsewhere and aim at greater exchange rate flexibility than has prevailed up to now, especially among DCs. The crisis of the international monetary system which followed the suspension of dollar convertibility into gold does not necessarily affect the relevance of this discussion: the international financial community is still likely to try to return to some sort of a parity system.

The 'Bretton Woods Code' is embodied in the Articles of Agreement of the International Monetary Fund and in the decisions of

[1] I should like to thank Brian Jensen for preparing the statistical tables. I am also greatly indebted to him and to Ricardo Arriazu, Bela Balassa, Otavio G. de Bulhoes, Luis Escobar C., Marcus Fleming, Isaiah Frank, Joseph Gold, Eduardo Gomes, Gottfried Haberler, Subimal Mookerjee, Alfredo Phillips O., Adelio Pipino, Marcos Sandoval and Ernest Sturc for advice on this paper.

[2] Completed in 1970. Some references have, however, been made to events of August 1971.

[3] See below for the definition of the Bretton Woods Code. The concept of balance of payments adjustment implies that of balance of payments equilibrium. For the understanding of this paper, I do not think it matters too much which concept of balance of payments equilibrium the reader has in mind. Balance of payments equilibrium is defined as the absence of a change in net reserve assets. But a zero rate of change of net reserve assets may be incompatible with dynamic overall equilibrium.

the Fund made under the Articles. The entire Code is reinforced to a considerable extent by the provisions of GATT which has to consult the IMF on balance of payments and exchange matters and accept its findings.[4] The term 'Code' means those rules which a country cannot infringe without exposing itself to some form of sanctions by the Fund.[5] The 'Fund's' actions reflect the views of its member countries expressed by the executive directors (and governors), and influenced powerfully by those held by the management and staff in a complicated and ever changing relationship.

I THE ORIGINAL CODE

Principal Items

Four items comprise the essence of the Code as regards balance of payments adjustment; they centre on what has been called the parity system.

First,[6] countries are required to co-operate to promote exchange stability, specifically by declaring a parity and maintaining effective rates for spot exchange transactions within 1 per cent of parity. However, the world is not envisaged as an optimum currency area and parities may be changed ('adjustable peg'), but only to correct a fundamental disequilibrium; the latter term has never been formally defined. Non-fundamental disequilibria are to be cured in other ways. Access to Fund resources is foreseen if disequilibrium is expected to be temporary; whether by nature, or because there is the expectation that a fundamental disequilibrium will be removed. The availability of the exchange rate instrument for correction of a fundamental disequilibrium means that great or even any sacrifices of employment and output may legitimately be avoided by opting for exchange rate adjustment. The conditioning of exchange rate changes on fundamental disequilibrium was, nevertheless, influenced by the desire to avoid competitive depreciation on the lines of the 1930s.

The Code determines not only the circumstances in which parities may be changed but also the manner in which they are to be changed. This is to be in discrete steps by specific decisions of monetary

---

[4] Article XV of GATT.

[5] Including non-material sanctions. This is the legal position but in fact a country infringing the Code might find itself exposed to unpleasantness on the part of individual member countries of the Fund (quite apart from sanctions imposed by them as contracting parties to GATT, by authorization of the CONTRACTING PARTIES).

[6] Articles I (iii) and IV (1)–(6); see also *Proceedings and Documents of United Nations Monetary and Financial Conference*, vol. 2, (New York, United Nations, 1970), pp. 1209–14.

authorities, not by the market,[7] and subject to prior consultation with (and, generally, concurrence by) the IMF.

The Fund can prescribe limits for forward discounts and premiums but has never done so, although forward rate flexibility can (in part) be an alternative to spot rate flexibility.

Secondly, several provisions are designed to ensure that parities are meaningful for current transactions, as defined in an extensive manner by the Articles. There are to be no restrictions on *current* payments and transfers and each member is to provide for convertibility of balances of its currency held by other members arising out of or needed for *current* transactions. Exceptions can, nevertheless, be approved (Article VIII, Sections 2, 3 and 4) by the IMF.[8] Also, multiple exchange rates in the narrow sense are proscribed (Article VIII); again, exceptions can be approved but any changes in them require Fund approval. Moreover, there are to be no currency arrangements discriminating among members (Article VIII, Section 3); exceptions can be approved.

Thirdly, and by contrast, there is no proscription of restrictions on capital movements (as such). In fact, the use of 'Fund resources'[9] to finance capital movements is prohibited under Article VI (unless they are neither large nor sustained). The implication is clear: capital movements are to be controlled rather than financed, if they become bothersome, and members are exhorted to help each other enforce exchange controls (Article VIII, Section 2).[10]

Finally, there is the 'scarce currency clause' (Article VII) which has never been applied. It authorizes discriminatory exchange restrictions against a country whose currency has been declared scarce by the Fund, because *its holdings* of that currency are about to be exhausted. A country could escape the invocation of the clause by appreciation or lending its currency to the Fund (both

---

[7] It is hard to imagine that competitive depreciation or other forms of disturbing rate policy could be safely prevented in any other way than by maintaining the parity system on the lines of the IMF's Articles of Agreement; see below p.216.

[8] Moreover, members claiming need for a post-war transitional period (Article XIV) are exempt from the need for IMF approval and prior consultation regarding the maintenance and adaptation to changing circumstances of restrictions existing at the time they became members. They were exempt as well from ex post consultation during the first years of the Fund's existence.

[9] This always excluded the so-called super gold tranche; since the 1969 reform of the Articles of Agreement, however, the equivalent of each country's gold subscription can also be used for financing capital movements.

[10] See J. Keith Horsefield (ed.) *The International Monetary Fund, 1945-65; twenty years of international cooperation*, (Washington, International Monetary Fund, 1969), vol. 1, p. 443.

would require the latter's approval). It could also escape the clause by inflationary policies or by lending its currency to other countries. Neither lending to the Fund nor to other countries need (depending upon the terms of the latter type of loans) imply removal of the underlying surplus. The clause was directed primarily against any country provoking or failing to remove a major depression but was also supposed to be useful in encouraging surplus countries to share with deficit countries any action addressed to balance of payments adjustment.

The Original Code and the LDCs

Compared to a Fund-less world, all countries (and particularly smaller nations, most of which are LDCs) benefited in so far as adjustment policies, including those of major countries, became, in the Fund, a matter for international discussion even if not international control. But discussion alone and the need to give explanations can be (and has proved to be) quite effective in inhibiting internationally harmful action even by major nations. Nor were the specific provisions of the original code likely to offset this advantage, even for LDCs.

Like other countries, the LDCs have an interest in being protected against competitive depreciation.[11] That the fear of attempts at competitive depreciation would prove essentially unfounded (so far), was not then foreseen. As a general rule, the adjustable peg is not less compatible with the needs of LDCs than with those of the developed countries (comments on the adjustable peg as compared to other systems are made below in Part IV). Since 'fundamental disequilibrium' has never been defined, parity adjustments were available to countries prone to suffering from pronounced export revenue instability even if the instability were less than long term in nature; moreover, the median instability for LDCs has not been particularly high in recent years.[12] Also, not many more LDCs than DCs exhibit that degree of inflation in excess of the world average which would be incompatible with the 'adjustable peg' system. In fact, to offset these few cases, there are quite a few more LDCs than DCs with very low rates of inflation, nor are the stable LDCs slowly-growing ones (Table 13.1). While LDCs might wish to restrict

[11] See *Proceedings and Documents of United Nations Monetary and Financial Conference*, vol. 2, (New York, United Nations, 1970), pp. 1209–14.

[12] 8 per cent *v.* 4 per cent for DCs, see '*The Problem of Stabilization of Primary Products*', in *Joint Staff Study*, IMF and IBRD (1969), part 1, chap. 3.

imports or subsidize exports in certain lines on a long-term basis, neither payments nor trade restrictions of a quantitative nature nor multiple rates (in the narrow sense) are the most effective means of doing so. In a world of convertible currencies, that is, the regime prescribed for Fund members, LDCs would probably have nothing

TABLE 13.1   *Rates of Inflation and Real Growth*

Cost of Living December 1969 (Dec. 1963 = 100)	More Developed Countries		Average Annual Growth Rate	Less Developed Countries		Average Annual Growth Rate
	Countries			Countries		
	No.	Per cent		No.	Per cent	
110 or less	0	0	—	7	21	6[1]
111–120	2	8	6	7	21	6[1]
121–130	13	52	5	7	21	6
131–140	5	20	6	1	3	6
141–150	3	12	5[2]	1	3	5
151–160	0	0	—	2	6	2
161–170	0	0	—	1	3	5
171–180	0	0	—	0	0	—
181–190	0	0	—	0	0	—
191–200	0	0	—	1	3	5
Over 200	2	8	5[3]	6	18	5
	25	100		33	100	

[1] Six countries.
[2] Two countries.
[3] One country.

Source: Inflation: *International Financial Statistics* (January 1971).
Growth: IMF Data Fund. Growth rates are unweighted averages of annual average growth rates of GDP (of GNP) for six-year periods, 1961/7 to 1963/9, whichever is the latest year available.

to gain, on balance, from discriminatory currency practices. Moreover, on all these matters (except parities) there is sufficient discretion to accommodate special cases.

The one exception, where the code is in theory not altogether well-suited to the LDCs' needs, is capital controls. The code would be more useful if it distinguished perverse flows, that is, generally, those from poor to rich, from other flows, and prohibited controls over the latter, that is, particularly over the outflow of long-term capital to LDCs. But the practical difficulties of making the distinction would be great.[13]

There is no suggestion that the code covers explicitly all aspects of policy relevant to balance of payments adjustment and no need that it should do so. Thus, nothing at all is said about the crucial problem of the manner in which financial policy designed to maintain or re-establish balance of payments equilibrium is to be pursued, for example, whether by monetary or fiscal measures. On the other hand, the Fund (like GATT) does provide, as mentioned, a forum for continuing consultation on all these matters and the Articles require co-operation of members with the Fund to achieve its purposes.

II THE FIRST MODIFICATIONS OF THE CODE: THE FIRST TEN YEARS (1946/7–1955/6)

The Changes

Almost as soon as the Fund started operations, the basis of the Code, the par value system, was breached and not only by multiple rates. This is paradoxical, for it is the only substantive item of the code from which the Fund cannot authorize any departure (except for multiple rates), although the Fund need neither invoke sanctions nor allow their automatic application against a deviating country. The lack of discretion to authorize departures refers to both aspects of the par value system, that is, that countries must (except for temporary multiple rate practices) conduct transactions within the margins around par values and that (therefore) changes in the latter should be made in discrete steps. The breach made was, of course, partial. In some cases, departure from par value was desired only for transitional purposes, where there was genuine expectation of an early return to a par value. In all cases except one, where par values were in effect abandoned in favour of floating rates for any length of time, the countries were LDCs. It was assumed that the latter were unlikely to disturb other countries by their rate fluctuations – there was perhaps a tendency to equate the harmlessness of such arrangements with a country's share in world trade.

In the immediate post-war years the Fund at first tried to enforce

---

[13] It would also infringe the principle of reciprocity, which was then dominant in monetary as well as trade matters. GATT (see Article XXXVI, Section 8) has formally abandoned it in trade matters as between developing and developed countries.

the par value system rigorously. Thus, in January 1948 the institution by a DC of multiple rate practices, involving broken cross rates and a limited free market of indefinite duration for convertible currencies, was explicitly rejected by the Fund.[14]

However, the attempt to enforce the Code on so rigorous an interpretation was soon abandoned. Already in June 1948, another country adopted a free rate as a transitional device[15] without formal Fund objection. In November 1949, another country adopted dual floating rates under the Fund's multiple rate jurisdiction and was able to maintain a single (formally) floating rate subsequently for many years without Fund objection.[16] The two countries mentioned were LDCs whose example was soon followed by others.[17] But they were not alone: the Fund did not object to the proposal of a developed country to adopt a floating rate in September 1949 in transition to a new parity (though the country did not implement the proposal).[18] Another developed country in 1950 introduced a free rate which endured until 1962;[19] in 1970, it again adopted a single floating rate.

Also, with the multiple devaluations of 1949 and numerous others of developed as well as less developed countries, there was certainly no rigidity of exchange rates.

One essential provision of the Code could not be implemented precisely as envisaged either then or later, namely, full-fledged prior consultation on rate changes (and restrictions).[20] The requirement was mostly observed in form. More important, in annual consultations the Fund staff has been able to give countries guidance as to exchange rate changes which would be considered appropriate by the Fund.

In the first case mentioned above,[21] where the Fund formally objected to a departure from the par value system, in the form of an unauthorized change in parity, the Fund allowed the (automatic) sanction of ineligibility to apply. In other cases, the Fund did not formally object and did not invoke any sanctions. Even at this early stage, the Fund soon tempered the expression of its inability to

[14] France: see *The International Monetary Fund, 1945-65* vol. 2, p. 44. All subsequent page references are to this volume unless otherwise noted.
[15] Mexico: pp. 153–4.   [16] Peru: ibid.
[17] Lebanon, Syria, Thailand: pp. 48–9.   [18] Belgium: p. 156.
[19] Canada: p. 44.
[20] This was particularly the case regarding rate changes since other departures from the Code were covered largely by Article XIV (see footnote 7).
[21] See vol. 2, p. 44.

approve a departure from the par value system by expressions which, for example, 'recognized the exigencies of the situation', although it could not approve the action taken. In those early stages of the evolution of its policy, the Fund would not have considered a country eligible to use its resources while it maintained floating rates.[22] Subsequently it went further and allowed access to its resources to a country with a fluctuating rate which asked for the Fund's assistance.[23]

While the attitude towards floating rates represented a first departure from the original Code, the acceptance of restrictions of various kinds on current transactions including discriminatory ones was in line with what had been foreseen for the post-war transitional period.[24] The acceptance of multiple rates was a corollary of the persistence of other restrictions. There was no occasion to invoke the scarce currency clause; the US, the only country whose currency could have become scarce in the IMF, was supplying dollars generously to the world.

An incipient departure of some importance from the original Code also occurred in this period in respect of the finance of capital movements by the Fund. Such a departure can be perceived in the attitude taken in 1948 and again in 1954, towards a proposed devaluation by an LDC. On both occasions, speculative capital flight played a role in the degree of devaluation of the currency in question which might otherwise, perhaps, have been less, if controls on capital movements would, and could have been instituted. Since the LDC in question claimed that this was impossible, the Fund did not object to the devaluation but one might say that the concept of fundamental equilibrium had thereby been extended, to include a disequilibrium partly prompted by speculative capital flights where the country, the currency of which was under attack, did not dispose of sufficient reserves or borrowing capacity or ability to institute controls.[25] On the other hand, also in 1954, when another LDC maintaining dual floating rates for (essentially) current and capital transactions, requested use of the IMF's resources, the standby arrangement specified that these had to be used only for support of the rate in the market for (essentially) current transaction.[26]

---

[22] It was understood, in the earliest case, that Mexico would be *de facto* ineligible while it was not making its parity effective: p. 153; the same was true at first of Peru: pp. 159ff.

[23] Peru: see p. 166.

[24] See Article XIV.

[25] Mexico: pp. 106–7.

[26] Peru: p. 166.

Effects on the LDCs

The changes in the Code during this first period were clearly beneficial to the countries directly concerned, with one exception, almost exclusively LDCs,[27] as well as to the world at large.

Abuse of floating rates did not occur. Considerations of social policy and the inflationary situation prevailing at the time in many countries had removed the principal incentive for competitive depreciation. For the LDCs which adopted them, one alternative to floating rates would have been more restrictions, which would have been distortive or ineffective. Another one would have been frequent changes in parities or nominally fixed exchange rates which in the extreme might not have been very different from floating rates. The single developed country maintaining a floating rate is believed not to have intervened to change the trend of its rates and the alternative would have been inflation or possibly a slower growth rate, if reserves had been accumulated at the expense of domestic investment.

After the 1949 multiple devaluations, the rates of industrialized countries were not much out of line and permitted a progressive liberalization of exchange transactions. More restrictions persisted among LDCs.

On the other hand, anything but an essentially flexible attitude towards quantitative restrictions, multiple rates and bilateral payments agreements was impracticable in a world emerging from the Second World War and soon plunged into another, if smaller, war.

III   THE NEXT TEN YEARS (1956/7–1965/6)

The Changes

During this period and particularly after 1958 the Code becomes in some respects even more flexible than during the previous period; in others it is more rigorously applied.

First, something of a dichotomy appears regarding the par value systems. The attitude of the IMF changes, under appropriate circumstances, from toleration to encouragement of floating rates for LDCs. An increasing proportion of them maintained fully effective parities or unitary rates (like practically all DCs at that time). But the Fund accepted, for LDCs, the fact that floating rates (or frequent small administrative rate changes, which would best be handled if the Fund did not insist on formally fixed rates) were the only practical solution in countries with prolonged inflation and could also be a

[27] The exception was Canada.

means of permitting the abandonment of multiple rates and quantitative restrictions earlier than might otherwise be possible. At the same time, the Fund recognized that it was necessary to give countries in this situation time (before they adopted parities) to undertake tariff and general fiscal reforms as well as other institutional changes. In fact, the emphasis of the Fund in many of these cases shifted to an insistence that the floating rates should not be prematurely pegged. It was only logical that the resources of the Fund should now be made available to LDCs to support exchange systems centred on fluctuating rates.[28]

If LDCs were reluctant to adopt such systems, the Fund did not refuse its assistance, but had no qualms about suggesting, or even insisting on, prior changes in fixed rates, whether parities or not. In fact, some LDCs have felt at times that the Fund was preaching too much floating and too much devaluation.[29] They have felt the Fund's attitude to be not so much permissive as overly enthusiastic. The Fund was able to make its point of view felt *vis-à-vis* the LDCs because it could not only dispose of its own resources, but could often influence syndicates lending jointly with an IMF standby.

For DCs, there is no similar encouragement of floating rates or devaluation; and the countries themselves (with the sole exception of Canada) took a negative attitude towards floating rates and, indeed, rate changes in general. In fact, the Fund helped and participated in establishing assistance schemes for financing capital flows from developed countries and in this way may have helped unwittingly to maintain not only the parity system but also exchange rate rigidity. Thus, the exchange rates of major developed countries remained fixed between 1956 and 1966 with only three exceptions. In only one rate change is the Fund believed to have taken an active role.[30] This passive attitude was, of course, entirely in accord with the letter and spirit of the Articles, much more so than the encouragement to make changes in the LDCs. The fact remains that even when tensions appeared which rather clearly suggested rate changes, they were not invariably undertaken.[31]

[28] See pp. 167–70.
[29] The Fund was formally within its rights in expressing opinions in informal consultations (p. 96) and its financial assistance outside the gold tranche is conditional; but LDCs sometimes felt that standards in granting assistance to different groups of countries were not always uniform; see also on a related problem *Annual Report* (1969), p. 146.
[30] The Fund had no active role in either the German or Dutch appreciations in 1961; the French devaluation in 1958 may have been an exception.
[31] For example, the UK in 1964.

The data presented (in Table 13.2) reflect the paucity of exchange rate changes in the period under review among DCs. The remarkable spurt in the number of rate changes after 1967 for DCs suggests

TABLE 13.2   *Number of Changes in Par Values and Fixed Unitary Rates According to Member Countries' Stage of Development*[1]

	1946–56	1957–66	1967[2]–70
DCs[3]			
1. Number which were members and had parity or fixed unitary rates throughout each period	10	17	19
2. Number of changes for above countries	10	7	9
3. a) Change per country	1	0·41	0·47
b) Change per country per year	0·09	0·04	0·13
LDCs[4]			
1. Number which were members and had parity or fixed unitary rates throughout each period	14	24	66
2. Number of changes for above countries	9	8	26
3. a) Change per country	0·64	0·33	0·39
b) Change per country per year	0·06	0·03	0·11

[1] Excluded in each period are countries which are not members throughout that period as well as those which, while members, throughout the period maintained a) multiple rates or unitary fluctuating rates through all or most of the three periods and, further, b) those which maintained multiple rates or effectively floating unitary rates in that particular period. Category (a) comprises presently sixteen LDCs; category (b) comprised two MDCs and four LDCs in the first period; one MDC and five LDCs in the second period; no MDCs and five LDCs in the third period.

[2] End of April 1970.

[3] The Group of Ten (United States, United Kingdom, Belgium and Luxembourg, France, Germany, Italy, Netherlands, Sweden, Canada, Japan), Austria, Denmark, Norway, Finland, Iceland, Ireland, Australia, New Zealand, South Africa.

[4] All other countries except socialist ones, other than Yugoslavia.

Source: IMF.

adjustment delays in the preceding periods. While the behaviour of parities or fixed unitary rates among LDCs was similar as among DCs, its significance is quite different. Almost all DCs had effective parities or unitary fixed rates at all times. A fair proportion of LDCs had multiple rates, some of which floated, or unitary floating rates during all or most of the period of Fund membership.

Secondly, the rest of the Code, in the period with which we are concerned, in a sense, was more valid than ever before since the Great Depression.

Restrictions on *current* payments had mostly been removed in developed countries by the late 1950s and were being abandoned in many LDCs.[32]

Simultaneously, however, there was a somewhat contrary development. A few countries which had already abandoned them felt the need at times to return to them to bolster doubtful parities by restrictions on current payments.[33] It is true that restrictions addressed to current transactions other than travel were mostly trade restrictions rather than exchange restrictions but the Fund advises the *contracting parties* on exchange matters, and GATT members are bound not to frustrate by exchange action the intent of the Articles of Agreement of the IMF.

Capital restrictions in the LDCs were of doubtful efficacy but survived none the less often in the form of separate legal or at least tolerated floating rates. In the industrialized countries they began to disappear after the restoration of external convertibility for current payments in 1958. There was, of course, no interference by the Fund with capital restrictions if a country desired to reinstitute them. But countries were quite reluctant to do so, even though their absence was one of the obstacles to the more frequent use of the option to change parities because of the flow of short-term capital which the absence of such restrictions permitted in anticipation of exchange rate changes. The reason was that large and important new means of financing capital flows were created in this period. As already mentioned, in serving this purpose, they contributed

[32] This situation prevailed whether countries formally abandoned their Article XIV status (see footnote 7) as most of the industrialized countries did, or whether they did not, as was the case with most LDCs. The difference between Article VIII and Article XIV countries became less important. On the one hand, Article VIII countries voluntarily submitted to annual consultations which were required by the Articles of Agreement only for Article XIV countries. On the other hand, the Fund became increasingly disinclined to regard changes in restrictions as adaptations to changing circumstances of existing ones and therefore increasingly inclined to demand prior approval for such changes from Article XIV countries (although it was still less exigent about the conditions for prior approval for the latter countries). Also, multiple rates became more popular than quantitative restrictions and these, being rate changes as well as restrictions, had always been regarded as requiring prior approval (see pp. 167–8), at least, if affecting payments for current transactions.
[33] For example, the United Kingdom, after 1963: *16th Annual Report on Exchange Restrictions 1965*, pp. 551ff.; or – less clearly – France after May 1968.

to rigidifying DC exchange rates (the clearest case is that of the UK).

Some of these means were entirely outside the Fund, like Central Bank swap arrangements. The General Arrangements to Borrow (GAB) were designed to help the Fund lend in connection with speculative capital movements, in view of the increased short-term capital flows due to the return to convertibility by Europe.[34] As a special borrowing arrangement for the IMF, the source and direct use of the resources of which is limited to the ten GAB members (whatever may be true of their indirect use), the GAB definitely does not fit into the universality which is the principle underlying the IMF concept. *More important, it led to the establishment of an international monetary decision-making centre in rivalry with the* IMF.

Great progress was made during this period with the removal of discrimination through bilateral payments agreements. The Fund promoted helpful joint consultations designed to remove them between partners to such agreements.

No application was made of the scarce currency clause. The occasion did not arise (two surplus countries revalued) and it was increasingly believed that it involved an excessively aggressive stance likely to provoke counter sanctions.

Also during the period, a potentially important change was made in Fund policies on drawings. This was the institution of the so-called compensatory financing facility to offset declines in export revenues, especially for primary producing countries. The idea was that the Fund's assistance should be available on relatively automatic terms in such cases. After a first start, the facility was liberalized somewhat in 1966 (and again in 1969).[35]

The Effects on LDCs

The Fund's encouragement or even over-encouragement of rate changes and its increasing enthusiasm for floating rates in LDCs did not encourage them to pursue inflationary policies which they would otherwise have eschewed; rather it encouraged them to eschew restrictions which they would otherwise have adopted in the intervals between formal devaluations.

Among DCs, detrimental *economic effects of exchange rate rigidity* or delays in exchange rate adjustment can be perceived in individual

---

[34] This is the meaning of the phrase 'the increasing volatility of balance of payments', p. 373. Whether the GAB also helped the Fund in adopting a more liberal attitude towards the use of its resources by LDCs, including the establishment of the compensatory financing facility, is another question.

[35] See pp. 417ff.

cases. The overall statistical evidence, however, is inconclusive. The trend of both DC and LDC Gross Domestic Product growth rates was upward since 1951. The two periods (1959–60, 1966–8) in which the DC growth rate of GDP fell, were periods of reduced US growth.[36] In the first period, nobody would have suggested that either the dollar should be devalued or other currencies revalued to relieve the US of a need for restrictive financial policies; in the second period of declining growth of DCs it would still be hard to claim that US restrictive demand policies were undertaken exclusively or even mainly for balance of payments purposes rather than for internal ones. The *quantum* of exports exhibited uninterruptedly rising growth rates for both DCs and LDCs since 1951 while the sharply upward trend of the *value* of exports for both groups of countries was interrupted only during one brief period (1965–8).[37] It should be noted that during the short period mentioned there was no overall rise in trade or payments restrictions. Of course, no statistical evidence of the kind adduced here could prove that the repercussions of the exchange rate policy pursued were harmless (or harmful), for the growth of world trade and income might well have been larger (smaller) if different exchange rate policies had been followed. Harmful effects of rigid exchange rates can probably be identified in the marked slowdown, during the 1960s, in the rise of official financial assistance.[38]

The attitude of the Fund in pressing for elimination of multiple

[36] The DC average annual GDP growth rate was 4 per cent in 1951/5; 3 per cent in 1956/60; 5 per cent in 1961/5, and 4 per cent in 1966/8. The corresponding figures for LDCs were 5 per cent for the first three periods and 6 per cent in the last one. *Source: United Nations Statistical Yearbooks*: 1969 Table 3, p. 9, Table 176, p. 534; 1968 Table 4, pp. 29–30, Table 183, p. 553; 1965 Table 4, pp. 27–8; 1959 Table 167, p. 449.

[37] *Volume*: growth rates rose as follows; for DCs from 5 per cent per annum in 1951/5 to 10 per cent in 1968/70; for LDCs: from 4 per cent to 7 per cent. *Source: United Nations Statistical Yearbooks*: 1969, Table 10, p. 44; 1968, Table 14, p. 67; 1962, Table 155, p. 447, and 1959, Table 154, p. 392. For 1968–70 estimated on basis of *International Financial Statistics* (March 1971), p. 36, and p. 32, respectively (for LDCs, the UN export price index excluding petroleum was used; for 1970 the change in export price index used was that between the second quarter of 1969 and the second quarter of 1970). *Value*: growth rates rose for DCs from 4 per cent to 12 per cent and for LDCs from minus 0·1 per cent to 8 per cent. *Source: United Nations Statistical Yearbooks*: 1969, Table, 12, p. 48; 1968, Table, 15, p. 70; and 1955, Table 146, p. 387. For 1968/70 estimated from *International Financial Statistics* (March 1970), p. 36.

[38] See *Partners in Development* (the Pearson Report), (Preager Publishers, 1969), Table 15; OECD *Development Assistance 1969 Review*, Tables 11.1 to 11.7; Annex Tables 1–13; also *1970 Review*, Tables 11–11. Restrictions on private capital flows affected mostly capital exports to DCs.

rates, quantitative restrictions and bilateralism was helpful to LDCs in so far as it led to liberalization by DCs and was at times not even felt as a hardship by the LDCs encountering such pressure. Sufficient time was allowed to replace by tariffs penalty import rates which were considered to serve a useful purpose, even after a reasonable devaluation. To replace subsidy export rates in excess of such devaluation and subsidy import rates by outright budgetary subsidies was

TABLE 13.3 *Proportion of LDCs[1] with Substantial Restrictions, by Type[2] (mid-1970)*

Type	Percentage
1. Quantitative import restrictions	30
2. Quantitative restrictions on current payments	24
3. Multiple currency practices	16
4. Any one of the foregoing type of restrictions	37
5. All of the foregoing types of restrictions	9

[1] See Table 13.2, footnote 4.
[2] The number of countries considered is eighty-nine.

Source: IMF

generally not attempted, while penalty export rates could be replaced by export taxes and where this was not done, the Fund proved understanding. The abolition of multiple rates did, of course, deprive countries with functioning representative institutions of administratively easy means of changing penalties and regards in connection with foreign trade. However, many legislations provide scope for executive action in the field of tariffs and exemptions. In any event, the International Monetary Fund adopted a lenient attitude towards multiple rates as long as exchange systems were being simplified rather than complicated.

The same practical considerations as in the case of multiple rates also explain the favourable attitude taken by developing countries in general to the elimination of quantitative exchange restrictions and other quantitative restrictions (see Table 13.3). In any case, at the time of writing, close to two-thirds of LDCs were free of substantial restrictions of any kind. This was recognition of a changed situation. The change was three-fold. First, the realization of the technical misfunctioning of these devices as compared to tariffs; secondly, recognition of the dangers of excessive protection; thirdly; better balance of payments performance, as the importance of export performance was recognized as an essential part of a successful development effort and a reduction in inflationary pressures took place due to the increasing recognition that inflation had hindered growth. At the same time, countries had become more sophisticated in the use of other policy instruments, as already mentioned above.

On aspect of the elimination of restrictions which deserves special mention is bilateral payments agreements. The widespread return to convertibility limited the interest of the developing countries in the maintenance of such agreements to a few Fund members which claimed to be able to discriminate through remaining quantitative restrictions and to countries of the Eastern bloc. However, even here there were frequent disappointments through the development of commodity arbitrage.

The return to convertibility in which in effect most LDCs participated[39] also put paid to the idea sometimes mentioned that integration among LDCs could be speeded up by the establishment of regional payments unions. What remained were some modest arrangements patterned on the European system of 'interim finance' or for the mutual extension of credit in convertible currencies with an increasing degree of conditionality and not limited to the appearance of intraregional deficits.

Along with the disappearance of restrictions on current transactions, those on capital transactions were also being removed. The removal of restrictions on short-term flows was perhaps more spectacular than that on long-term transactions. Thus, one of the world's major capital exporters on private account, the UK, had all through the time of its inconvertibility maintained a considerable flow of long-term capital exports. What characterized the period under review was the greater ease of short-term movements and the opening up of markets for bond floatation.

IV   THE LATE 1960s

Changes Accomplished and Contemplated
As rates of inflation continued to diverge in industrialized countries,[40] several of their parities had to be changed during the period. The Fund took a discreetly advisory role in some of these cases. These changes were preceded by exceptionally severe speculative crises.

[39] Although they formally maintained Article XIV status.
[40] As well as the relationships in them between export prices on the one hand and prices in general on the other hand.

There is no indication that in this period any country which was not in fundamental equilibrium was forced into a rate change by speculative flows.[41]

The delays in rate changes noted led to a search for making them easier. Since a large part of the payments problem of the late 1960s consisted in an excessive balance of payments deficit of the US, attention was paid particularly to means of easing revaluation of (other) countries.

While the politics may point in a different direction than economics, an indirect devaluation of the US dollar[42] became technically less necessary and attractive after March 1968, when the two-tier gold price was introduced. Another objection to the indirect approach is that a major country can have large, enduring deficits which are not reflected in large or persistent surpluses of specific trading partners so that the incentive to appreciate for any one of these may be weak.

Nevertheless, the problem of revaluation retained its importance because it would often be preferable to share rate changes against a common denominator like gold between surplus and deficit countries in order to relieve (many) third countries from following in the steps of one or the other countries changing rates.

Also, easier revaluations were believed to be needed in order to promote a 'more equitable sharing' of the 'burden' of balance of payments adjustment, in favour of deficit countries (other than the reserve centre).

The concept of 'burden' as used in these discussions is an ambiguous one. It refers partly to the *political* burden, that is, the need to take an explicit, unpopular decision. It is clear that a surplus country can escape (at an economic cost) the need of taking any explicit decision in order to restore equilibrium,[43] while the deficit country cannot do so. Easier rate changes may make it easier to share the explicit decision-making, a political advantage.

[41] UK, 1967; France, Germany, 1969; Canada, 1970; to mention only the principal currencies. The same may not be true of the changes in May 1971, depending on the interpretation given to the word 'forced'.

[42] As well as the 'Marris heresy', that is, the idea of expressing parities not in gold but in SDRs.

[43] Equilibrium is defined as zero net change in reserve assets. The latter concept is slightly ambiguous. More serious is the fact that equilibrium so defined will almost necessarily be incompatible with overall equilibrium in a nonstationary economy so that balance of payments equilibrium in the usual sense is hardly to be aimed at. One should really aim at 'reasonable' equilibrium or disequilibrium – it does not matter which – the rate of change of net reserve assets compatible with overall economic equilibrium.

'Burden' also refers, however, to the economic cost of the process of adjustment where the situation is less clear.[44] Whenever adjustment requires changes in the real demand and supply functions involved (the opposite case would be trivial) a restructuring of *all* the economies concerned will be necessary.[45]

In the presence of imperfect price (and wage) flexibility everywhere, both unemployment and inflationary distortions may accompany the restructuring process.[46] But there is no reason why the deficit country should be worse off than the surplus country. In fact the opposite may be the case depending upon which is considered the greater evil, inflation or unemployment. The deficit country must act but can choose between deflation and devaluation; even in the latter case, it will not normally escape all unemployment but at the expense of larger internal price rises it can escape much of it; the surplus country must suffer a downward pressure on prices and employment in either case.

Where we have been talking of inflation and deflation, we have of course been doing so in relative terms; the deflationary or inflationary moves which are the result of the adjustment process will neutralize the pre-existing deflation or inflation or add to it according to whether we are in the presence of a dilemma case or not. While the rate change option distinguishes the present system from the gold standard, the protection of the policy initiative taken by any country from an offsetting action by any country in the opposite situation of fundamental disequilibrium distinguishes it from the conditions which prevailed in the 1930s.

This assurance marks great progress over the pre-IMF situation. Moreover, difficulties of decision-making ensure in practice that the adjustment process chosen by whatever country takes the first step will be the one that will prevail: for example, if that country chooses a not too lengthy disinflation policy to cure the deficit, it is unlikely to have a more rapid adjustment thrust upon it by somebody else's appreciation. In sum, easier rate changes including revaluations are

[44] As distinct from a process of adjustment, which can assume alternative forms, accomplished adjustment can in no sense be a burden, because there is no alternative to it in the long run.

[45] This will be true even if the balance of payments disequilibrium is removed mainly by a change in the capital account, which cannot leave the structure of the economy unaffected.

[46] If all prices were perfectly flexible upward, downward price inflexibility – under exchange flexibility – would not matter: all relative price changes would take place by instantaneous upward adjustment (except for the exchange rate) so that the price rises would have none of the effects of inflation.

desirable but not because of economic burden sharing as usually envisaged.

For the purpose of making exchange rates more easily changeable, freely floating rates were rejected at an early stage of the international discussion among officials. Even after the crisis of August 1971 there does not seem to be any official enthusiasm for them.

The substantive reasons usually given for rejecting freely floating rates as a 'normal' system may be more or less convincing. But the procedural reason can hardly be questioned. This is, that it is hard to imagine international control ex ante of exchange rates without the parity system and that ex ante control is preferable to ex post control. But the parity system has not, in my opinion, any frequency requirement other than that exchange rate changes cannot be continuous or so frequent that ex ante control becomes impossible. Individual exceptions to the parity system in particular circumstances are tolerable and have been tolerated without harm.

The need for effective control over exchange rates is particularly great because there is no guarantee that 'free' rates would not, in fact, be mostly subject to official intervention for more than 'smoothing' purposes. The exchange rate is simply too important a price for most countries to leave it to the market unless the market happens to behave in the way in which authorities want it to. The effective choice therefore is not between parities and freely floating rates but between intervention according to the rules of the parity system and intervention without rules. It is hardly possible to formulate rules for intervention outside the parity system which would be practicable and acceptable.

It is, however, legitimate to ask whether ex ante control exists in fact under the parity system. Nobody can claim that in practice exchange rate changes are substantively decided upon by national authorities only after formal concurrence by the Fund. Sometimes they are even announced before a formal decision of the Fund has been made.

The contact between the IMF and its members means, however, that the latter presumably know the former's opinion of their exchange rate and give it weight in their substantive decisions. One must also assume that ex ante control increases that weight as compared to what it would be under ex post control. Ex ante control carries with it at least the possibility of a condemnation of a rate change by the Fund simultaneously with its announcement by the national authorities. The mere possibility of such a simultaneous or swift condemnation, which would hardly be possible under ex post control, is a strong incentive for countries to pay regard to the views of the international financial community.

Moreover, what would be gained by replacement of the parity system even if one could be confident that governments would not intervene in nominally floating rates more than in a merely smoothing fashion? After all, what is the harm of sticking to the parity system in 'normal' circumstances? There is no proof (or reason to believe) that it could not have been worked without the delays in parity adjustments which are attributed to it as due to the fear of major speculative capital movements if the expectation of more frequent rate changes were to become established. It is these movements, of course, and the consequential fear and rate rigidity which the Bretton Woods rule for control of capital movements was, *inter alia*, designed to avoid. But, in the meantime, we have developed substitutes and are taking a second look at limited capital controls.

In addition to freely floating rates (so-called), greatly widened margins were also rejected as a 'normal' option, because they were felt to be substantially equivalent to freely floating rates. The 'crawling peg' was rejected in both its forms, the 'discretionary' crawl as well as the 'automatic' crawl. The first was again rejected because of the lack of ex ante approval; the second, because the arguments of the formula could be manipulated, so that it would become equivalent to the discretionary form of crawl.

What other ways are there to ease changes of effective exchange rates? Essentially two different orders of measures are relevant to this problem.[47] The first is substantive, whether to establish new forms of flexibility. The second is procedural, whether to encourage flexibility by legalizing certain kinds of it which already exist but have so far only been tolerated.

[47] Wide margins would generally be expected to induce governments to intervene well before the extremes were reached. Thus, while movements which went as far as the extreme would be extremely effective in evoking stabilizing speculation, any movement which stopped short of the extremes might be likely to be interpreted as being the result of intervention rather than of market forces, even if the latter were in fact responsible. Therefore, it would be necessary, in order to get advantage from the system, to intervene so as immediately to push the effective rate to the extremes for otherwise the suspicion of intervention could lead to increased destabilizing speculation. If wider margins were associated with a sliding peg system there might be additional reason to believe that, under certain conditions, the combination would lead to increased rather than reduced destabilizing speculation, see Stephen Marris, *The Burgenstock Communique: Essays in International Finance*, (Princeton, New Jersey, August 1970), no. 80, pp. 23–4.

The discussion originally centred on three proposals:

1. slightly wider margins
2. the encouragement of more frequent parity changes (i) without change in the present Articles of Agreement or (ii) by exempting limited adjustments from prior Fund concurrence
3. temporary and transitional floats outside narrow margins

Of these only (1) and (2) (i) and (ii) and more clearly the latter would represent substantive change. (3) would be procedural only – it is already tolerated.

The Interest of the LDCs

The LDCs have taken an open-minded but cautious attitude on these proposals. One of their preoccupations is that the legalization of departures from the par value system likely to be practised by DCs might be combined with continued illegality for the type of departures practised mainly by LDCs, for example, short-term floats *v.* long-term floats, even where the latter were justified by difficult inflation problems. Mainly, however, while greater flexibility for DCs may offer LDCs potential advantages (fewer restrictions) the extent of the advantages is not always clear and there may be disadvantages which outweigh them. These fears have been strengthened rather than relieved by the crisis of August 1971.

Let us now examine these proposals in turn.

Wider margins. Apparently, the most innocuous one is a slight widening of margins around parity, the figure most frequently mentioned being 2 to 3 per cent.

Fluctuations of 2 to 3 per cent around parity are believed, other things being equal, to affect less the current account than the capital account, and particularly speculative capital flows between the DCs; slightly widened margins should not be expected to induce major equilibrating movements even of capital in primary-producing countries because their money markets are often narrow, there are controls, or fears of controls on capital movements or fear of extended pressures on balance of payments. Also relatively few are in the habit of making use even of the present margins of permissible fluctuations. Thus, a majority of IMF members, including most LDCs, will derive no direct benefit from wider margins. But they may suffer more or less damage.

Before discussing the latter one should ask how useful slightly wider margins would be. One may legitimately doubt the need for them since, as we have already seen, their main function of reducing disruptive flows between DCs can be replaced by other means short of controls (credits), which could be further developed. Controls are also now viewed with less abhorrence than a short time ago. Furthermore, the effects of slightly wider margins in discouraging disruptive capital flows may be quite small not only when speculation has taken hold but even with respect to flows induced by interest rate differentials. The German experience before May 1971 casts doubts on the effectiveness of forward rate policies in affecting interest induced flows and similar doubts apply to slightly wider margins. On the other hand, if governments were prepared to rely more on fiscal and less on monetary policy in dealing with the business cycle or with inflationary spurts, short-term capital movements, in response to interest rate differentials, would be greatly diminished. Thus there seems to be dilemma: slightly wider margins may not be very helpful and greatly widened ones would be the end of any effective parity system.

Let us, however, turn to the possible dangers posed by even slightly wider margins.

First, and most important, there would be a difficult or embarrassing choice for many IMF members, especially – but not only – LDCs to which major currency to peg, if those major currencies fluctuated more against each other than at present, even within the limits of a slight widening of margins.[48] This aspect becomes particularly frightening in view of the possibility that exchange blocs will develop into trade discrimination even where the conditions for customs unions or free trade areas that are conducive to welfare are not present.

Secondly, under greater exchange rate flexibility there would be increased reliance on monetary policy for control of *self-generated*

[48] That small countries follow independent exchange rate policies under the present system is evidenced by the following examples:

1. Independent par value on joining, or soon after: Yugoslavia, Ghana.

2. Par value not changed when there was devaluation of major currency: Algeria, Morocco, Tunisia, Iraq, Zambia, Libya.

3. Par value changed independently although still formally tied to major currency block: Jamaica, Ghana, Zambia, India.

4. Countries not following neighbours: small European countries in relation to German revaluation.

5. Countries re-orienting exchange rate policy: South Africa, with Botswana, Lesotho and Swaziland.

inflations or deflations (as distinct from *imported* ones). This increased emphasis on monetary policy is a consequence of the well-known fact that under exchange rate flexibility the effects of fiscal policy tend to be offset by exchange rate movements. By contrast, monetary policy under greater exchange rate flexibility would not lead to neutralizing capital flows, as at present (or to less of it).

An exchange rate system which increased the effectiveness of monetary policy might even be considered a good thing if fiscal policy were in any case too slow or too rigid. But since the final story on the lags of monetary policy has not yet been written, an exchange rate system which reduced the effectiveness of fiscal policy would bring no benefit and might bring a good deal of damage.

Thirdly, from the particular point of view of smaller countries, especially LDCs who peg to a major currency, there might be a special disadvantage deriving from even slightly wider margins: namely, increased debt management problems due to the increased interest rate fluctuations which would prevail if greater use were made of monetary policy by the issuers of major currencies in attempting to neutralize self-generated inflations (or deflations).

One might ask whether this disadvantage is not offset by the fact that where an industrialized country was protecting itself against *imported inflation*, it might under slightly wider margins leave the task to the exchange rate and therefore need less of either fiscal or monetary restrictions. Under these conditions it could maintain more stable interest rates which would be an advantage to those borrowing-LDCs which pegged to its rate. It might also be asked whether a further offset would not derive from the fact that the situation of countries not pegging to a country adopting wider margins for dealing with self-generated inflations and deflations but interested in borrowing in its markets, would tend to be different; exchange rate movements (spot and forward) would tend to neutralize interest rate fluctuations. The problem is that in most cases smaller countries will tend to peg to the currency of the country in whose markets they do most of their trading and borrowing while major countries will increasingly be concerned with dealing with their self-generated cyclical movements rather than with imported ones.

As can be seen, the slight widening of margins offers no discernible direct advantages and under certain circumstances discernible indirect risks to the LDCs. Perhaps one should not overrate them, but one cannot be indifferent to them.

Prompter parity changes. Since the Executive Directors' Report was written, interest has subsided in the proposal to exempt parity changes of a limited extent from the requirements of advance Fund concurrence but it has increasingly seemed to some that no further clarification would be necessary to encourage prompter parity changes, beyond that already given in the Report.

What about the economic effects of prompter changes in parities, which would, of course, still have to remain justified by fundamental disequilibrium? I shall assume that prompter changes in parities will, over any period of reasonable length, make average exchange rates differ from what they would have been otherwise, rather than produce wider fluctuations. On that hypothesis, one must initially weight the effects on LDCs of the substitution of restrictive policies of various kinds (including fiscal and monetary ones) by DCs against those of exchange rate changes.

On the *initial* impact of exchange rate changes *vice* restrictive policies, no general judgement is possible. For instance, in so far as trade restrictions fall on imports of manufactures, but not on primary products, a primary producing LDC may see no immediate advantage in greater rate flexibility of the industrialized countries but the same attitude would not be taken by an industrializing LDC. These examples could be multiplied endlessly.

Eventually, however, the main effect on LDCs will be indirect, via the impact on the comparative growth rates and economic structure of the industrialized countries under more flexibility *v.* more restrictive policies. Specifically, one will have to ask whether prompter parity changes would bring about a more rapid growth rate or less protectionist attitudes on the part of the great trading countries. The evidence so far, as already mentioned, is, in general, inconclusive, although official financial assistance to LDCs appears to have been inhibited.

The encouragement of more frequent parity changes, though it is not an equivalent of the so-called discretionary crawling peg is a step in the same direction and can presumably have the same advantages (and apply to the same situations provided the relative rate of inflation or deflation compared to that of the world is not too high), without the disadvantage of exemption of the changes from ex ante international control; in particular it would be quite illegitimate to suggest, as has been done by some critics of the Executive Directors' Report, that it would lead to the same large speculative movements as a parity system operated with infrequent and delayed adjustments. The interest rate weapon could be used in a very similar manner – to the extent that this was preferable to re-cycling or other measures – to avoid these flows under a system of more frequent changes in parities as it could be to avoid them in an automatically or discretionary crawling peg.

Deviations from the parity system. The apparently most radical proposal concerns temporary deviation from the par value system. This deviation can be *either* for the very short term, as in Germany in 1969, *or* for a medium term, as originally (that is, before the monetary crisis of August 1971) envisaged for the second Canadian float of 1970, and the German and Dutch floats of 1971 and those of various less developed countries. The economic effects of the first type or 'transitional' floats are identical with those of prompter parity changes, which have just been discussed. More prolonged floats refer to cases where the changes in effective exchange rates would simply have to be too frequent to qualify even formally as parity changes.

Here, however, we go from the substantive to the procedural. Both transitional and prolonged floats (and wider margins) are already tolerated in exceptional circumstances and on analysis it appears that there can be no reason why they have to be legalized in order not to be eschewed by other countries than those which have practised them in the past. It is hard to accept the argument that those other countries exhibit a greater sensitivity to the difference between acquiescence and full legality. Nor is it true that in order to improve the surveillance of the Fund over countries deviating from the Articles, there is need for legal changes; the Fund can, where necessary, exert close surveillance even where these deviations are not legalized.

But there is an additional problem. There seems to be some disposition in the international financial community to legalize everything up to and including transitional floats but, not even in exceptional cases, floats of indefinite duration although they have been tolerated in the past. On the ground of equity, however, it would be wrong that certain kinds of deviation from the present letter of the Articles which have been tolerated should be legalized (for example, transitional floats), while others which had been equally tolerated should remain illegal, even if they continued to be tolerated (for example, temporary but non-transitional floats). Nor would it seem appropriate to legalize deviations from the present Articles which have not been tolerated in the past, while refusing to legalize others which have been tolerated.

Access to balance of payments finance. Providing for additional financing of balance of payments deficits (over and above what is now available) is a temporary alternative to greater rate flexibility, in so far as widening the adjustment options available to countries is concerned. Here there is a real iniquity, not between surplus and deficit countries, but between different groups of the latter.

As a result of developments over the last ten years or so, the world presently has three types of liquidity. First, there is owned liquidity consisting of gold and foreign exchange holdings, gold and super gold tranches in the Fund and SDRs. Secondly, there is access to the IMF's credit tranches and thirdly, there is a considerable amount of other credit in the form of central banks' swap arrangements and so on, limited, however, essentially to some DCs.

I have referred earlier to the usefulness of credit facilities as a welcome means from everybody's point of view, for offsetting speculative capital flows between DCs, the alternative to which might otherwise have to be capital controls. The fact, however, is that these non-Fund credit facilities can be used and have been used not only for, as it were, re-cycling flows but also for ordinary balance of payments support. Thus, an obvious differentiation is introduced into the working of the international adjustment mechanism as between countries which do and those which do not have access to these extra Fund credit facilities. It means that the former countries, and not only the reserve centres among them, have access to considerably wider options for their adjustment policies than other countries.

What makes the situation even more undesirable is the fact that these borrowing facilities, accessible to only one small group of countries, completely escape the control of the international financial community via the IMF. The IMF sometimes, in fact, bails out over-generous lenders under these facilities. The delays and rigidities which have often been blamed on the parity system are just as often a consequence of the existence of these credit facilities accessible to few and exempt from control by the IMF.

A reform of the credit system outside the IMF which is growing up alongside owned reserves and the Fund would have two effects. It would contribute to re-establishing greater equity among the beneficiaries and other countries, especially LDCs, and it would contribute to a better working of the international adjustment process. It should be part and parcel of any reform which may be thought necessary in that system (see Table 13.4).

TABLE 13.4   *Distribution of Balance of Payments Finance*

	Reserves[1] (including SDRs, Reserve Positions in IMF)	Quotas[1]	Non Fund[2] Credit Lines
MDCS	73	21	17
Group of ten	58	18	16[3]
LDCS	19	8	0·4

[1] 31 December 1970.

[2] 31 March 1971; excluding Switzerland. See *Federal Reserve Bulletin* (March 1971), p. 190.

[3] Includes US $1 billion equivalent of unspecified European currencies. See *Federal Reserve Bulletin*, vol. 1, p. i.

Source: IMF (unless otherwise quoted).

V.   CONCLUSION

The preceding sections of this paper have shown that the Bretton Woods Code has proved extremely flexible. In particular, the Code has not inhibited members from adopting those exchange rate practices with or without the IMF Articles of Agreement which their condition made to appear advisable to them, provided they were justified by the need to remove fundamental disequilibrium and were not unnecessarily harmful to others. Even when the Fund has not formally authorized certain practices because it could not legally do so, it has not invoked sanctions, even if the practices were contrary to the core of the Articles of Agreement, the par value system. In fact, some LDCs have been encouraged, where appropriate, to adopt floating rates and received financial assistance to do so. What complaints there have been have been preferred by some LDCs complaining of excessive encouragement to devalue (parities, fixed rates and rates subject to frequent administrative adjustment); or they have referred to complaints of lack of encouragement to DCs who were reluctant to change parities or have, at least on a few important occasions, delayed exchange rate adjustment. The expansion of bilateral borrowing arrangements between DCs (as well as the creation of the IMF-connected GAB) have contributed to these delays. In this way, also, multilateral surveillance over these countries by the Fund has been seriously weakened; nor can one say that it has been replaced by effective multilateral surveillance by the participants in the GAB, in which, in any case, the LDCs do not participate directly.

The available statistical evidence is inconclusive on the effects of rate rigidity among DCs (as compared to LDCs) in the early 1960s on the growth rates of GDP or of trade. The fact is that performance in all these respects (except for the growth rates of official financial assistance to LDCs) has been rather good throughout the post-war period. But it is true that the main balance of payments disequilibrium of recent years has been that of the United States. The same degree of disequilibrium elsewhere could have led to more restrictions and more pronounced detrimental effects; but it is more likely that it would have been cured by parity changes (or perhaps by a more radical reduction of international responsibilities than that undertaken by the United States).

Nevertheless, the crises of the late 1960s have given rise to the discussions presently under way on building greater exchange rate flexibility into the international monetary system, or, more exactly, of legalizing existing forms of exchange rate flexibility, for the benefit of those DCs which have claimed that unlike others, they cannot live with merely tolerated but not legal flexibility. Events in 1969/71 cast some doubts on this requirement. For it has become evident that to an increasing extent, DCs have been prepared to avail themselves of the Fund's tolerance in adopting exchange rate practices involving greater flexibility even where these are contrary to the present Articles of Agreement.

It is not clear whether the changes which have been discussed (ranging from more frequent use of the Bretton Woods Code's provision for parity changes to willingness to 'acquiesce in' deviations from the Articles of Agreement to amendment of the latter) would be helpful, on balance, to the LDCs. Since most forms of flexibility now under serious discussion are already practised and tolerated by the IMF, the question, of course, refers to the likelihood of their wider adoption by DCs than at present, if they were legalized or if their toleration were more explicitly stated. One thing is clear: it would be harmful to the LDCs if any new or presently tolerated forms of flexibility were to be legalized which are of no direct interest to LDCs while others which they do use and which are presently tolerated would remain illegal.

The burden of this chapter is that the present system, which has been associated with unprecedented growth rates of the world economy, has also served the LDCs well, in view of the flexibility which the system has shown.

There is no suggestion that the present system is ideal from the point of view of the LDCs. While it does not inhibit them from using exchange rate flexibility as a policy instrument, it does not offer them an adequate substitute for the bilateral borrowing to which developed deficit countries have access and which enables some of the latter to evade to a large extent the choice between rate changes and financing of deficits. As a result, the International Monetary Fund's multilateral surveillance is less effective in them than in LDCs.

While a reasonably favourable judgement of the essentials of the present system at this time characterizes most members of the international financial community, the system is now seriously threatened. It is still likely and to be hoped that the essence of the system, as an on-the-whole successful experiment in international co-operation, will survive.

CHAPTER 14

International Capital Movements, Fixed Parities, and Monetary and Fiscal Policies

F. MODIGLIANI

I INTRODUCTION

There is a broad measure of agreement among professional economists on the proposition that the free movement of long-term international capital, just like the free movement of commodities, is highly desirable since it contributes to a more efficient use of resources, besides its likely contribution to a closer knit and a more peaceful world. There is, however, far less agreement as to what kind of international settlement system and what type of domestic policies are best suited to foster the international movement of capital.

One widely-held view is that the goal can best be served by retaining and strengthening the present system of permanently fixed official parities and forsaking any form of 'interference' with capital movements. Such interferences include not only direct controls but also the use of tax measures aimed at influencing the incentive to private capital movement by modifying the relation between the net private yield from, and the net private cost of, domestic versus foreign uses and sources of funds. The support of fixed parities rests on the consideration that variations in the rate of exchange between currencies increase the risk and, hence, have the effect of discouraging long-term capital movements. The opposition to any form of interference rests on the seemingly obvious proposition that it would prevent or reduce the flow of capital from where its productivity is lower to where it is higher. Since one of the most forceful and articulate expounders of this point of view in recent years has been C. P. Kindleberger, we find it convenient to refer to what follows as the 'CPK position', without necessarily implying that Kindleberger himself would endorse all that we ascribe to that position.

The basic purpose of this paper is to argue that the CPK position,

239

despite its apparent cogency and attractive simplicity, suffers in reality from a number of fatal flaws and, as a result, its policy recommendations are inconsistent with the basic purpose they are supposed to serve.

The major conclusion of our analysis can be summarized in the following propositions:

1. Under a system of fixed and rigid parities, once proper allowance is made for widespread wage–price rigidities, complete freedom of capital movement may not only fail to achieve significant movements of real capital, but, in addition, tends to be inconsistent with domestic stability.

2. The above inconsistency can be eliminated through a 'co-ordinated monetary and fiscal policy approach'. It is shown, however, that under this approach fiscal policy is used not to *facilitate* the transfer of real capital, but rather to *eliminate the need* for a real transfer by removing the incentive for private investors to avail themselves of the freedom to move capital. Thus, the modern supporters of freedom of capital movements together with fixed and rigid parities are sacrificing the end to the mean: instead of wanting an open door so that capital can flow through it they want to remove the incentive for capital to flow so that the door can be kept open.

3. If freedom of capital movements is to achieve the intended purpose of bringing about a flow of real capital to those areas where its productivity is highest, then fixed and rigid parities must give way to a fuller and more systematic use of changes in parities.

4. Even with greater flexibility in exchange rates, it may be appropriate on occasions to modify the private incentive to the movement of capital. This result may be achieved through the use of conventional fiscal policy tools. It is argued, however, that contrary to the position taken by the CPK school, the use of tax incentives and related devices, aimed at modifying the relative cost and return of domestic versus foreign uses and sources of funds, provides an alternative approach which is preferable in most, if not all, relevant dimensions.

II FOUNDATIONS OF THE CPK POSITION AND THEIR SHORT-COMINGS

As indicated in Section I, the support of the CPK position for a system of fixed and rigid parities, free of any interference with private capital movements, rests on the ground that such a system maximizes the response of private capital flows to differentials between domestic and foreign private yields. But in order to conclude that such a response is 'socially' desirable it must be assumed that the movement of private capital in search for the highest private yield (or the cheapest source of funds) will redistribute the flow of *real investment*, without reducing its volume, towards those areas where its productivity is highest. We suggest that this assumption is subject to question on at least three major counts:

1. It presumes that differentials in private yields imply similar differentials in net social returns.

2. It presupposes that differentials in yields, with freedom of private capital movements, will lead to flows or transfers of *real* resources, as distinguished from international reserves, in predictably short order.

3. It neglects the possibility that under fixed and rigid parities, the transfer of real resources, if and when it occurs, may be achieved at significant economic and social costs, including reductions in output and in the overall flow of investment, through a fall in the rate of utilization of resources.

Let us examine each of these points more closely.

i. Private versus social returns. As has been pointed out by many authors, in a world in which net yields to private investors are affected in very large measure and in very complex ways by the entire fiscal system of the country as well as by direct controls, and in which the structure of capital markets and the intermediaries operating therein exhibit vast differences, there is not even a *prima facie* case for the proposition that differences in private yields can be taken as meaningful indicators of differences in social returns. On the contrary, the relation between private and social yields could be estimated only by a painstaking comparative analysis of fiscal and capital market structures, country by country. Thus, until such time as fiscal and capital market structures have been made reasonably uniform, there is no sound basis for arguing that freedom of capital to move where the private yield is greatest necessarily contributes to an improved allocation of world resources.

ii. Movements of private capital and transfer of real resources under fixed parities. It is generally agreed that, in a system of fixed exchanges, a movement of private capital from, say, country A to B, in response to an emerging difference in private yields will, in the first place, generate transfers of international reserves. But will these movements in turn soon give rise to corresponding transfers of real resources? For this to happen, there must eventually occur an increase in the current account balance of country A and a shrinkage in that of country B equal to the flow of capital to be transferred. These changes in turn will generally require a rise in the price level of B and a fall in the price level A – at least if we assume away the possible but unlikely case of perverse elasticities.

This change in relative price levels is precisely what is expected to happen under the idealized textbook version of the gold standard, through the working of two well-known mechanisms: a) the commitment of the monetary authorities of each country to respond promptly to changes in its international reserves with roughly proportional (or more than proportional) changes in its monetary base; plus the assumption that a change in the monetary base will, in short order, produce corresponding changes in the actual money supply; b) a high degree of flexibility, both upward and downward, in the entire structure of wages and prices. Under these idealized conditions the initial flow of reserves from A to B would cause first a contraction of money supply in A and an expansion in B, which, in turn would give rise to movements in the opposite direction in the interest rates in each country, tending to wipe out the differential and to put an end to the movement of reserves. The rise in interest rates in A, in turn, reduces investment (and possibly consumption), and hence aggregate demand, tending to create an excess supply of labour. However, because of the assumed flexibility, the excess supply promptly results in a fall in wages and prices. Meanwhile, the same sequence is occurring in B, with 'sign reversed'. Finally, the change in relative prices expands net exports of A and reduces those of B, bringing back aggregate demand to the initial level, so that price levels stop changing. In the new equilibrium, the rate of investment has fallen in A and has risen in B to the point where the yields are equal in the two countries, and a portion of the unchanged saving flow in A, no longer needed to finance the lower investment, finances the larger investment in B, through the rise in net exports. (The equalization of yields need not actually occur in the context of growing economies. It is conceivable that some yield differential and, corresponding to it, some flow or real capital, may persist for a long time, even indefinitely.)

So much for the textbook version of the gold standard. Consider now what would actually tend to happen under the present kind of managed gold exchange system, and with marked wage and price rigidities, at least in the downward direction. As long as there are no interferences with movements of private capital, the first step – that is, the transfer of international reserves–will still tend to occur. But what effects this will have on the money supply and aggregate demand in country A and B are now a matter of the response that the central banks choose to adopt. If country B does not like inflation, and especially if it does not welcome the foreign investments, it can offset the larger demand for domestic assets by foreigners by selling some of the assets it owns, leaving the monetary base, the money supply and the structure of interest rates largely unchanged. It will replace in its balance sheets the original income-yielding assets with international reserves, which, if kept in the form of gold, will yield nothing, and even if invested in eligible market instruments of country A will have a relatively 'low' yield since, by assumption, yields in A are lower than in B. By following this course, the central bank of B will also prevent the operation of any mechanism tending to reduce the incentive to the capital flow, and thus may keep accumulating reserves. (If country A happens to be the reserve currency country, B may also complain that that country is, in effect, buying up profitable assets in B and financing the purchase with 'forced' cheap credit from the central bank of B.) If, on the other hand, the receiving country B permits an expansion of the money supply – whether because it is consciously and willingly playing according to the rules of the game or because of inaction or lack of adequate institutions to offset the inflow of reserves – it will create some inflation at home, though very likely complaining that A is 'exporting inflation' through its deficit in the balance of payments.

Similarly country A may, at least initially, react to the loss of reserves by offsetting it in order to avoid domestic deflation. This will again tend to hinder the transfer of real resources, for any given policy of country B, by hindering accommodating changes in interest rates and in the balance on current accounts, thus contributing to the continuing flow of international reserves.

Suppose, on the other hand, country A did undertake a policy of monetary restraint either because it was following the rules of the game, or, more likely, because it was forced to do so to stem the continuing loss of reserves. How far would this really help? It is very likely that, initially, interest rates would tend to rise in A and this would help by reducing the incentives to capital exports. In addition, as in the idealized version, the contraction in money supply and rise in interest rates would reduce aggregate demand and, hence, the demand for labour. But because of rigidities, wages and prices would fail to respond promptly and thus generate a rise in net exports to offset the fall in domestic demand. Instead there would be a tendency for employment and output to fall – unless monetary restraint is adequately offset by expansionary fiscal policy, a possibility which will be considered separately below. In this process some improvement in the net exports of A and, hence, some real transfer may take place but not so much through the probably sluggish relative decline in prices as through the fact that the depressed level of income and employment would tend to reduce imports and possibly somewhat expand exports. In any event, the fall in investment in A will be offset only very partially by a rise in net exports and instead will mostly result in a fall in saving through the fall in income. Furthermore, the fall in economic activity in A, by generating excess capacity and depressing profits, is likely, in short order, to put downward pressure on market interest rates, unless the central bank is sanguine enough to keep contracting the money supply even faster than income and the demand for money is falling. It is, therefore, entirely possible that after an initial rise, the entire level of interest rates may sag even below the starting level, rekindling the inducement to capital exports.

The upshot of all this is that under the present system of fixed and rigid parities and widespread wage–price rigidities, there is no reliable mechanism that ensures the prompt transfer of real resources to match the movement of private capital. Furthermore, in so far as the transfer occurs, this comes about through a mechanism which interferes with the domestic goal of maintaining price stability and full employment. Under these conditions, complete freedom of capital movements may not only fail to achieve significant movement of real capital, but in addition, tends to be inconsistent with domestic stability.

III   FISCAL POLICY AS THE CURE FOR ALL

Quite recently it has been suggested that the apparent inconsistency between freedom of private capital movements and domestic stability can be eliminated through a 'co-ordinated monetary and fiscal policy approach'. The goal of balance of payments equilibrium with complete freedom of capital movements, it is asserted, is not inconsistent with the goal of price stability and full employment because the *two* goals can be reconciled by the appropriate use of *two* tools, namely the monetary tool and the fiscal tool. Indeed, by suitably combining an 'expansionary' or 'contractionary' fiscal policy with a 'tight' or 'loose' monetary policy, it should, in principle, be possible to make full employment and price stability consistent with any desired level of interest rates – at least within sufficiently wide limits.

This possibility opens up new vistas. Clearly, under complete freedom of capital movements, interest rates must tend to be the 'same' in all countries (up to appropriate risk and liquidity differentials) or can differ at most by very moderate differentials accompanying a flow of real resources between countries. But this requirement of uniform interest rates at a somehow determined world level can be made consistent with the maintenance of full employment even in the face of inter-country differences in the propensity to accumulate and in the domestic 'marginal yield' that would correspond to a given flow of saving. In essence, this result would be achieved by varying government expenditure and by manipulating consumption, through taxation, so that the sum of expenditure and consumption fills the gap between full employment income and the level of domestic investment consistent with the given world level of interest rates. An alternative, and for present purposes, more enlightening formulation is to say that fiscal policy should aim at making full employment net domestic saving – the sum of private saving and government surplus – equal to the rate of domestic investment consistent with the uniform yield across countries (plus the historically given current account surplus). Monetary policy can then be relied upon to supply the quantity of money needed to transact a full employment income with a level of interest rates consistent with the 'world level'. This same concept is sometimes expressed by saying that monetary policy must be aimed at balance of payments equilibrium and fiscal policy at the maintenance of full employment. This formulation is somewhat misleading since, in reality, both monetary and fiscal policy must be determined simultaneously in view of both goals. It is true, however, that with perfect international mobility of capital, monetary policy loses much of its power to control interest rates; any attempt at maintaining rates to a level inconsistent with the world level would tend to create offsetting capital flows and surplus or deficits in the balance of payments of such dimensions as to make the goal an unrealistic one.

We have no significant disagreement with the above analysis and its implications for the consistency of domestic full employment and price stability with balance of payments equilibrium, in the presence of complete freedom of capital movements. We would only point out that two important changes in present institutions would be required:

1. We would need far greater short-run flexibility in fiscal policy than is consistent with the present institutions, at least in the US. Hence, if our policy-makers are inclined to opt for a mechanism of this type they ought to be much more active than they now seem to be in educating Congress and the public in the necessity of delegating discretionary power to the administration and also in the necessity of shaping US fiscal (and not just monetary) policy to accommodate the rest of the world.

2. Mechanisms and procedures would need to be set up for the main countries to agree on just what the level of interest rates should be for the world as a whole. For, in the last analysis, the world level would be determined by the average overall degree of fiscal tightness or looseness through its effects on the average world level of resources available for capital formation. This aspect of the problem is generally referred to as the necessity for all countries to adopt a co-ordinated monetary-fiscal policy mix. In the absence of explicit co-ordination, as has been pointed out repeatedly, for example, by Tobin, there would be a continuous danger of interest rate escalation with the overall level being swayed in the direction of levels prevailing in those countries opting for the highest level of interest rates. This situation is well illustrated by the experience of the 1960s when the US was pushed towards a high-interest-rate full-employment regime by the behaviour of its European partners.

IV   A VITAL SHORTCOMING OF THE CPK POSITION

While we are prepared to concede that the above system could conceivably be made to work tolerably well, we see very little ground for arguing that such a system would be very desirable or economically efficient Quite the contrary, we suggest that it would be inferior in all major relevant respects to a system allowing at least some flexibility in exchange rates and relying on specific tax measures to control private incentive to the movement of capital.

Freedom of capital movement basically implies equality of yields across countries Now, as far as one can see, the only sound economic argument in favour of freedom of capital movement is that the equality of yields is brought about by a transfer of real capital from where its yields would otherwise be lower to where it would be higher. The transfer of real capital, in turn, requires surplus and deficit in the current account balance through which countries with 'surplus saving' – that is, saving in excess of the rate of domestic investment called for by the common yield – finance the excess of investment over saving of the countries 'short of saving'. Under the pure gold standards, the required rate of net exports is achieved primarily through changes in the relative price levels.

The obvious alternative mechanism to bring about transfer, without sacrificing price stability and full employment, would be recourse to suitable adjustments in the rate of exchange. Such adjustments, in fact, permit changing the relation between domestic and foreign price levels without requiring changes in either domestic or foreign price levels measured in terms of the domestic currency. The CPK school rejects this approach on the ground that changes in parities increase the risk incurred by investing or borrowing abroad and, hence, would sap the incentive to the movement of private capital. They advocate instead relying on co-ordinated fiscal policy to make changes in parity unnecessary to maintain equilibrium in the balance of payments, while retaining freedom of capital movements. But, paradoxically enough, by embracing this approach they are, in effect, *sacrificing the very feature that makes the freedom of capital worth having*. For, the purpose of the fiscal policy they recommend is not that of providing an alternative mechanism to *achieve the transfer* of the difference between domestic saving and investment at the common yield, but quite the contrary that of forcing saving into equality with domestic investment, thus *eliminating the need for the transfer*. Looked at from the point of view of private investors, this policy *removes* the incentive to take advantage of the freedom to move capital. Thus, the modern supporters of freedom of capital movement together with fixed and rigid parities are in effect sacrificing the end to the mean: instead of wanting an open door so that capital will flow through it, they want to remove the incentive for capital to flow so the door can be kept open!

V THE RELATIVE MERITS OF GENERAL FISCAL POLICY VERSUS SPECIFIC INSTRUMENTS AS DEVICES FOR REMOVING THE INCENTIVE TO CAPITAL FLOWS

Once it is clearly realized that the purpose to be achieved through the so-called 'co-ordination' of monetary and fiscal policies is that of controlling the incentive for capital to move, it is but natural to ask whether there are any other methods that will achieve the same purpose and how the available alternatives compare in terms of other effects.

Clearly, an alternative way of removing or controlling the incentive for private capital to move between A and B, consists in offsetting the difference between the private yields prevailing in A and B by fiscal devices aimed at a) equalizing the *private* returns a national of A can obtain from domestic and foreign investments and b) equalizing the private cost a national of B has to incur by raising funds in A as compared with B. The most obvious examples of such devices are the so-called 'interest equalization taxes' and the differential taxation of domestic versus foreign corporate profits. Both devices are presently being used to some extent in the USA, the first to reduce and the second to *enhance* the incentive to capital exports.

In our view, a strong case can be made to support the contention that the 'equalization of private returns' approach is preferable to the 'co-ordination of fiscal policies' in most, if not all, relevant respects: a) easiness of application, b) required degree of inter-national agreement, c) dislocation of existing economic structures, and last but not least, d) the freedom it leaves to each country to pursue policies of more or less rapid expansion of the domestic stock of productive physical capital.

Of these various claims, the easiest to demonstrate is the last one. Obviously, under the 'co-ordination' approach a country loses the freedom to use fiscal policy to restrain or stimulate consumption (private and public) and thus to stimulate or restrain national saving and capital formation. It must instead use fiscal policy to enforce a level of national saving consistent with exogenously determined investment. In particular, it might be forced to thwart the thrift of its population by running a budget deficit on current account, thus 'artificially' increasing private disposable income and consumption, and satisfying the accumulation propensity of the community with government bonds instead of income producing addition to the stock of physical capital. This loss of freedom to manage the rate of capital formation, which can be clearly avoided through the equalization approach, seems particularly objectionable since it is hard to see how or why its use could significantly harm any other country.

Claim a) seems also fairly straightforward, though it involves, in part, considerations of a 'political' nature But, at least to a naïve observer, it would appear that it is generally easier to secure modifications of specific tax measures affecting a relatively minor sector of the economy–as required under the 'incentive equalization' approach–than to secure changes in broad-based levies as required under the 'fiscal co-ordination' approach We also suspect that, in the case of specific tax measures, it might be easier to institute fiscal devices involving some degree of automaticity, or delegation to the executive to vary the rate of taxation, within some limits.

As for claim b), while the 'co-ordination' approach, by its very nature, requires an appreciable measure of explicit international agreement, at least among the major financial powers, the 'equalization' approach would not seem to require much agreement, though undoubtedly co-ordination would help to make it work more smoothly and would avoid the possible danger of retaliatory measures. But we suggest that the danger of hostile retaliation is not really too serious, for the initiative for taking specific measures would normally fall on a country which was losing reserves because of excessive capital outflows not matched by corresponding surplus on current account – witness the instance of the USA. It is hard to see why other countries would want to go out of their way to pass legislation designed to thwart the effort of the losing country to re-establish equilibrium in its international accounts. It might be optimistic to expect other countries to pass legislation or regulations that will *help* the country in difficulty, but to suppose that a significant number of countries would go out of their way to *hinder* the adjustment process seems to be unwarrantedly pessimistic. In short, then, the 'co-ordination' approach requires *active co-operation*, whereas the 'equalization' approach can get by as long as we can count on the absence of *active obstructionism* – though co-operation would, no doubt, improve its workings.

Claim c) is probably the hardest to substantiate, especially since it involves two distinct aspects: dislocations of the domestic economy and dislocations imposed on foreign partners. In so far as the domestic effects are concerned, the claim can be defended at least with respect to one typical cause of difficulty. Suppose that, for a given country, the international accounts are initially balanced and now, for some reason, the returns to investments and, hence, the demand for funds, tend to shift markedly down (or up) without a similar shift occurring in the 'rest of the world'. In a closed economy, the natural response to this situation would be to pursue an easy monetary policy with a view to reducing market rates of interest in line with the reduced anticipated profitability of investment. Such a policy aims at maintaining aggregate demand and employment while, at the same time, also largely maintaining the distribution of output between consumption and capital formation. But with an open economy, if there is freedom of capital movements, the attempt at easing credit and lowering interest rates will tend to result in large outflows of capital, without even succeeding in reducing interest rates as much as desirable. The 'equalization' approach would handle the difficulty by fiscal devices aimed at reducing the *private* return from *foreign* investments to a level commensurate with the reduction desired in domestic rates, thus making it possible, by and large, to pursue the domestic monetary-fiscal policy mix that would have been available to a closed economy. By contrast, the 'co-ordination' approach would require stimulating consumption and reducing full employment saving to match the decreased flow of investment expenditure consistent with the maintenance of the initial level of domestic interest rates required by the unchanged level of world rates. But this approach, if successful in maintaining the aggregate level of output, still implies that the composition of output tends to change from investment goods towards consumption goods, causing a dislocation which can be avoided by the equalization approach. To be sure, if the initial shift in country A were due to a downward shift in the propensity to consume, the implications of the two approaches would be reversed. Now the composition of output would change if full employment were maintained by an easing of monetary policy, while the change would be avoided by relying on fiscal stimuli to consumption. But, in the first place, it is generally agreed that disturbances to equilibrium are much more likely to originate in shifts in the investment schedule than in the consumption function; and, in the second place, under the equalization approach the country would have the option to respond differently to different sources of disturbances so as to minimize dislocation, using, for example, fiscal policy to respond to disturbances originating in consumption and monetary policy to counteract changes originating in the investment sector. Under the co-ordination approach, by contrast, the country would have no choice but to respond primarily with fiscal stimuli, whether or not this would produce dislocations.

The comparative dislocation effects on foreign partners are more difficult to assess. To a first approximation, it would appear that the two approaches would have similar effects since they both endeavour to prevent changes in flow of capital or to contain them within the limits of concurrent changes in the current account balance. But admittedly, this aspect of the problem requires further exploration, both to understand the comparative implications and to see how disturbing dislocations might be minimized.

VI CONCLUSIONS: THE ALTERNATIVE TO FIXED AND RIGID PARITIES AND CO-ORDINATION OF FISCAL POLICIES

In summary, the 'CPK approach' suffers from a basic flaw: for the sake of achieving the purely formal goal of freedom of capital movement, it advocates a system which, paradoxically enough, tends, in effect, to stifle the flow of real capital – the only real justification for advocating freedom of capital movements. In addition, it also requires individual countries to give up the freedom of managing the rate of capital formation.

We have shown that, in so far as one wishes to influence the incentive to private capital movements, this result can be achieved at least as effectively, and generally more effectively, by relying on the equalization of yields rather than on the co-ordinated fiscal policy. However, both approaches are designed to minimize the need to transfer resources by removing the incentive for private investors to take advantage of the freedom to move capital. Clearly a yet better approach would be to adopt mechanisms to permit the flow of capital by facilitating the matching transfer of real resources, whenever differences in private yield were an indication of corresponding differences in social returns. As already noted, the obvious mechanism is that of changes in the exchange rates which result in changes in relative prices and thus in current account balances without relying on the costly and unreliable device of actual changes in price levels.

The adoption of greater exchange rate flexibility would also reduce, but not necessarily eliminate, the desirability, at least occasionally, to modify the incentive to private capital movements. Aside from the fact that differences in private yield may not be a reliable measure of differences in social yields, one must also remember that changes in net exports to accommodate the transfer of real capital are not costless, since they involve internal reallocation of resources. A good case can therefore be made for limiting the speed with which changes in parities are allowed to occur, and the case is further reinforced by the consideration that rapid changes in parities may give rise to disturbing speculative movements. Whether such limitations are best handled by crawling pegs or other devices is for present purposes a mere detail. The important point is that, with such limitations, there may arise a need, at least in the short run, for holding private capital movements in line with the achievable transfer of real capital. To achieve this goal, without outright limitations on the freedom of capital movements, countries could rely on general fiscal policy as one of the possible devices for influencing incentive to capital movements. But they should also be allowed to opt, just as freely, for the alternative approach relying on specific tax and related incentives, which, we have argued, is likely to be superior under most circumstances. Under this alternative, specific tax measures would be used by a country to control the relation between the return obtainable by its nationals from domestic and foreign investments and the cost incurred by foreigners by raising funds in its market as compared with other markets.

It is possible that greater reliance on changes in parities as a method of controlling balance of payments disequilibria might increase the uncertainty of return or costs from international lending or borrowing, and this result, in turn, might give rise to a somewhat smaller flow of funds for any given differential between foreign and domestic rates. But we suspect that the CPK position greatly exaggerates the significance and undesirability of this phenomenon. Without entering into lengthy details, it might be pointed out that, for short-term lending, the parties could always hedge through forward markets. If a system of gradual changes in parities were accompanied by a sufficiently broad band of permissible fluctuations around the parity, one might expect that the incentive to short-term capital movements, in response to transient changes in short-term rates, might be largely eliminated through movements in the spot and forward rates. But it is generally agreed that this is a desirable development as such movements contribute little, if anything, to the channelling of long-term capital to where it has larger social returns, while their elimination allows countries greater freedom to use monetary policy for short-term stabilization.

For long-term capital movements, on the other hand, the size of changes in parities required to accommodate the transfer of real capital may be expected to be small enough to have but a minor effect on the return or cost from long-term investments, especially when compared with the many other sources of risk associated with foreign operations. Note also that under the alternative of fixed parities, in so far as the capital movements had not been stifled by the use of general fiscal policy or specific tax measures, the transfer would require changes in the price level of each country; but this means that the reduction in the risk of foreign lending and borrowing would be achieved at the expense of a commensurate increase in the risk of real returns from *domestic* lending and borrowing operations, which are presumably much larger in volume than the international operations.

To be sure, changes in parities may come also from differential rates of price movements in different countries. But under these conditions, even the CPK school would have to accept the inevitability of changes in parities. Furthermore, with differential rates of inflation, offsetting changes in parities might well reduce the risk of the *real* return, if the contract were denominated in the currency with greater price stability. Quite generally, the real risk from both price level movements and variations in exchange rates could be minimized by denominating contracts in some numeraire having stable purchasing power; while no such numeraire exists at present, it could be created by escalator clauses or by appropriate reforms of the international payments system which we have suggested elsewhere.[1]

Last, but not least, it is by no means obvious that the moderate increase in risk from foreign lending that might arise under the proposed alternative might not, on the whole, have a salutary effect, like any other device that blunts the *incentive* to movement of capital without curtailing the *freedom* of movement. Indeed, why is this particular method of reducing the incentive to capital movement any less desirable than the 'co-ordinated fiscal policy' approach advocated by the CPK position? On the contrary, just like the use of specific fiscal instruments, it contributes to allow greater freedom to individual countries to pursue somewhat different interest rate and capital formation policies without curtailing the freedom of capital movements.

[1] Two alternative reforms which would result in an international numeraire with stable purchasing power have been suggested in Modigliani and Kennen, 'A Suggestion for Solving the International Liquidity Problem', *Banca Nazionale del Lavoro, Quarterly Review* (March 1966), and Modigliani and Askari, 'The Reform of the International Payments System', *Essays in International Finance* (Princeton, New Jersey, September 1971), no. 89.

V

COST-BENEFIT ANALYSIS

CHAPTER 15

Further Reflections on the OECD Manual of Project Analysis in Developing Countries

I. M. D. LITTLE AND J. A. MIRRLEES

I INTRODUCTION

The genealogy of the OECD *Manual of Industrial Project Analysis*, volume 2 (hereinafter often referred to as the *Manual*)[1] goes back to the authors' experience in India with the MIT Mission, organized by Paul Rosenstein-Rodan who thus originated their interest in developing countries.

The authors have now had some experience of audience reaction to lectures and seminars on the subject of the *Manual*, and hope that they can, as a result, clarify their views on some points.[2] It has also been suggested by some economists that, in the *Manual*, a lot of foliage obscured what we hope is the hardwood of the analysis. We therefore start with a compressed reformulation of the economics. Only in the last section do we consider an extension of the analysis to agricultural projects.

II THE SOCIAL PROFIT

This is our measure of the net social benefit of a project in any one year.

a. *The System*

Solely for the sake of simplicity of exposition, we first assume a) that we are dealing with a public sector project, and b) that the

---

[1] *Manual of Industrial Project Analysis in Developing Countries*, vol 2: *Social Cost-Benefit Analysis* (OECD, 1969).

[2] The authors are particularly indebted to Maurice Scott for many criticisms and suggestions.

project employs no skilled labour. The numeraire used is *government savings expressed in terms of foreign exchange* of constant value. This involves the use of 'border prices'. 'Prices' are to be regarded as marginal costs or revenues whenever appropriate 'Border' prices mean the c.i.f. or f.o.b. prices of the developing country. When we write investment, consumption, etc., these magnitudes must be taken to be measured in border prices.[3]

Using the assumptions, the savings of a project can be expressed as

$$(1) \qquad\qquad \text{Savings} = V - LC,$$

where V, L, and C symbolize respectively value-added, labour, and the consumption of a worker All prices are taken net of indirect taxes.

But the savings cannot usually be regarded as the whole 'social profit' of a project, for the following reasons:

1. In a developing country more employment generally causes more consumption, because the consumption level of industrial workers is higher than their alternative product (this is further elaborated below).

2. Extra consumption is valuable.

Therefore, in order to arrive at the social profit, we need to add a term which expresses the value of this extra consumption, in terms of savings which is our numeraire.

The authors take it that income in the hands of the government may be more valuable than extra consumption by industrial workers.[4] There is evidence for this in the statements of governments, and more generally in the importance attached to development; although governmental behaviour is sometimes difficult to reconcile with what is said. Where this is the case, and we do not suggest that it must be the case, a rupee of consumption by industrial workers cannot be given the value of a rupee of expenditure by the government, whether on investment or on some form of public consumption which is held to be as valuable as investment. We suppose the S units of consumption equal one unit of government revenue. Where S differs from unity it will normally exceed it. In the *Manual*, we expressed the extra consumption caused by a

---

[3] We used the term 'world prices' in the *Manual*: but the term 'border prices' is more descriptive, and less likely to arouse prejudice.

[4] In the *Manual*, we contrasted investment with consumption. But where a public sector project is under consideration, government or public income may be more appropriate.

project as $L(C-M)$, where M is the marginal product of labour in agriculture.[5] The rationale of this is that although a man newly employed in industry may well come from the urban unemployed or underemployed, nevertheless another man may well be drawn from agriculture. This seems a reasonable supposition for many developing countries, but it is not an integral part of the analysis: a different and, perhaps, more complicated model for the estimation of the extra consumption may be more appropriate in some countries. The value of the extra consumption, in terms of savings, is thus $L/S(C-M)$. This must be added to the savings of the project to give the 'social profit'. Hence,

Social profit = Savings + savings equivalent of consumption

$$= (V - LC) + \frac{L}{S}(C - M)$$

(2)
$$= V - L\left[C - \frac{1}{S}(C - M)\right].$$

Finally, we want an expression for a shadow wage, W^*, such that if labour is valued at this wage then the simple expression $V - W^*L$, which is clearly analogous to profit, will correctly measure social profit. Obviously then

(3)
$$W^* = C - \frac{1}{S}(C - M).$$

Having reached this point, let us return to the two initial assumptions made. The first was that we are dealing with a public-sector project, so that the savings of the project do not go to increase private consumption. With a private-sector project, it is necessary

[5] In more detail we supposed that the extra consumption of a man moving from agriculture to industry is $C-A$ where A is the average per head consumption of a poor peasant family. The consumption of the family is in turn raised by A, the share of the departing member, but reduced by M, the marginal product of the departing member. We recognize that this too is a crude model, which may not be applicable to all countries, and which should in any case be improved as more knowledge is acquired of all the ramified effects of increased industrial demand for labour. It has, for instance, been argued that the additional employment of one man in a town may pull in more than one man from agriculture, which would raise the shadow wage. As against this we have allowed no multiplier effect on employment arising from workers' purchases of non-traded goods, which would tend to reduce the shadow wage. We hope to go into these and other complications on another occasion: but it is not clear to us at present that they would make any significant difference to any practicable estimation procedure for the shadow age.

to allow for consumption out of profits, and to put some value on such consumption.[6] It is also necessary to recognize that private savings, while they increase the consumption of workers by increasing investment and employment, will also partly go to increase the private consumption of the rich, and may therefore be considered to be less valuable than income in the hands of the government. We do not go further into these particular valuation problems here. The second assumption was simply designed to simplify the algebra, and evade a discussion of how to assess the social cost of skilled labour, a subject on which we have nothing to add here to the admittedly rather sketchy discussion in the *Manual*.

Before proceeding in Section III to a discussion of 'present social value', which is the final arbiter of a project's desirability, we turn first to a consideration of the rationale of using border and producer prices, and of the methods employed to arrive at them; and, secondly, to further consideration of S.

b. *The Justification*

Why border prices? We believe, on the one hand, that prices in many developing countries have become seriously distorted (that is, not reflecting social costs and benefits), and, on the other, that the price a country receives for an export product, or the price it has to pay for an import, can be conveniently and correctly used as a basis from which to arrive at a substitute set of accounting prices for commodities which measure reasonably well their true relative social costs and benefits. The greater the extent to which the output of a project either increases exports of that commodity, or replaces imports, and the greater the extent to which an input of the project increases imports or reduces exports of that input, the more exactly is this true. In short, the greater the extent to which it affects only trade, the better will border prices measure its social costs and benefits.

A high proportion by value of the inputs and outputs of most industrial projects are in fact traded, that is, the same or very similar goods cross the frontier. This does not, however, entail that the project under consideration will mainly affect trade. For instance, there might be a fixed and filled import quota implying that use of that commodity as an input could affect trade, even if it was actually bought from abroad. In general, only trade – rather than domestic production or consumption of the commodity – will be affected if

[6] The *Manual* suggested that the value might be set as zero as an approximation – but this is clearly disputable.

internal prices are not changed as a result of the project. At least we can say that many industrial projects in developing countries are intended to be mainly import substituting or export promoting.

If the use or production of some commodity by the project does not affect trade at all, then we clearly cannot correctly value it by direct appeal to border prices. In that event, it is deemed to be 'non-traded', and valued as described below. When commodities are 'non-traded' we suppose that the predominant effect of a change in demand or supply is a change in the output of such goods.

A third possibility is that the project, by demanding certain inputs, affects neither trade nor production, but reduces the use of the input by another producer. This is, of course, most likely to happen in the short run. In this case, we should in principle value the input by estimating its marginal productivity in terms of foreign exchange. In principle, also, the output of the project might affect production or consumption rather than trade. In the *Manual*, we did not consider at great length projects to produce non-tradables, since we considered that the output of industrial projects could almost always be treated as tradable (we were not primarily considering 'infrastructural' projects, but manufacturing industry).[7] But it was presumed that, in general, the project output would not displace production of the same commodity elsewhere, unless it were already socially unprofitable.

It is clear that the production or use of some goods will partly affect trade, and partly domestic production or consumption. In such cases it is not clear whether the commodity should be treated as traded or non-traded, and it is part of the art of project analysis to make convenient but reasonably realistic and accurate assumptions as to this division. We discuss this point again below.

[7] Where the government produces a non-tradable such as electricity, it is a truism to say that it should extend production to the point where marginal social cost equals marginal social benefit. The m.s.c. will be reckoned in accounting prices, say dollars. What then is implied about domestic pricing policy? Suppose that the m.s.c. is one dollar, and that the official rate of exchange is one rupee to one dollar. Then if the electricity is sold to another undertaking which has been evaluated in the manner of the *Manual*, and which should therefore operate in terms of accounting prices, the charge for electricity should be one rupee (in equilibrium). When the electricity is sold to any part of the private sector, which pays no attention to accounting prices, then a first approximation to the price to be charged would be the 'standard conversion factor' which is an average relationship between accounting and actual domestic prices (see *Manual* 12.4). But other considerations could arise, such as the desirability of relating the price closely to other fuels, or the desirability of imposing a tax, especially perhaps for domestic users.

With industrial projects, experience suggests that the most common case of clearly non-traded goods and services will be inputs of construction, power, transport, and other services. Our normal method of valuing such items is to break them down into their inputs, with similar iterative treatment of non-traded inputs into non-traded inputs, until one is left only with traded goods and labour or land (including minerals etc.). In short, input/output methods are resorted to for non-traded goods.[8] In the extreme case, if all inputs and outputs were deemed non-tradable, and valued in this manner, our methods would not differ from those of some other exponents of the art of project analysis, who break down goods by use of the input/output table into the primary factors of production, foreign exchange, and labour, and then use a shadow exchange rate to value the former in terms of the latter. The fact that we revalue labour in terms of foreign exchange, instead of foreign exchange in terms of labour, is a mere difference of numeraire. Both methods are really aiming to estimate the value of non-tradable goods by their marginal social costs of production, short- or long-run depending on circumstances. In neither case is this meant to deny the 'rationing' function of prices: that is, in the very short-run the market should normally be cleared, and the market clearing price is then the proper accounting price (after adjustment by some conversion factor, if necessary, to make the domestic price comparable with border prices).

Thus the essential difference is that we advocate valuing many goods by direct appeal to c.i.f. or f.o.b. prices. This method is very closely related to the 'semi-input/output method', invented and advocated by Professor Tinbergen.[9]

A theoretical justification for this advice is easy to offer. If the economy were trading non-optimally, but was moving to an optimum foreign trade policy, the relative prices of traded goods at the port (and industrial projects tend to be in or near ports, which makes things easier) would become equal to relative c.i.f. or f.o.b. prices.

---

[8] We also discussed other short-cuts, in particular a 'standard conversion factor' to be applied to all internal prices which were not treated in a more sophisticated manner. This SCF is the inverse of a foreign exchange premium.

[9] The best account of this method which we have seen is in Bent Hansen, 'Long- and Short-Term Planning in Underdeveloped Countries' (North Holland, 1967). In these de Vries Lectures, Professor Hansen discusses semi-input/output more fully as a method of planning than of project evaluation. But the theoretical rationale of how the methods of the (subsequently published) Manual fit in with (more or less) optimal planning, is so clearly explained that the present authors would like to regard it as a theoretical introduction to the Manual.

If we correctly guess which goods will be imported and exported (or neither) in such an optimum situation, then we have the correct relative prices for traded goods. There can be no doubt, in such a situation, that the limited input/output method would give superior results. A historical input/output table would show wrong import and export coefficients for traded goods. In reality, we do not expect countries to adopt ideal policies, and such a knock-down proof of superiority would be disingenuous. However, a naïve use of input/output methods would be correct only if the government saw to it that coefficients did not change as a result of development: and this is, perhaps, a still less plausible assumption than that governments will permit trade to develop along reasonably rational lines.

The use of the limited input/output method is clearly justified provided there are at least *some* commodities whose production or use would mainly affect trade, and this is surely unquestionable. So it remains only to suggest guidelines for what we believe is the essential division into traded and non-traded goods and services. We advise that evaluators should lean over backwards to deem commodities to be 'traded', whenever they or very similar goods are in fact traded; and, in particular, we advise that the distinction as to whether a commodity is actually bought or sold at home or abroad is often a most misleading indication of whether trade is affected or not. Several reasons can be given for this guideline. First, if there is no quota and if imports or exports of the commodity are in perfectly elastic supply, then internal prices are determined by the exchange rate, the trade-tax structure, and internal transport costs (provided the latter costs can be assumed to be constant). Domestic production of traded goods is therefore determined independently of domestic demand; and increased demand or supply by the project will affect only trade in these goods.

Secondly, where this is not quite true, full capacity working will ensure that increased demand by the project spills over into imports, or reduces exports. Of course, when there is some inelasticity of foreign trade, or where economies of scale are significant, domestic production may increase as a result of an increase in demand, even in the absence of quotas; but this takes time, and the early years are the least discounted. However, where the project is long-lived, the rate of discount is not very high, and the effect on prices of increased local production can be predicted, then this effect could be allowed for.

Thirdly, if domestic production does expand, and if such expansion is socially desirable, then the predicted c.i.f. price will still not usually be a bad estimate of the social cost of such expansion. That the social cost should be higher than the c.i.f. price is ruled out if the expansion is worth while. It might be lower and could be significantly lower if increasing returns are such that marginal costs are well below the average cost which justifies domestic production: but it cannot be lower than the f.o.b. price.

Lastly, it is often much easier for the evaluator to assume that a good is 'traded'; this is an important point, since the amount of research that can be done for any particular project analysis is limited. Although border prices may be difficult to find and to predict, and it is often difficult to know whether continuous supplies at a particular price will be available, nevertheless they are very often easier to establish than internal prices.

We recognize that the above arguments are not conclusive. Trade in some commodity may be significantly inelastic – possibly as a result of controls. Domestic production which is socially undesirable may then be increased as a result of the project: or it might not, with the result that other projects would be starved of the input in question. The output of the project might cause a fall in socially desirable production elsewhere, rather than be substituted for imports, etc. Occasionally one may know that such things, however irrational, will in fact be likely to happen. As we have already indicated, where the input or output is very important, such possibilities should be considered – and, on occasion, it may then be necessary to treat an apparently traded good as 'non-traded'. Examples of this were given in the *Manual*.

Why, in general, producer prices? In the *Manual* all prices are taken net of indirect taxes for the purposes of project evaluation. This appears to be the normal practice in cost–benefit analysis, though exceptions occur. But there is sometimes some confusion as to the justification for this. People may accept rather readily that an excise tax on, say, petrol can hardly constitute a real cost to the country, as it flows into the Exchequer. But should one not count as a benefit an indirect tax on a final good, especially if one is assuming that savings are more valuable than consumption? The answer is still 'no', although it is a little harder to see why.

The basic point to remember is that one must try to use a set of relative prices which reflects the welfare potential of the various goods and services. At a theoretical level it can be shown, on certain assumptions, of which the most important are that the administrative costs of taxation are negligible and that commodity taxes are well chosen, that 'productive efficiency', which implies using prices net of indirect taxes, does yield the maximum welfare potential of a set of inputs.[10] But let us try to spell out some of the argument in a prosaic way.

First take traded inputs. Now it is *not* always the case that indirect taxes should in theory be excluded. For intermediate goods, the distinction lies between taxes that are distorting and those that are corrective. A case of a distorting tax is one that is levied for revenue purposes despite the fact that it causes a divergence between the price and the real social cost of the input: or one that is mistakenly levied to correct such a distortion, in fact creating one. Our view is that most indirect taxes on inputs are of one or other of these kinds. But there are some cases of corrective taxes. Examples are taxes on inputs whose use results in external diseconomies, or an 'optimum' tariff. It would be correct to include such taxes in the price. But there is an alternative, which comes to the same thing. In the case of a tax which purports to be levied because of an external diseconomy, one can still net off the tax and try to measure the external diseconomy directly. In the case of an optimum tariff, we recall the fact that where there is an inelasticity of supply then our border prices are to be taken to mean marginal import costs: this, of course, comes to the same thing as allowing an optimum tariff in the price, such as optimum tariff almost never corresponding to any actual tariff. We think that the procedure of disallowing all indirect taxes on inputs, and only then correcting the price for any supposed import inelasticity or other social affect is certainly best.

Now take taxes on traded outputs. If the output is purely an intermediate (and this term can cover capital goods as well as all exports), then it is clear that the argument of the above paragraph, about inputs, applies. But suppose the output is a final good, say cigarettes. Should not the tax be included on the grounds not only that it is corrective (against cancer) but also perhaps because it is useful to have such a taxable commodity produced? But, again, the right answer is 'no'. First, imported cigarettes can equally well be taxed, and so the taxability argument is irrelevant. Secondly, in the case of final consumer goods, corrective taxes or subsidies are applied precisely because the amount consumers are willing to pay

[10] Peter A. Diamond and James A. Mirrlees, 'Optimal Taxation and Public Production', forthcoming in *American Economic Review*.

is not regarded as a good measure of social welfare. Taxed cigarettes have a high price because the government thinks them evil, not good. There is certainly no argument here for including the tax. But now suppose the tax on the final consumer good is purely for revenue reasons. Can it not be argued that the high price denotes high marginal utility, so that the tax should be included? Certainly, the high price denotes high marginal utility for some people, but it does not follow at all that production should therefore be encouraged (relative to, for example, untaxed intermediates and capital goods) if the amount consumed is independent of the amount produced, which will usually be true, or nearly true, in the case of traded goods.

Now let us turn to non-tradables. Suppose there is a tax on electricity, and some project is evaluated costing electricity net of tax. Then, if the project is to operate as designed, the government may actually have to remit the tax. It may also have to remit tariffs for similar reasons. Our argument, in effect, is that such tax remissions on inputs, where necessary, are worth while in the interests of productive efficiency. Where the project is in the public sector, there is, of course, no difficulty: the government can afford not to pay its own taxes.

Finally, consider the example of a sales tax on final consumers of electricity. If one were to count in the tax as a benefit of an electricity-producing project, one would tend to promote the production of electricity to the point where it could be sold only at a price which, net of tax, would show a loss. Private producers would obviously not do this, so one is here considering a public supply. We feel that it must obviously be presumed that the government, in designing the tax system, would not want the tax on consumers to be offset by what is in effect a negative tax (the difference between marginal cost and price) by the public undertaking. This is what we meant by saying, in the *Manual*, that projects must not fight against the tax system. Another way of putting what is essentially the same point is that while a high consumers' price does indicate high utility, it is also true that satisfying this highly valued marginal demand implies reducing public revenue (which may be more valuable than consumption), unless the tax was previously set so high that a reduction would have increased revenue – and the Finance Ministry does not often make this mistake.

It may be said that we are in general assuming that taxes levied on final consumers are rational, and that taxes on intermediates are not rational: we would not quarrel with this. But the 'in general' should be noticed. Also, in saying that one should not, in project analysis, fight the tax system, we do not mean that project appraisers can never suggest to the government that the output of the project might be a suitable candidate for increased or reduced taxation: which is another way of saying that the government might wish to consider whether the existing net of tax value of the output truly measures its benefit.

Why value savings more than consumption? This was discussed at length in the *Manual*, and we here do little more than put the same points succinctly.

It is obvious from equation (3) above that if savings and consumption are equivalent ($S = 1$), then the shadow wage is the marginal product of labour. If, on the other hand, extra consumption is deemed to be valueless, then $S = \infty$ and the shadow wage is the actual wage. The shadow wage (W^*) is also, of course, the actual wage (W), if $W = M$. We take $W > M$ as normal for industry in developing countries, and think it absurd to suppose that extra consumption is valueless; or, what comes to the same thing from an analytical point of view, to suppose that any government would want to adopt an investment programme which maximized growth.[11]

The possibility that $S = 1$, and that the shadow wage should be set equal to the marginal product of labour has to be taken more seriously. If S is taken to be greater than 1, then the investment programme (or that part of it to which the advocated criterion is applied) is designed not just to maximize immediate income, but partly to help the government increase savings and hence, normally, raise the rate of growth. It can be, and has been, argued that there is no need for the investment programme to be diverted from the job of maximizing income, when government revenue and hence investment can be more efficiently increased, if need be, in other ways – especially by taxation. It is difficult to be dogmatic about this, for the strength of the administration, and inherent difficulties of raising taxes, as well as the existing level of investment, vary markedly among developing countries. So also do governments'

---

[11] Some economists have emphasized that extra consumption by very poor people may be actually productive: in which case, an increase in savings might not increase the rate of growth of output, if it was obtained by reducing the wage.

expenditure patterns. Some undoubtedly waste money, and it finds its way into the hands of relatively rich people, and it then becomes very difficult to argue that the consumption of workers is less valuable than money in the hands of the government.

One may also come to rather different views depending on whether a) one simply tries to do what the government says it wants, or b) one tries to interpret the government's actions, which may be inconsistent with what it says it wants, or c) whether one adopts a more detached and independent attitude, and tries to promote a criterion which will maximize the present value of welfare, taking into account the probable behaviour of the government. Thus most governments dislike raising taxes, and would probably opt for using project selection to help raise revenue which implies $S > 1$. As against this, adopting approach (b), one can argue that some governments use a lot of actual or potential revenue for the purpose of increasing immediate employment and consumption, for instance by over-staffing public services, and paying rice subsidies; and that they often encourage high industrial wages. Taking viewpoint (c), one can argue both ways: for instance one may maintain that, even although more taxes could be raised, nevertheless the government is unlikely to do it, and it is therefore best to advocate a criterion which will increase revenue; or one can argue that if the government's revenue is increased by public profits, it will raise less in taxation, in which case there is little or no point in making $S > 1$ – a view which would be reinforced if it were believed that public expenditure, whether on investment or consumption, was so ill-planned that it did little or nothing for development.

The issue also depends on whether the criterion is to be widely or narrowly applied. If it were very widely applied, then it is plausible to suggest that, if the shadow wage were made equal to the marginal product, which was itself very low, then the result would be to encourage employment and consumption so much that the government would have genuine difficulty in maintaining both a desirably high level of investment and avoiding excessive inflation. Partly for this reason, and partly because we suspect that many governments would say 'yes' to any way of raising revenue which is less obvious than taxation we took the view that S should usually be deemed to be greater than one, with the shadow wage rate higher than the marginal product in agriculture. But we do not believe that this is necessarily the case in all developing countries. For instance, some governments may be faced with a situation in which unemployment is as politically embarrassing as any increase in taxation would be.

Can S be measured? Our view is that it must be – somehow! It is well known that administrators like to put extreme values on things. Many administrators would probably like to have S equal to infinity, and many well-meaning humanists would put it equal to 1, or even less than 1.[12] Governments often vacillate: sometimes profits, sometimes employment, is given more implicit weight in decisions, implying that S implicitly fluctuates, from decision to decision, somewhere between 1 and infinity. Choosing a value is a way of getting more consistency into investment decisions.

It is clear in a general way what considerations are relevant. Investment today provides profits, therefore savings, and so the opportunity for further investment, tomorrow and beyond. Consequently, the value one would put on investment today depends upon the value of investment to be done in the future, which itself depends upon the value of investment in the further future, and so on. This infinite regress does not prevent a theoretical solution to the problem. If future investment opportunities, the savings behaviour of the economy, and the value to be put on consumption in different years, were all known, it would be possible, in principle, to calculate the value of investment relative to consumption at all times, including now.[13] This theoretical solution requires that present and future values of S should all be calculated simultaneously; and indeed that some approximation to the optimum development of the economy throughout the future should be obtained.

Although the considerations that arise naturally do lead quite logically to complicated optimizing analysis, it is surely true that no practical argument about S can yet be mounted in these terms. As so often happens, the connections between values, facts and policies, when logically pursued, become too complex for those who decide the policies, or have to obtain agreement about them. Some kind of short-cut is required. Indeed, we should expect to be able to provide

[12] In certain circumstances, S could be held to be less than unity. But this implies the existence of some shibboleth on the part of government, for if some private consumption is worth more than public money, it should not be difficult to increase S to unity by subsidizing that consumption.

[13] One must mention the proviso that the existence conditions, discussed by authors on the theory of optimum growth (for example, F. Hahn and M. Farrell (eds), *The Theory of Infinite Programmes* (Oliver and Boyd, 1967)), are satisfied. Also, the phrase 'in principle' refers to the very considerable mathematical difficulties that might arise in an attempt to do such a computation.

short-cut methods of estimation that would be accurate enough for practical purposes. After all, the further future cannot be very relevant to the decisions to be made now: therefore the shadow wage rate cannot be very sensitive to our assumptions about it. In the *Manual*, we introduced a 'time-horizon', T, deemed sufficiently long for it to be fair to assume that consumption and investment will by then be of roughly the same value (at the margin). T should not be too long, lest an estimation of the values of the social discount rate, investment opportunities, and reinvestment opportunities up to then, be too difficult to make. Common sense should be able to suggest a reasonable compromise. A crude formula based on such assumptions is suggested in the *Manual*. It was not anticipated that an unreasonably great amount of effort would be devoted to estimating the various parameters appearing in it.

The chief justification for such a crude formula is the presumption – which might turn out to be wrong – that the shadow wage rate will not in fact turn out to be very sensitive to the particular estimates of the parameters, so long as they are reasonable. If the estimate of the shadow wage rate is in fact sensitive, to a significant degree, to the parameter assumptions, it seems inevitable that the choice of S and hence the shadow wage rate will be rather unreasoned. One would hope that the scope for unreason would become less as economists find out more about economic possibilities, and about ways of explaining more clearly the meaning of the value judgements required. However, this may be rather far in the future, and in the meantime a shadow wage rate has to be chosen. At present, practical project evaluators place it anywhere between the actual wage and zero – often, but not always, at one extreme or the other. Moreover, policy-makers and project choosers are seldom presented with any arguments concerning its value or its significance. We believe that, in general terms, the significance of our formula $C - 1/S(C - M)$ can be explained to policy-makers and administrators, even if the formula presented in the *Manual* for estimating S is likely to be useful only to economists.

Do these rules assume the world is perfect? Although in the above discussion we have tried to talk about the world as it is, the reader may be suspicious that we are too eager to apply the rules of classical welfare economics, and therefore likely to have forgotten important imperfections. Naturally, any system of project appraisal, or planning, or economic control, must be simplified if it is to be practicable: it will not be exactly right for any particular situation, because there will be many particular complications most of which will have to be ignored. The question is, whether the aspects we ignore are likely, at all frequently, to be of great importance.

One way of assessing this is to consider under what circumstances our rules would be *exactly* right.[14] In doing this, we draw together the various arguments that have been presented in the preceding sections. Think of the economy as consisting of a controlled sector and an uncontrolled sector In the controlled sector, what the government wants to happen happens, while the rest of the economy can be influenced only indirectly – through prices, taxes, quotas, licences, etc. In this uncontrolled sector there may be monopolists, many different income levels, fragmented markets, and other imperfections. Nevertheless, we can assert the general principle that, if the government acts in all spheres consistently with its overall objectives, it will want productive efficiency within the controlled sector. The argument is, roughly, that a government willing to vary taxes, public utility prices, etc., in an optimal way will be able to make good use of any extra production, or reduced inputs. Therefore, if a way can be found of making more without making less of anything else, it should be done. It follows that productive efficiency is desirable, and this implies, as we have already mentioned, that it makes sense to use the same accounting prices for all production decisions to be taken within the controlled sector.

The proviso, that the government acts in all spheres consistently with its overall objectives, is a strong one. It does not claim that the government will do things that are impossible for it, but it does claim that it will adjust taxes, quotas, and so on, in optimal ways. Otherwise, particular production decisions might influence these other, non-investment, decisions in desirable ways. For example, a decision by one department to build less electricity capacity combined with a decision, perhaps by a second department, to encourage its use within the controlled sector by setting a relatively low accounting price, could force what might be a beneficial decision (perhaps by a third party) to take measures to reduce private consumption. But if private demand were already optimally controlled, this would not be desirable. We must add that we do not know of a

[14] Diamond and Mirrlees, op. cit., discuss the general theory of a world in which the government has only incomplete control over the economy and, in particular, is unable to levy the lump-sum taxes and subsidies it would ideally wish. We here apply it to the kinds of economies we had in mind in writing the *Manual*.

system of project appraisal that can satisfactorily take account of differences in the good sense and efficiency of different government departments in this way, and doubt whether such a system would be very acceptable to governments. But in particular cases, these considerations might form an important part of a project report.

In any case, the proviso is unduly strong. For it may be that in certain spheres, although the government is not acting optimally, the way that it is influencing the uncontrolled sector (deliberately or otherwise) is independent of the production decisions being taken in the controlled sector. An obvious case of this is where the price charged by a public utility, although not optimal, is fixed arbitrarily, and is unlikely to be affected by project decisions. It is clear that in such a case, there is no advantage to modifying our decision rules.

The power of the argument for productive efficiency is seen most clearly when we regard international trade as part of the controlled sector – as, in developing countries, we frequently may. For then we see at once that the rates of transformation of commodities through trade should equal their rates of transformation of production in the controlled sector. In other words, the accounting prices should be the border prices. It is, as the above discussions have made clear, in the case of non-traded goods that the determination of accounting prices is harder, and sometimes very hard. This is because, where marginal costs vary with the scale of production, the relation between the accounting price and the terms of sale to the uncontrolled sector have to be considered for a theoretically correct determination of the accounting price. In practice, one is naturally forced to use crude short-cuts and approximations in many such cases.

It does seem to us, however, that the above framework provides a natural framework for improving estimates of accounting prices, even when the assumptions that would justify them completely are not satisfied. Then we have to ask ourselves whether existing tax policies, and the like, lead to an apparent overvaluation or undervaluation of the commodity in question. If, in the present state of knowledge, such a question can only occasionally be given a convincing answer, that is in part because the bias can go either way, and there is no general presumption that it goes one way or the other. Since good investment appraisal requires the use of unbiased accounting prices, it seems to be good sense to use those implied by the assumption of optimal government control (within given limits) as the first approximation.

III PRESENT SOCIAL VALUE

The present social value is obtained by discounting social profits by what we call the 'accounting rate of interest' (ARI). Projects are to be undertaken if and only if they have positive social present value: thus we can think of the ARI as the social rate of return on the 'marginal' project. It is the maximum rate of interest at which it would be sensible for the government to borrow from abroad. It is also the rate of fall of the weight given to social profits, that is, public income.[15]

Usually the ARI differs from the consumption rate of interest (CRI), sometimes referred to as the 'social rate of discount'. The consumption rate of interest is the rate at which society wishes to discount consumption, that is, roughly speaking – private income. The ARI and CRI differ because the relative weights of public and private income – their ratio is S – change. Where W_G and W_P are the weights of government and private income, we have the identities

$$(4) \qquad S = W_G/W_P$$

$$(5) \qquad -\frac{\dot{S}}{S} = \frac{\dot{W}_P}{W_P} - \frac{\dot{W}_G}{W_G} = \text{ARI} - \text{CRI}.$$

Our reasons for thinking that the CRI and ARI are likely to be rather different are as follows. The CRI must be rather directly related to the consumption levels that people are going to have: extra consumption will be given less weight when people are in any case going to be richer. The CRI will – in general – be greater the faster we think that consumption levels are going to rise. It has nothing – directly – to do with the probable effectiveness of new investment, or the resources that are likely to be available for new investment.

Suppose, for example, that the prospects for consumption growth

---

[15] This is true only if the government behaves rationally. To make the point, we could define the government rate of interest (GRI) as the rate of fall of the weight given by the government to its income. It is then possible that the government *says* this rate is, say, 7 per cent. But it is also possible that the social return on the marginal government project (the ARI) is, say, 10 per cent. This, however, implies that the government is not investing enough. The reason may, of course, be that it cannot or will not tax enough. But, in that event, it should be placing a higher weight on its income in the present. In other words S should be higher, and so also should be the rate of fall of S. But this is only to say that its announced rate of 7 per cent is wrong. So we do not, in the text, distinguish the GRI and the ARI as defined in this footnote. Finally, of course, rational government behaviour implies equating the marginal social value of a rupee's worth of government investment with that of government consumption on defence, health, etc.

(during the next decade, say) are rather poor, but that new opportunities for investment seem rather good. We might well choose a low value of the CRI – 5 per cent, say. If we used the CRI to discount the profits from these investment projects, we might obtain large positive present social values – and find that many more projects qualified than there were funds available. This is a clear sign that the value of investment now is greater than the value of consumption now: thus $S > 1$. Even with the relatively high shadow wage rate that this may indicate, the CRI may still be too small a discount rate. The ARI ought to be greater than the CRI; and S should be falling over time. Since S will eventually be close to 1, it will have to fall over time if it is now greater than 1.

The CRI, the ARI, and S are all related to one another. Even when one can make a good guess at the CRI, the ARI and S have to be worked out together, and the relationship between them is quite complicated. But that would not be a good reason for supposing, as a matter of convenience, that S is a constant, and the CRI a suitable discount rate for the evaluation of investment projects. *If* one were going to work out the effects of the project on consumption, both directly, and indirectly through the further projects that would be financed by the savings arising, the CRI would be suitable: but that is not a very convenient way of conducting cost–benefit analysis. It is much more natural to measure the benefits in terms of public income, since the investment costs themselves are a charge on public income. Then, conveniently, the discount rate is the rate of return on a marginal project. This procedure is all the more convenient if we can take it that the SWR will be more or less a constant proportion of the actual wage during the life of the project. We think that that will often be a sufficiently good approximation. For, usually, either the marginal product of labour elsewhere will be quite close to the consumption of wage-earners, or S will be rather high. In either case, the SWR will not be very much less than consumption out of wages; and as S falls, one would expect marginal productivity to be rising. Thus the SWR should not change at all rapidly.

While we think that the normal case of development is that where S is high initially, and falls over time until it is approximately unity, the opposite could happen, for a time. If, for instance, savings (domestic or foreign) were abundant relative to domestic investment opportunities, then S might start at unity (or, conceivably, below unity). Improvement in investment opportunities might then bring about a rise in S. This would entail that the CRI rose above the ARI.

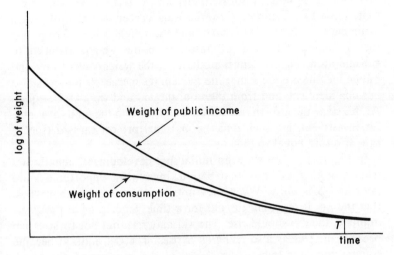

Figure 15.1

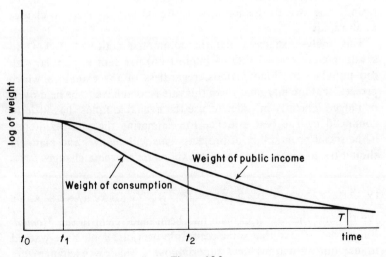

Figure 15.2

These two cases are illustrated in Figures 15.1 and 15.2. In the first case, S is initially substantially above 1. Even with the SWR quite close to consumption by the wage-earner, the rate of return available is high: the ARI is high, and the weight assigned to public income should fall, and fall faster than the weight assigned to consumption. This continues until, at T, the weights of private and public income are the same: the two curves merge, their slopes also become identical, and from then on, the ARI and the CRI are equal. At this stage the growth rate of consumption, and the funds available for investment, are such that the marginal project earns a (social) rate of return equal to the CRI.

In Figure 15.2, we show an initial 'pre-development' equilibrium from t_0 until t_1. During that period, investment opportunities are poor and S is unity. When they improve, S must rise above 1 so that the ARI is *less* than the CRI for a time. Since growth prospects improve, the CRI should rise. The ARI may rise, but not by so much because the SWR is also rising as S rises. The CRI and ARI become equal again at t_2 where the slopes of the two curves are equal. From t_2 on, the situation is the same as in Figure 15.1. In this second case, one would begin with quite a low SWR, equal to the opportunity cost of labour to the industrial sector. The SWR would then rise towards the wage-earner's consumption level during the period t_1 to t_2, rising faster than the actual wage rate. But from t_2 on, the ratio of the SWR to the actual wage would not be likely to change at all rapidly.

This analysis suggests that the common practice of sticking to a rather conventional rate of interest (10 per cent is popular – all too popular) for long periods, regardless of the extent to which projects that are marginal when this rate is used have to be held over, or judged leniently in order to use the available funds, has little to commend it. The best evidence for estimating the rate of interest is the social profitability of projects. This will change, and planners should try to make changes in the ARI to reflect these changes.

IV THE BALANCE OF PAYMENTS AND THE EXCHANGE RATE

We thought that our approach had been made clear in the *Manual*. But we have found that some confusion prevails; some have wanted to use our valuations, *and* superimpose a shadow exchange rate if the country was in balance of payments difficulties.

When high protection, by quota or tariff, is so prevalent, one of the most important functions of a shadow price system is to get the relative prices of domestic and foreign resources right. Having tried to do this by revaluing domestic resources, it should be obvious that there is no case for using a shadow wage in addition. Take a very simple case. A project imports machines against a loan, combines them with local labour, and exports the result – there being no other costs. The alternative occupation of labour is to grow rice, which substitutes for imports, and there is no case for valuing labour at a higher figure than its marginal product.

Suppose the loan cost in foreign exchange is 100F, the domestic cost is 100D, and the export proceeds 200F. The exchange rate is 1:1, and so the operation has zero profit. But the required labour saves by import substitution only 50F, whereas this project would permit it to earn 100F, net of all costs.

Assuming for simplicity that $S = 1$, our approach is to value labour at 50, thus correctly stating the social profit. An alternative approach is to use a shadow exchange rate of 1:2, so that the relative costs become loan 200, labour 100, and the sales 400 – which gives, of course, the same profitability as on our approach. The introduction of non-traded goods, other than labour, complicates the procedure without altering the very simple principle which is that everything depends on relative prices. If the relative prices of all goods are optimal, then that is the best one can do for the balance of payments.

But, it may be objected, the above example makes no allowance for increased consumption, which will also have a balance of payments effect. This is true. If we want the total balance of payments effect, when consumption is inevitably increased as a result of the project, then it is necessary to use a shadow wage rate equal to C – that is, the actual consumption of labour revalued at border prices. Using the symbols of Section II(a), and assuming that all accounting prices have been correctly estimated, then the production effect on the balance of payments is $(V-LM)$, while the consumption effect is $-L(C-M)$. Together these add up to $(V-LC)$ which we saw in Section II(a) to be an estimate of the savings, in terms of foreign exchange, resulting from the project.[16] It should be no surprise that

[16] It must, however, be recognized that this estimate may be rather a mixture of short- and long-run effects. The purchase or sale of traded goods will have an almost immediate impact. But where, for instance, non-traded goods have been valued in terms of the foreign exchange cost of increased supply, this expenditure of foreign exchange would be delayed for a considerable time. In the meantime, there might be a shortage of the non-traded goods concerned which would also

that is the same result as is arrived at by setting S equal to infinity. For setting S equal to infinity implies that the country is concerned only to increase savings (measured as always in terms of foreign exchange). In other words, improving the balance of payments has absolute priority over increasing consumption.[17]

We can thus say that when the government chooses S, it has also chosen the weight to be attached to an improvement in the balance of payments. The greater this weight, the *higher* must be the shadow wage. But, if anyone, nevertheless, wants to see a separate balance of payments calculation, it becomes very easy to re-do the calculations with a shadow wage rate equal to C.

Apart from showing that it is folly to try to use both approaches simultaneously, the above example points to an advantage which we would claim for our method. We can cost the particular inputs relevant to our project directly in terms of foreign exchange. For any particular project this is likely to be more accurate than applying a global shadow exchange rate. Where, for example, the divergence between wages and marginal product differs for different parts of the country, our method can take direct account of this in a way which a shadow exchange rate cannot. The example shows what happens when the exchange rate is actually changed. It brings relative actual prices into line with the relative shadow prices, and so makes socially profitable projects actually profitable. The actual exchange rate is a means of implementing good micro-economic planning decisions: neither it, nor any single shadow exchange rate, is necessary for good central investment planning.[18]

People often think that changes in the exchange rate are made in order to change the balance of payments. We do not think this is usually the case in developing countries. In fact, the balance of payments can be and is kept manageable by quotas, tariffs, export subsidies and borrowing. But, the time comes when, as a result, relative prices become so badly distorted that the need for a change of policy becomes obvious. A devaluation makes domestic resources more competitive, which permits the restoration of a system in

have balance-of-payments effects, but ones that might well not coincide with those estimated. A precise and accurate time phasing of the foreign exchange effects would be exceedingly difficult to estimate, and would depend anyway on many doubtful behavioural assumptions.

[17] Earlier we said, that setting S equal to infinity implies that growth is the sole objective. These statements are not really in conflict: for savings of foreign exchange can be applied either to investment or to improving the balance of payments. If either has absolute priority, extra consumption is set at nought.

[18] This point has also been made by Bent Hansen, op. cit.

which actual costs and prices better reflect social costs and prices, and which should therefore encourage more effective investment and a better growth rate.

Once domestic resources have been made adequately competitive, the balance of payments should, in the short term, be managed by the use of reserves and by borrowing; and, in the longest term, by fiscal and financial measures acting on private expenditure, as well as by adjustments in public investment and consumption, which would involve changes in the accounting rate of interest.

V AGRICULTURAL PROJECTS

As we have stressed, the *Manual* was written with manufacturing projects primarily in mind. Since then, quite a lot of work has been done on agricultural projects using the same method. In due course we hope that some of these results will be published. In the meantime it is worth making the following few preliminary observations. Some, perhaps many, agricultural projects differ in no essential respect from industrial projects. A good example is an estate producing an export crop. But where there are important differences they can probably be categorized as follows:

1. The technological relationships are harder to guess.

2. The state of affairs if the project is not done is sometimes harder, and may be almost impossible, to define.

The above differences affect any method of appraisal. Others which more closely concern *Manual* methods are,

3. The proper value to put on family or hired labour in settlement projects may involve rather different methods of estimation from those suggested in the *Manual*.

4. Where the project is very far from a port, or a substantial part of the output is not *prima facie* traded, then the use of border prices may well become futile, since trade may be insignificantly affected. We have not actually come up against such a case, but they must exist. But, even when trade is probably affected to a significant extent, it may be very difficult to decide what trade and how much. This is because the project may well affect local prices significantly, and hence the pattern of consumption. Thus in agriculture there is probably a continuous spectrum between the pole of trade being predominantly affected, where *Manual* methods apply excellently, and the pole of local prices and consumption being predominantly affected. In the latter case it might be more straightforward to work

in terms of consumption benefits, using a CRI and an investment premium, while putting more stress on consumer surplus and distributional affects, in the manner of the UNIDO *Guidelines for Project Evaluation.*[19]

[19] UNIDO, Mimeo (May 1970).

VI

LABOUR PRODUCTIVITY: INTERNATIONAL DIFFERENCES AND SHORT-RUN BEHAVIOUR

CHAPTER 16

Labour Productivity and Other Characteristics of Cement Plants – An International Comparison[1]

C. DIAZ-ALEJANDRO

I INTRODUCTION

This paper compares labour productivity and other characteristics of cement plants in Latin America with those in Australia, Canada and the United States, and tries to explain and quantify the sources of productivity differences in this industry. It also attempts to measure the degree of capital–labour substitution that exists in this activity. The major data were obtained from answers given to mailed questionnaires sent to all plants listed in the 1963 *World Cement Directory*[2] for the region and countries indicated.

Cement is a relatively homogeneous output, produced by a straight-

[1] This study was supported at different stages by grants from the Social Science Research Council (Latin American Collaborative Research Summer Grant), the John Simon Guggenheim Foundation, and the Ford Foundation. I am grateful to them, and to the cement plants which answered the questionnaires.

James Gough, John Simpson and Steven Kadish provided valuable help with the computations. Mr Kadish, in particular, did some very unusual things with the computer, allowing not only a fast pace of work during the summers of 1970 and 1971, but also making possible the 'frontier' experiments described towards the end of this paper. He also made many useful suggestions and criticisms.

An early version of this paper was presented at seminars in Princeton, Minnesota, Harvard, the Inter-American Bank, and Yale, where helpful comments were received. I am especially grateful to Richard Nelson, Robert Evenson, Yoav Kislev and Howard Pack for their extensive and detailed comments. Thanks are due also to Nathaniel Leff, Richard S. Eckaus, Frances Stewart, James Simler, Anne O. Krueger, Zvi Griliches, David Felix and Howard Kunreuther for helpful observations. Miss Mary Downey graciously typed this and earlier versions. But responsibility for any kind of remaining errors is mine only.

[2] *World Cement Directory* is published by the European Cement Association (CEMBUREAU). The plants listed include clinker grinding plants (excluded from this study), as well as cement plants under construction, and some which have gone out of operation since 1963. Two rounds of questionnaires were sent, roughly six months apart.

283

forward, vertically-integrated production process, with most plants being sited next to their own quarries. The questionnaire, therefore, referred mainly to physical amounts of inputs and gross output (for example, metric tons of cement produced, number of employees, etc.). International comparison is facilitated by this approach.

The questionnaires asked for 1963, 1964 and 1965 data for each plant; in most of the subsequent discussion these years were averaged. In some cases, as when a plant was starting operations, the early years were dropped; in a few cases, 1966 was included in the averages.

Questionnaire data for 1963 which overlapped with that given in

TABLE 16.1 *Comparison of Sample with Universe Characteristics for 1963*

	(1) Sample	(2) Universe	(1) as a Percentage of (2)
Cement output (million metric tons)			
Latin America	8·86	20·39	43·50
United States, Canada and Australia	9·48	68·46	13·80
Number of plants			
Latin America	41·00	117·00	35·00
United States, Canada and Australia	26·00	218·00	11·90
Average plant output (thousand metric tons)			
Latin America	216·20	174·30	124·00
United States, Canada and Australia	364·50	314·00	116·10

Sources and Method: 'Universe' obtained from CEMBUREAU, *World Cement Directory*, for 1963. It was assumed that all plants for which *capacity* data were given in the *Directory* were in operation during 1963, as not all plants listed in that publication reported their output. Total output obtained from the *Directory*, pp. ix–x. 'Latin America' is defined to include, besides the twenty Latin American Republics, the Bahamas, Jamaica, Puerto Rico and Trinidad. Therefore, Puerto Rico is excluded from US totals. The sample includes plants which did not report 1963 data; they are excluded from this Table, but will be used below. This table underestimates the size of the non-Latin American sample; eleven US plants, owned by the same company, answered in two questionnaires, giving averages, *each of which was treated as a single plant*, even when obtaining total output.

TABLE 16.2   *Major Characteristics of the Sample (mostly 1963–5)*
(Average per Plant per year)

	(1) Latin America	(2) Non-Latin America	(1) as a Percentage of (2)
Total employment (persons)	432·4	189·4	228·3
In quarries	60·5	24·3	249·0
Elsewhere in plant	385·6	165·1	233·6
With university and technical diplomas	19·1	9·7	196·9
With university degrees	7·4	5·3	139·6
Output (thousand metric tons)	227·9	390·8	58·3
percentage of portland in output	96·1	97·2	—
Output per employed person (metric tons)	565·5	2,277·7	24·8
Capacity (thousand metric tons)	276·5	505·0	54·8
percentage capacity utilization	84·6	78·8	—
Horsepower installed (thousand)	13·4	19·3	69·4
Horsepower of electrical motors (thousands)	11·3	18·1	62·4
Kilowatt-hours consumed (million)	28·4	46·7	60·8
Percentage of electricity purchased	37·6	94·7	—
Percentage of output shipped in bags	82·3	19·0	—
Number of kilns	2·8	2·5	112·0
Average age of kilns (years)	14·1	13·3	106·0
Average surface of kilns (square meters)	827·4	1,557·4	53·1
Percentage of plants using wet process	65·1	77·8	—
Percentage of plants with own quarries	86·8	92·6	—
Sales value per cement ton (US dollars)	23·24	23·16	100·3
Total wages and salaries as a percentage of sales value	18·4	16·9	—
Annual wage and salary bill per employee (US dollars)	2,238·6	6,762·3	33·1

Sources and Method: 'Averages' for magnitudes such as output per employed person have been generally obtained by averaging the corresponding data for *each plant*.

the *Directory* were checked for consistency; no significant disparities were found for the common data. Table 16.1 compares some characteristics of the sample with those of the universe for 1963. The sample for non-Latin America (NLA) is a bit thin,[3] but on the whole the response was satisfactory, and much better than expected. Not all questions were answered by those responding; in what follows, the size of the sample will fluctuate depending on what variables are discussed (and minor discrepancies will appear in the averages).

The major characteristics of the sampled plants are presented in Table 16.2, and will be briefly reviewed in this introductory section. The average Latin American (LA) plant has more than twice the number of employees as the NLA plants, but produces less than 60 per cent of the output of those plants (nearly all output is of portland cement in both regions). Average labour productivity in Latin America, therefore, is only one-quarter the average for the sample of industrialized countries.[4] LA annual wages and salaries per employed person, however, are one-third those of industrialized countries. LA plants have on average a higher share of employees in quarries, and a smaller share of their labour force with diplomas and university

---

[3] This led a cynical wag to remark that Latin American productivity was lower because its entrepreneurs spent their time answering questionnaires sent by silly academics. While on the topic of wags, I should warn the wit that scores of colleagues and friends have already told me that they expected concrete results from this study.

[4] The average labour productivity data of Table 16.2 may also be compared with those given by the Organization for Economic Co-operation and Development (OECD) for the cement universe of some countries (all data is metric tons of cement per employee for the average of 1963, 1964 and 1965, excepting Australia):

		Index
Netherlands	2,175	100
Canada	2,063	95
United States	1,784	82
Switzerland	1,777	82
Sweden	1,657	76
United Kingdom	1,470	68
France	1,464	67
Federal Republic of Germany	1,370	63
Italy	1,183	54
Australia (1963 Only)	1,094	50
Greece	986	45
Ireland	888	41
Spain	692	32
Latin America (sample)	566	26
Turkey	428	20

For basic data see OECD, *The Cement Industry* (several annual issues). Australian data from the *World Cement Directory* for 1963.

degrees. The share of wages and salaries in total sales is higher in LA plants, but the difference is small and the standard deviations (not shown) are very high.

If all plants for which output and total employment are given in the 1963 *World Cement Directory* are also taken into account, the resulting average labour productivities for 1963 are as follows:

	Number of Plants	Metric Tons Per Employed Person
Latin America	92	503·4
Australia, Canada and the US	94	1,724·0

Richard R. Nelson has suggested that it is likely that the range of average labour productivity will be greater in less developed than in developed countries.[5] A similar hypothesis would postulate that the ratio of standard deviation to the mean average labour productivity for a given industry will be greater for a less-developed than a developed country. If our sample is divided just into NLA and LA, this hypothesis is rejected. The data are as follows for average labour productivity (expressed in metric tons of cement per employed person):

	Number of Plants (a)	Mean (b)	Standard Deviation (c)	(c) as a Percentage of (b)
Latin America	42	565·5	300·9	53·2
Non-Latin America	27	2,277·7	1,291·0	56·7

Results more favourable to the hypothesis are obtained taking additional 1963 data from the *World Cement Directory*, introducing more geographical sub-divisions, and excluding the two Puerto Rican plants from Latin America:

	Number of Plants (a)	Mean (b)	Standard Deviation (c)	(c) as a Percentage of (b)
United States	69	1,727·2	653·8	37·9
Canada	13	2,135·0	1,100·0	51·5
Australia	11	1,111·0	239·5	21·6
Mexico	18	677·0	330·0	48·7
Argentina	14	333·9	152·8	45·8
Brazil	25	417·2	218·8	52·4
Other Latin American Countries	33	458·7	202·2	44·1

[5] See his pathbreaking, 'A Diffusion Model of International Productivity Differences in Manufacturing Industry', *American Economic Review*, vol. 58 (December 1968), no. 5, part 1, p. 1231.

Surprisingly (in view of much recent literature), capacity utilization in the sample is higher, on average, in Latin America. 'Capacity' in the cement industry is traditionally estimated on the basis of the size and number of kilns, which are assumed to work continuously (three shifts), except during an annual shut-down for repairs.[6] But adding all plants from which output and capacity data are given in the *World Cement Directory* for 1963, the results are as follows:

	Number of Plants	Percentage Capacity Utilization
Latin America	100	85·1
Australia, Canada and the US	102	86·9

Furthermore, the standard deviations of the means given in Table 16.2 for percentage capacity utilization are high (13·6 per cent for Latin America and 16·6 per cent for Non-Latin America) relative to the sample gap in average capacity utilization. We cannot say that a significant difference emerges between the capacity utilization rates of LA and NLA plants, a result which may be typical for continuous process industries.

An indirect measure of capacity utilization is given by the relationship between kilowatt-hours of electricity consumed and horsepower of electrical motors installed. Table 16.2 data show that ratio to be roughly the same in LA and NLA, the average for the latter being only 3·2 per cent higher than for the former.[7]

---

[6] The correlation coefficients (Rs) between capacity and total kiln volume for the sampled plants are as follows:

	Number of plants	R
Latin America	40	0·85
Non-Latin America	21	0·88
Pooled	61	0·89

The duration of the annual shut down is likely to depend on market conditions and other variables, but this point was not researched.

[7] Kilowatt-hours of electricity consumed per horsepower of electrical motor installed are as follows:

LA	2,502
NLA	2,584
All US Manufacturing (1954)	2,349

The last line was obtained from Murray F. Foss, 'The Utilisation of Capital Equipment: Post-war Compared with Pre-war', *Survey of Current Business*, vol. 43 (June 1963), no. 6, p. 11. This article used US data for electric power consumption and the horsepower of electric motors together with assumptions, to estimate the average number of hours per year that electric-power-driven equipment was utilized. It makes the point that most production equipment in manufacturing is powered by electric motors and suggests that '. . . there is probably a fairly good

It was thought unwise to ask in the questionnaire for the 'capital' of each plant. Rather, physical proxies were sought. These include installed horsepower (for electricity and other motors), kilowatt-hours used (from sources both inside and outside the plant), and number, size and age of kilns. Kilns are generally regarded as the main component of capital costs in cement plants, especially when the wet process is in use.[8] There is, furthermore, evidence linking the price of this kind of equipment to the area of its surface.[9] These proxies, unfortunately, fail to capture such things as differences in installation costs, inventories and buildings and structures. More importantly, they will not reflect the degree of use of new types of control equipment, like computers, which are increasingly being installed in new cement plants in industrialized countries.

Horsepower of electrical motors, kilowatt-hours consumed and total kiln surface in the average LA plant hover around 60 to 64 per cent of the mean for NLA plants, not far from the 58 per cent corresponding to output comparisons. LA kilns, on the other hand, are on average slightly older than those in NLA plants. Our proxies fail to show substantial differences in capital–output ratios between LA and NLA plants, even though the difference is marked for capital–labour ratios. More on this below.

Table 16.2 shows that the average plants being compared produce in fact different bundles of goods and services, even though both apparently specialize in portland cement. The LA factory is really a combination of electric plant (only 38 per cent of its electricity consumption is purchased outside, compared with 95 per cent for NLA), bagging operation (82 per cent of output shipped in bags v. 19 per cent for NLA), and cement production. Comparison of labour productivities has to take this fact into account. Non-electrical motors, for example, appear closely linked to the plant generation of electricity.[10]

positive correlation between the horsepower of a machine and its dollar cost' (p. 11).

[8] See, for example, Leonard A. Doyle, *Inter-Economy Comparisons: A Case Study* (Berkeley and Los Angeles, University of California Press, 1965), p. 21.

[9] See John Haldi and David Whitcomb, 'Economies of Scale in Industrial Plants', *Journal of Political Economy*, vol. 75 (August 1967) no. 4, part 1, pp. 373–86. 'The amount of material required for containers (tanks, furnaces, kettles, pipes and so on) depends principally on the surface area, whereas capacity depends on the volume inclosed' (p. 375). A check (which I have not carried out for lack of data) would be to see how close a correlation exists between the indicated capital proxies and book value of plant and equipment in cement in countries where all those data are available.

[10] For forty-nine plants (LA and NLA), the correlation between horsepower

The variety of services and processes carried out under the label of a 'portland cement plant' suggests that for some types of analysis plant data may be too aggregated, while for others it may be too micro and incomplete. If, as Yoav Kislev notes, the construction industry of a country lacks facilities to handle cement in bulk, cement plants will have to install bagging operations, regardless of other economic parameters. Under these circumstances, one may attribute low productivity to plants which simply reflect extra-plant conditions. A more accurate picture could be obtained by comparing the combined production *and* distribution systems for cement across countries. Similar considerations would apply to the combination of infrastructure services (of which electricity is only one example) and cement production. On the other hand, for the purpose of isolating exactly where within the plant the possibilities of capital–labour substitution are greatest, more disaggregated data on the input uses of different intra-plant processes would be desirable.

To complete the review of Table 16.2, one may note that average cement prices, obtained by dividing sales values (excluding bags) by sales in metric tons, are similar in LA and NLA, even though unit labour costs appear higher in LA. Here is a Latin American industry whose prices do not appear grossly out of line with those of 'world' markets, even at going (often overvalued) exchange rates.[11]

installed in non-electrical motors and kilowatt-hours produced in the plant is $+0·68$. For the NLA plants by themselves the correlation is $+0·80$, and it becomes $+0·68$ again for just the LA plants.

[11] Sales values in local currencies were translated into US dollars by using average merchandise exchange rates. The latter were found by dividing the sum of exports and imports valued in local currencies by the same variables expressed in US dollars, for the relevant years. Basic data obtained from International Monetary Fund, *International Financial Statistics*.

The secular progress of Latin American import substitution in cement may be seen in the following table, showing for the major countries cement imports as percentages of total apparent domestic cement consumption:

	1920–4	1935–8	1951–4	1960–4
Argentina	67	6	16	nil
Brazil	100	13	27	nil
Chile	51	2	nil	1
Colombia	82	28	1	nil
Cuba	54	6	28	8
Mexico	20	4	2	nil
Peru	86	34	10	2
Uruguay	13	7	16	nil
Venezuela	68	70	10	nil
Central America (six)	90	88	40	22

Basic data obtained from CEMBUREAU, *World Cement Market in Figures* (Paris, 1967). Between 1920–4 and 1962–6 Latin American cement output has grown at

The rest of the paper will use plant data, in spite of their limitations, to investigate productivity differences between LA and NLA, and the degree of capital–labour substitution which exists in cement production. It will be seen that differences in capital–labour ratios and scale explain significant shares of the productivity gap. But a large part of that gap remains unexplained either by those two variables, or by any other variable which could be unambiguously labelled.

II AVERAGE LABOUR PRODUCTIVITY AS THE DEPENDENT VARIABLE

Multiple regression analysis has been used for untangling various

TABLE 16.3 *Regressions 'Explaining' (log. of) Average Labour Productivity. Data for LA and NLA Pooled*

	(1)	(2)	(3)
Constant	1·817	2·737	1·928
	(3·69)	(6·10)	(5·36)
LKL1	0·588	—	—
	(7·59)		
LKL2B	—	0·404	—
		(6·63)	
LKL3	—	—	0·706
			(10·33)
LCAP	0·590	0·381	0·262
	(8·57)	(5·09)	(4·35)
CAPU	0·915	0·988	0·324
	(4·32)	(4·32)	(1·78)
LKILNS	−0·447	−0·202	−0·191
	(5·06)	(2·26)	(2·97)
SKILL	3·192	2·480	1·483
	(3·78)	(3·19)	(2·37)
WET	−0·200	—	—
	(2·67)		
AGE	0·007	—	—
	(1·90)		
LA	−0·286	−0·594	−0·200
	(2·19)	(5·05)	(1·98)
R^2	0·94	0·93	0·95
Observations	55·00	54·00	65·00
F-test	86·90	99·60	168·90

an average annual rate of 10 per cent, while apparent cement consumption (production plus imports minus exports) grew at about 7 per cent per year.

TABLE 16.4   *Regressions 'Explaining' (log. of) Average Labour Productivity. Data for* LA *only*

	(1)	(2)	(3)
Constant	1·368	1·620	1·721
	(2·90)	(3·12)	(4·27)
LKL1	0·537	—	—
	(6·00)		
LKL2B	—	0·307	—
		(4·44)	
LKL3	—	—	0·607
			(6·58)
LCAP	0·607	0·473	0·338
	(8·51)	(5·10)	(4·19)
CAPU	1·156	1·265	0·290
	(4·12)	(3·75)	(1·02)
LKILNS	−0·466	−0·207	−0·209
	(4·28)	(1·53)	(2·23)
SKILL	3·384	3·999	2·357
	(3·67)	(3·62)	(2·62)
WET	−0·207	—	—
	(2·51)		
AGE	0·004	—	—
	(0·92)		
R^2	0·88	0·82	0·86
Observations	36·00	28·00	39·00
F-test	28·60	20·20	41·10

influences on average labour productivity. No attempt has been made to fit particular production functions to the data. Empirical opportunism was also followed in deciding which variables, and in what form, were used in the regressions. The best results are presented in Tables 16.3, 16.4 and 16.5. In all cases, the dependent variable is the logarithm of annual average labour productivity, defined as tons of cement per person employed in the plant.[12]

The independent variables listed are those which survived, or came close to surviving, significance tests based on *t*-statistics, which are given in parentheses under the coefficients. The variables are defined as follows:

LKL1:   logarithm of the capital–labour ratio, where the surface

[12] Most, but not all, plants also provided data on hours worked per year per employed person. The averages were as follows:

	Number of plants	Hours
LA	35	2,127
NLA	26	2,021

TABLE 16.5   *Regressions 'Explaining' (log. of) Average Labour Productivity. Data for* NLA *only*

	(1)	(2)	(3)
Constant	1·120	2·966	1·553
	(0·87)	(4·59)	(2·65)
LKL1	0·911	—	—
	(4·62)		
LKL2B	—	0·733	—
		(7·28)	
LKL3	—	—	0·924
			(9·40)
LCAP	0·545	0·120	0·111
	(2·44)	(1·04)	(1·28)
CAPU	0·668	0·844	0·460
	(1·70)	(3·35)	(2·23)
LKILNS	−0·340	−0·079	−0·140
	(1·56)	(0·78)	(1·82)
SKILL	4·258	0·648	0·371
	(1·64)	(0·67)	(0·47)
WET	−0·180	—	—
	(0·82)		
AGE	0·014	—	—
	(1·82)		
R^2	0·83	0·86	0·89
Observations	19·00	26·00	26·00
F-test	7·80	23·60	31·70

area of all kilns is used as a proxy for capital. Labour refers to total employment in the plant.

LKL2B: as LKL1, except that the horsepower of electrical motors in the plant is used as a proxy for capital.

LKL3: as LKL1, except that total kilowatt-hours consumed are used as a proxy for capital.

LCAP: logarithm of maximum output capacity of the plant, expressed in tons of cement.

CAPU: actual output expressed as a percentage of capacity.

LKILNS: logarithm of the number of kilns installed in the plant.

SKILL: number of employees with university and technical diplomas expressed as a percentage of total employment.

WET: dummy variable, with a value of 1 when the wet process is used, and zero when the dry process is used.

AGE: average age of kilns used in the plant, in years. Age is measured from installation date. The average is unweighted.

AGESQ: the variable AGE squared.

LA: dummy variable, with a value of one for Latin American
             plants, and zero for the rest.

   Several other variables were used, including a dummy for whether
or not the plant has its own quarry, the share of portland cement in
output, etc., with mixed or poor results. As expected, multi-collinearity presented problems. For example, a variable expressing for
each plant output shipped in bags as a percentage of all output
performed well in equations using pooled data (as those shown in
Table 16.3), but was 'killed' when the dummy variable LA was
introduced. The simple correlation coefficient between the LA
dummy and the variable for the share of cement shipped in bags is
+0·84 (with sixty-nine observations). The corresponding figure for
the correlation between the same dummy and the percentage of
electricity each plant purchased from outside sources is −0·62
(with sixty-seven observations). It may be noted, however, that even
when the LA dummy was not introduced, the variable for share of
electricity purchased did poorly in most equations. (Other interesting
failures will be reported below.)

   A fuller idea of the multi-collinearity problems present in the
regressions of Table 16.3, and in other regressions to be shown below,
is given by the following correlation matrix for some of the independent variables (see page 295). AWR stands for average wages
per employee, BAGS for the share of output shipped in bags and
PKWHP for the percentage of total electricity consumed purchased
outside the plant.

   Table 16.3 presents regressions using both LA and NLA data, while
Tables 16.4 and 16.5 show the same regressions but using just LA
or NLA data. (Note that the regressions for each group use slightly
different samples.) The R^2s are quite high (bearing in mind we use
cross-section data). The coefficients for 'capital'–labour ratios all
have a high degree of significance, but show a high range of estimates
for the elasticity of output with respect to 'capital'. (When Table
16.3 regressions were run without the LA dummy, the range was
even higher.) Furthermore, such elasticity is uniformly *higher* for
NLA than for LA.

   The result closest to *a priori* expectations is obtained with LKL2B,
using the horsepower of electrical motors as a proxy for capital,
and which yields the lowest coefficient. This variable also performs
best in other regressions to be discussed below. On the other hand,
LKL3, using kilowatt-hours consumed (from all sources) as a capital

	KL2B	CAP	CAPU	AGE	LA	AWR	BAGS	PKWHP
KL1	0·54	0·43	−0·16	−0·13	−0·80	0·71	−0·69	0·59
KL2B	—	0·41	−0·06	−0·20	−0·50	0·61	−0·52	0·56
CAP	—	—	−0·23	0·05	−0·39	0·49	−0·41	0·24
CAPU	—	—	—	−0·08	0·19	−0·06	0·27	−0·11
AGE	—	—	—	—	0·05	−0·22	−0·04	−0·03
LA	—	—	—	—	—	−0·82	0·84	−0·62
AWR	—	—	—	—	—	—	−0·78	0·41
BAGS	—	—	—	—	—	—	—	−0·48
PKWHP	—	—	—	—	—	—	—	—

proxy, performs in a sense 'too well'. Electricity consumption is so closely related to output that other variables tend to lose significance (especially capacity utilization), while the *a priori* case for relating electricity consumption to capital is weaker than with the other two proxies.

The consumption of kilowatt-hours is the variable with the highest simple correlation with cement output, and that correlation remains very high whether LA, NLA or pooled data are used:

Pooled	+0·95
LA	+0·90
NLA	+0·98

A similar statistical problem would arise if the proxy chosen refers to a plant activity which, though relatively unimportant, is registered accurately and is closely bound to output (for example, number of paper bags consumed). Horsepower and kiln surface area proxies, in that order, can be considered, therefore, as more reliable than electricity. It may be noted that results very similar to those obtained using kilowatt-hours as an independent variable were reached when the calories provided by electricity were added to the calories provided by fuel consumption, to create a new independent variable to act as capital proxy.

The coefficients for the capacity variable indicate substantial economies of scale, especially for Latin American ranges, although once more the estimates show great variability depending on the proxy used for capital. For the Latin American observations, a 1 per cent increase in capacity would yield, *ceteris paribus*, an increase in average labour productivity of between 0·34 and 0·61 per cent. These figures, combined with those discussed above, again show the difficulty of separating the results of capital-deepening and scale expansion.

Attempts were made, in a Cobb-Douglas spirit, to measure scale by the number of employees. The results were uniformly poor.

The capacity utilization variable has the expected sign and is in most cases significant. The coefficients for other variables were little affected whether or not this variable was introduced into the regressions; that experiment (not shown) was motivated by the fear that the introduction of CAPU biased the results obtained for other coefficients.

An interesting result is the significance of (log of) the number of kilns in the plant in all regressions of Table 16.3 and in two of those in Table 16.4. The results indicate that the larger the number of kilns, the lower the average labour productivity, for any given level of capital density and scale. As LKL1 uses total kiln surface as a capital proxy, the results in the first columns of Tables 16.3 and 16.4 are better than the rest. More fundamentally, this variable could be picking up productivity differences between plants which achieved a given capacity by a gradual process of adding new kilns, and those which from the start adapted their (smaller) number of kilns to the desired (and observed) plant capacity. Presumably, the latter have a higher productivity than the former, among other things because the larger number of kilns for a given output will require a greater amount of raw material and final product handling. It may be noted that a fairly high positive correlation exists between the number of kilns in each plant and a simple measure of dispersion of the age of those kilns. A (lower) positive correlation also exists between that measure of dispersion and the average age of kilns.[13] Finally, plants faced with greater fluctuations in demand may have adapted by having a larger number of kilns.

The skill variable yields significant results for the Latin American and pooled data, but not for NLA. For the latter, better results (not shown) were obtained using a variable expressing just the number of employees with university degrees as a percentage of total employment; but this variable did worse than SKILL for LA and pooled data.

The dummy variable for the process used in production gave mixed results, often insignificant, but generally showing lower labour productivity in plants using the wet process.

Considerable experimenting was carried out with variations on the AGE variable, but with disappointing results. Often when the variable yielded significant or near-significant coefficients (as that shown in Table 16.3), the sign was unexpected, implying that the older the kilns, the higher the plant's labour productivity. It is noteworthy

[13] Measure of dispersion for each plant is:
$$\frac{\Sigma|x_i - \bar{x}|}{n}$$
where:

x_i = age of kiln i
$\bar{x}$ = average age of kilns in plant
n = number of kilns.

The R^2 between this measure of dispersion and number of kilns is 0·50; the relationship is positive. When the measure of dispersion is correlated with the average age of kilns in plant, the R^2 drops to 0·20 (the relationship is also positive).

that the simple correlation for the pooled data between number of kilns in the plant and the average kiln age is +0·43 (see also footnote 13). Variables limiting the maximum age of kilns to twenty-five years, and weighting the average age of kilns in each plant by their size were tried with mediocre results. Note also that the variable, as defined, fails to take into account frequency of repairs.

It is possible that the variable AGE picks up two offsetting influences: equipment vintage, on the one hand, and the accumulated experience and learning of the plant's workers and management, on the other. To test this possibility, both AGE and AGE squared were introduced in several regressions, with the supposition that the former would pick up the vintage effect, and the latter the learning effect. The signs came out as supposed, but the coefficients were insignificant. Some of these experiments will be reported below.

The significance of the LA dummy can be interpreted as meaning that LA and NLA plants operate on different production functions; in other words, there appears to be a (neutral) efficiency difference, with the LA plants producing less output than the rest for given capital–labour ratio, scale, skill, etc. Such an interpretation is reinforced by the results of Table 16.8 (to be discussed). But this straightforward interpretation is clouded by the multi-collinearity among the LA dummy, the percentage of output shipped in bags, the percentage of electricity purchased from outside the plant, and similar variables. It is difficult, then, to separate apparent productivity gaps arising from the fact that cement plants in LA and NLA include different processes and activities, from those which result from 'true' efficiency differences in the handling of the basic factors of production. The LA dummy, however, performs so much better than the other variables (of less ambiguous interpretation), that one is left with the general efficiency difference as the major interpretation.

III A QUANTIFICATION OF THE SOURCES OF THE PRODUCTIVITY GAP

The previous section has provided us with equations which, in spite of several weaknesses, appear to explain a very high share of the variability in average labour productivity across plants, and isolate several independent variables which are significant in that explanation. One may ask about the quantitative importance of each of those variables.

The pooled data regressions of Table 16.3 predict the following average labour productivities (in metric tons of cement), when their coefficients are used, first with the average LA values for the different independent variables, and then with those for the NLA sample:

	Regression (1) (Using LKL1)	Regression (2) (Using LKL2B)	Regression (3) (Using LKL3)
Predicted LA Productivity	500·4	493·5	497·1
Predicted NLA Productivity	1986·1	2080·5	1921·1
Predicted LA Productivity as a percentage of predicted NLA Productivity	25·2	23·7	25·9

The question may be asked as to what would happen to the predicted productivities and to the productivity gap if using the same Table 16.3 regression coefficients, we combine them with all *but one* of the average NLA values for the independent variables. For example, in Table 16.6 the entry under Column (1), Row LKL1, says that if in

TABLE 16.6 *Ratio of* LA *to* NLA *average labour productivity if indicated variable takes the average value for* LA *data, while all other variables take the average values for* NLA *data, using regressions of Table 16.3*

	(1)	(2)	(3)
LKL1	0·496	—	—
LKL2B	—	0·549	—
LKL3	—	—	0·377
LCAP	0·609	0·758	0·841
CAPU	1·057	1·080	1·020
LKILNS	0·958	0·959	0·972
SKILL	1·050	0·997	1·007
WET	1·047	—	—
AGE	0·997	—	—
LA	0·752	0·552	0·819

regression (1) of Table 16.3 we use NLA average values for all variables *except* LKL1, for which we use the LA average value, the predicted average labour productivity would be 984·5 tons, or 49·6 per cent of the NLA productivity.

The results shown in Table 16.6 indicate that the capital–labour ratio, scale and the LA dummy variable (or general efficiency differences) dominate the explanation of the gap. Other variables, although significant for inter-firm labour productivity differences, contribute little to explaining the LA/NLA productivity gap, and in several cases (for example, CAPU, SKILL and WET in the first column) indicate that LA plants have average values which yield higher productivity, *ceteris paribus*, than NLA plants. (It should be remembered that the sample used changes from column to column.)

Taken at face value, the results of Table 16.6 attach great importance to the LA dummy as a drag on average labour productivity; even if LA plants had the same capital–labour ratio, scale, etc., as NLA plants, their labour productivity would remain at between 55 and 82 per cent of that of NLA plants. Even greater importance is attached by this method to low LA capital–labour ratios as drags on average labour productivity.

TABLE 16.7   *Gains in productivity obtained by introducing NLA average values, one at a time, into Table 16.3 regressions, using LA average values for all other variables (Columns (a) expressed in metric tons of cement; Columns (b) as percentages)*

	(1)		(2)		(3)	
	(a)	(b)	(a)	(b)	(a)	(b)
NLA productivity	1986·1	—	2080·5	—	1921·1	—
LA productivity	500·4	—	493·5	—	497·1	—
Productivity gap	*1485·7*	*100·0*	*1587·1*	*100·0*	*1424·0*	*100·0*
LKL1	509·1	34·3	—	—	—	—
LKL2B	—	—	405·1	25·5	—	—
LKL3	—	—	—	—	823·3	57·8
LCAP	321·7	21·6	157·8	9·9	94·1	6·6
CAPU	−27·2	−1·8	−36·5	−2·3	−9·8	−0·7
LKILNS	21·8	1·5	21·1	1·3	14·5	1·0
SKILL	−23·7	−1·6	1·7	0·1	−3·5	−0·2
WET	−22·6	−1·5	—	—	—	—
AGE	1·3	0·1	—	—	—	—
LA	165·4	11·1	400·0	25·2	109·9	7·7
Residual	539·9	36·3	637·9	40·2	395·5	27·8

An alternative, and more natural procedure is presented in Table 16.7, using LA average values for the independent variables as bases in the regressions of Table 16.3, and observing by how much the predicted average labour productivity is increased (or decreased) by introducing NLA values for variables, one at a time. The columns marked a) show the net change in productivity, measured in metric tons, obtained by introducing the NLA value for the variable in the corresponding row, while all other variables keep their LA values.

The b) columns show the share that such a net change represents of the observed total productivity differences between LA and NLA. As before, differences in capital–labour ratios, scale and the LA dummy, appear as key explanatory variables. Note, however, that even in regression (3) these three variables leave a substantial part of the productivity gap unexplained; that residual, which did not appear in the exercise of Table 16.6 , is also left unexplained by the other variables. It is now seen that raising the LA capital–labour ratio to NLA levels, leaving other variables unchanged, would only eliminate between 26 and 58 per cent (more reliably: between 26 and 34 per cent) of the productivity gap. If both the capital–labour ratio and the scale of LA plants were brought up to NLA levels, the two more reliable equations of Table 16.3 would still predict an LA average labour productivity between one-half and two-thirds that of NLA.

A final exercise (not shown) with the regression results consisted of taking, say, LA mean values for the independent variables and introducing them into the regressions of Table 16.5, that is, those with coefficients estimated using NLA data The average labour productivity predicted by combining LA mean values with coefficients obtained using NLA data can then be contrasted with those obtained with NLA coefficients *and* mean NLA values, and with those obtained with LA mean values *and* LA coefficients. A similar exercise was carried out with the NLA mean values combined with LA coefficients. Relatively little difference was made to the predicted LA average labour productivity whether LA or NLA coefficients were used, and the results were similar to, although usually lower than, those obtained using coefficients derived from the pooled data. The same cannot be said for NLA productivity; here LA coefficients applied to NLA mean values for independent variables yielded productivities between only 49 and 71 per cent of those obtained by NLA mean values combined with their own coefficients (those of Table 16.5). It may also be noted that the predicted LA/NLA productivity gap is smaller when LA coefficients are used; but the larger gaps predicted by NLA coefficients correspond better to the true gap, as reflected in the sample. In both cases, the trouble lies with the abnormally low predicted NLA productivity when NLA independent variable average values are used together with LA coefficients (those of Table 16.4). One may speculate that the coefficients estimated using only NLA data are attributing to the most important independent variable, that is, the capital–labour ratio, responsibility for higher productivity which arises elsewhere. But this may not be the only difficulty involved in the use of capital–

labour ratios as explanatory variables for average labour productivity. To those additional difficulties we now turn.

IV OUTPUT AND AVERAGE CAPITAL PRODUCTIVITY AS DEPENDENT VARIABLES

The results obtained in the previous section are, on the whole, somewhat 'neo-classical', in the sense that they attribute a significant share of the explanation for productivity gaps to differences in capital–labour ratios. In other words, by yielding high elasticities of output per employee with respect to capital per employee, they imply considerable substitution possibilities between capital and labour in cement production. (However, the importance they give to scale economies and general efficiency differences make them less 'neoclassical'.)

Although the technique of making average labour productivity a function of, among other things, the capital–labour ratio, is used widely in the literature, it is easy to see that it could yield misleading results. Consider the following extreme hypothesis (adapted from arguments often given by knowledgeable 'practical' men). Take an activity with L-shaped isoquants, or no substitution possibilities at all between capital and labour. Now suppose that plants differ in the efficiency with which they use labour, or simply differ in hiring practices, so that some plants have the 'right' amount of capital but more than the minimum labour which is technically necessary to produce a given output. In other words, their 'X-inefficiency' is not neutral with respect to labour and capital, but is concentrated in the use of labour. This may be due to custom, which requires that each skilled worker be aided by a bevy of unskilled ones, socio-political pressures inducing padding of pay-rolls, or by a desire of entrepreneurs to have within the factory a reserve of trained employees, even if they are not fully occupied. (It is sometimes argued that more workers are used in LA plants for repairs; this is likely to be the case, but it would be just one way to substitute labour for capital, unless the argument refers to in-plant v. outside repairs.) Under the hypothesized circumstances, one could get a good fit between average labour productivity and the capital–labour ratio, yielding a spuriously positive elasticity of output per employee with respect to capital per employee. By dividing both output and capital by the same variable, which is subject to influences not foreseen in pure neo-classical theory, we may get an apparently good relation between productivity and capital intensity.

Consider the following simple numerical example, where capital and output are the same in all plants (say they are both equal to 10), but where the labour employed differs as follows:

	Labour Employed	Average Labour Productivity	Capital–Labour Ratio
Plant 1	1	10	10
Plant 2	2	5	5
Plant 3	3	3·3	3·3
Plant 4	4	2·5	2·5
Plant 5	5	2·0	2·0

The fit between the last two columns is obviously good, and the (apparent) output–capital elasticity is one. But changes in the capital–labour ratio occur while the capital–output ratio remains unchanged.

A direct way to check on the previous hypothesis, relating output to each of the inputs and to other independent variables, is plagued by multi-collinearity in a worse fashion than for previous results. The best streamlined results of this approach are given in Table 16.8 where the new variables are defined as follows:

LK1:   logarithm of capital, where the surface area of all kilns is used as a proxy for capital.

LK2B: as LKL2B, except that the horsepower of electrical motors in the plant is used as a proxy for capital.

LK3:   as LK1, except that total kilowatt-hours consumed are used as a proxy for capital.

LEMPTO: logarithm of total employment in the plant.

As before, the more sensible results are given by the groups (1) and (2). Output elasticity with respect to 'capital' is significant and quantitatively important in all regressions; the corresponding elasticity with respect to labour is significant for both the pooled and the LA samples in groups (1) and (2). The fact that LA regressions yield significant coefficients for both labour and capital, while those for NLA show significant coefficients only for capital, casts doubt on the general validity of the hypothesis sketched in the previous paragraph.

As in Tables 16.4 and 16.5, the output–capital elasticity is higher for NLA than for LA; if the average output–capital ratios implied in Table 16.2 are added to this information, one concludes that the marginal productivity of capital is higher in NLA (presumably capital-abundant) than in LA (presumably capital-poor). For regres-

Table 16·8 Regressions 'Explaining' (log. of) Output

| | (1) | | | (2) | | | (3) | | |
	(P)	(LA)	(NLA)	(P)	(LA)	(NLA)	(P)	(LA)	(NLA)
Constant	-2·306 (3·42)	-3·543 (3·65)	-3·807 (2·83)	0·828 (1·66)	-1·693 (1·63)	2·185 (5·06)	2·135 (8·15)	1·837 (3·98)	2·410 (7·51)
LK1	0·668 (6·11)	0·581 (4·44)	1·156 (4·51)	—	—	—	—	—	—
LK2B	—	—	—	0·536 (7·50)	0·472 (4·94)	0·753 (8·04)	—	—	—
LK3	—	—	—	—	—	—	0·894 (14·98)	0·875 (11·04)	0·938 (10·45)
LEMPTO	0·448 (3·29)	0·628 (3·31)	-0·031 (0·14)	0·531 (5·40)	0·789 (5·13)	0·179 (1·76)	0·065 (0·90)	0·112 (1·09)	-0·021 (0·22)
CAPU	0·558 (1·73)	0·696 (1·39)	0·399 (1·00)	0·907 (3·23)	1·196 (2·50)	0·838 (3·43)	—	—	—
SKILL	4·106 (3·04)	4·815 (2·74)	6·064 (2·22)	2·370 (2·33)	4·430 (2·43)	0·713 (0·76)	—	—	—
AGE	-0·024 (1·43)	-0·027 (1·16)	-0·026 (0·98)	—	—	—	—	—	—
AGESQ	0·0006 (1·50)	0·0006 (1·13)	0·0010 (1·41)	—	—	—	—	—	—
LA	-0·731 (4·09)	—	—	-0·765 (5·30)	—	—	-0·082 (0·78)	—	—
R^2	0·83	0·80	0·86	0·85	0·83	0·90	0·91	0·89	0·91
Observations	55·00	36·00	19·00	54·00	28·00	26·00	65·00	39·00	26·00
F-test	33·40	19·10	12·20	54·60	28·60	48·70	204·60	145·20	122·60

sions in group (2), in fact, the implied NLA marginal capital productivity is 72 per cent higher than that of LA.[14]

The results of Table 16.8 also confirm the presence of economies of scale, particularly in LA plants; the coefficients for capital and labour in LA regressions (1) and (2) add up to 1·21 and 1·26, respectively, while those for the pooled sample add up to 1·12 and 1·07. Note that the coefficients for capital in Table 16.8 are always higher than those for the corresponding capital–labour ratios in Tables 16.3, 16.4 and 16.5; this is due (at least in part) to their picking up scale effects directly in Table 16.8.

The coefficients for the capacity utilization variables maintain their significance only in the group (2) regressions, while those for SKILL hold up better. The AGE and AGESQ coefficients came close enough to significant levels in group (1) regressions to be of some interest. For groups (1) and (2) the LA dummy is not only highly significant, but its introduction into the regressions also improved markedly the significance of other coefficients. This result confirms the view that there are (neutral?) efficiency differences between the LA and NLA production functions.

There is another way to check on the validity of the extreme hypothesis sketched above. If the good fit between average labour productivity and the capital–labour ratio is due partly or totally to the indicated spurious reasons, one should obtain much poorer results when making average capital productivity, or its inverse, the capital–output ratio, the dependent variable. The poorer results will be reflected in the size of the correlation coefficient, of the F-test, and of the t-statistics for the capital–labour ratio. If the extreme hypothesis is correct, variations in the capital–labour ratio would have no significant effect on the capital–output ratio.

[14] The ratio of NLA to LA output–capital elasticities may be written as follows:

$$\frac{[\partial 0/\partial K]_{NLA}}{[\partial 0/\partial K]_{LA}} \cdot \frac{[0/K]_{LA}}{[0/K]_{NLA}} = \frac{0\cdot753}{0\cdot472}.$$

From Table 16·2, using horsepower of electrical motors as capital proxies, we have that:

$$\frac{[0/K]_{LA}}{[0/K]_{NLA}} = 0\cdot93.$$

Therefore, we get

$$\frac{[\partial 0/\partial K]_{NLA}}{[\partial 0/\partial K]_{LA}} = \frac{1\cdot60}{0\cdot93} = 1\cdot72.$$

Note, however, that the coefficients to be obtained in the new regressions are linked to the old by the identity:

$$\frac{K}{Y} = \frac{K/L}{Y/L}.$$

Suppose one has estimated coefficients for the following regression:

$$\log(Y/L) = B_0 + B_1 \log(K/L) + B_2 \log CAP,$$

and then estimates:

$$\log(K/Y) = \alpha_0 + \alpha_1 \log(K/L) + \alpha_2 \log CAP.$$

Because of the identity shown, it will be true that:

$$B_1 = 1 - \alpha_1$$

and,

$$B_2 = -\alpha_2.$$

Table 16.9 presents the major differences between these two types of regressions; the results for variables LCAP, CAPU, LKILNS, SKILL, WET, AGE and LA were identical with those shown in Tables 16.3, 16.4 and 16.5 for the corresponding regressions (that is, same numerical value for the coefficient and for its t-statistic), but with a different sign. They are not shown in Table 16.9.

With one exception, the R^2s and the Fs in Table 16.9 are lower than the corresponding ones in Tables 16.3, 16.4 and 16.5. The t-values for the constant terms in Table 16.9 are higher than the corresponding ones in the earlier tables; but only two t-values for independent variable coefficients share that characteristic. For regressions using kilowatt-hours consumed as a capital proxy, the collapse of the R^2s, Fs and ts is quite sharp; on the other hand, regressions using horsepower of electrical motors as the proxy hold up well, and in some cases show improvements in explanatory power in Table 16.9. On the whole, the results shown in Table 16.9 indicate that the link between labour productivity and capital-intensity is not simply due to the spurious reasons sketched in the extreme hypothesis.

V PLANTS ON THE 'EFFICIENCY FRONTIER'

Another way of approaching differences between LA and NLA plants, as well as characteristics of the whole sample, is to deal just

TABLE 16.9   *Regressions 'Explaining' (log of) the Capital–Output Ratio*

	Constant	LKL1	LKL2B	LKL3	R^2	F-test
Pooled data						
(1)	5·091	0·412	—	—	0·74	16·30
	(10·34)	(5·32)				
(2)	4·171	—	0·596	—	0·72	20·40
	(9·30)		(9·79)			
(3)	4·980	—	—	0·294	0·32	4·49
	(13·84)			(4·31)		
LA data						
(1)	5·540	0·463	—	—	0·81	17·10
	(11·75)	(5·18)				
(2)	5·287	—	0·693	—	0·85	24·40
	(10·18)		(10·00)			
(3)	5·187	—	—	0·393	0·43	5·00
	(12·87)			(4·26)		
NLA data						
(1)	5·788	0·089	—	—	0·64	2·80
	(4·47)	(0·45)				
(2)	3·942	—	0·267	—	0·51	4·10
	(6·10)		(2·65)			
(3)	5·355	—	—	0·076	0·31	1·80
	(9·15)			(0·77)		

with 'efficient' observations. Efficiency is here defined in a technological sense, that is, the attempt tries to isolate points on an isoquant.[15] For a given capacity range, a plant with a higher capital *and* labour requirement per unit of output than another one is eliminated, until only undominated or 'efficient' plants remain, for which, say, a higher per unit capital requirement is offset by a lower unit labour use. This procedure in effect traces out isoquants made up of the most efficient plants in the sample.

Table 16.10 presents the outcome of such an exercise, which is, of course, very sensitive to extreme observations (sometimes of doubtful reliability). Ranges were selected somewhat arbitrarily, but experiments with different ones did not change the results significantly. It may be seen that 'efficient' LA plants have, on the whole, lower

[15] This approach was pioneered by N. J. Farrell, 'The Measurement of Productive Efficiency', *Journal of the Royal Statistical Society*, Series A (General), vol. 120 (1957), part 3, pp. 253–81. See also D. J. Argner and S. F. Chu, 'On Estimating the Industry Production Function', *American Economic Review* (September 1968), pp. 826–39. I am grateful to Peter T. Knight for calling my attention to this approach.

TABLE 16.10 *Capital and Labour Inputs per Unit of Output of Plants on the Efficiency Frontier*

(Starred plants belong to LA; per unit inputs of Labour and capital expressed as indices, with averages for all efficient plants equal 100; TMT stands for thousand metric tons)

	Using Kiln Surface Area as Capital Proxy		Using Horsepower of Electric Motors as Capital Proxy	
	K/O	L/O	K/O	L/O
Range 0 to 110 TMT	[*] 95	288	[*] 107	179
Range 110–175 TMT	[*] 92	87	[*] 69	200
	190	81	[*] 93	54
			118	50
Range 175–250 TMT	[*] 55	145	[*] 54	130
	104	80	101	20
Range 250–350 TMT	[*] 56	147	[*] 78	244
	93	69	[*] 82	239
	106	41	98	26
Range 350–550 TMT	127	75	[*] 52	130
	133	64	79	24
	148	39		
Range 550–700 TMT	[*] 61	244	[*] 83	70
	96	84	110	17
	97	37		
More than 700 TMT	47	18	[*] 105	192
			[*] 111	84
			112	29
			247	11
Average LA	72	182	83	152
Average NLA	114	59	124	25
(Average NLA/ Average LA)	(158·3)	(32·4)	(149·4)	(16·4)

unit capital requirements, and higher labour use than NLA plants, whether kiln surface or electric horsepower is used as the capital proxy. Unit capital use in NLA plants is on the average 58 or 49 per cent higher than in LA plants, while labour inputs are 68 or 84 per cent less.

As could be expected from the methodology used, positive evidence on capital–labour substitution is stronger here than when all plants were taken into account, but the opposite is the case on scale economies. Indeed, looking at efficient LA and NLA plants separately, when electric horsepower is used as the capital proxy, capital unit requirements first tend to decline, but then increase for plants

TABLE 16.11   *Average excess of unit capital and labour requirements compared with 'efficient' plants, when horsepower in electric machinery is used as capital proxy: single range*

(Unit requirements in 'efficient' plants equal 100)

Relative to 'efficient' plant:	K/O		L/O	
	NLA plants	LA plants	NLA plants	LA plants
#(1) (LA)	274	308	35	141
#(2) (NLA)	178	200	187	747
#(3) (NLA)	140	157	224	891
#(4) (NLA)	128	144	267	1066
#(5) (NLA)	57	64	411	1640

Note: There are twenty-two plants in the NLA average and twenty-eight in the LA average. 'Efficient' plant (1) is the most labour-intensive; (5) is the most capital-intensive.

in ranges higher than 550 TMT. No clear pattern emerges for labour requirements, nor for capital use when kiln area is the proxy. When all ranges are pooled together in just one group, the biggest plant dominates all others when kiln area is used as the capital proxy, but five 'efficient' plants (4 NLA, 1 LA) remain when horsepower in electrical motors is used for that proxy.

Taking these five 'efficient' plants (and working with a single capacity range), Table 16.11 estimates how LA and NLA plants exceed, on average, the minimum unit labour and capital requirements. In other words, Table 16.11 presents a rough calculation of the 'X-inefficiency' for the group of plants in the sample. The excess of unit capital use in LA plants relative to each 'efficient' plant is only about 12 per cent above the corresponding excess of NLA plants, but the excess of unit labour requirements in LA plants is about four times the corresponding 'X-inefficiency' of NLA plants. This evidence is compatible with previous results showing that LA plants operated with different, and less efficient, production functions than NLA plants. But it now suggests that such efficiency difference is not neutral, but biased towards the relatively less efficient use of labour than of capital. In other words, it hints that there is a kernel of truth in the extreme hypothesis of the previous section, and highlights the greater variation in labour productivity than in the capital–output ratio. Given available data, it appears difficult to settle the issue as to whether the LA 'X-inefficiency' is neutral or labour-using; indeed, it may be as difficult to settle this issue as it is to determine whether technological change is neutral or biased towards the greater use of one or another factor of production.

Returning to Table 16.11, it may be noted that 'efficient' plants #2, #3 and #4 clearly dominate the averages for 'inefficient' LA and NLA plants. But comparing LA 'inefficient' plants with the most capital-intensive 'efficient' plant (#5), one observes a (rather expensive) trade-off between capital and labour use. Trade-offs can also be detected comparing NLA 'inefficient' plants with 'efficient' plant #1, and (in the opposite direction) with 'efficient' plant #5.

When the characteristics of the ten LA 'efficient' plants shown in Table 16.10, using horsepower of electrical motors as the capital proxy, are compared with those for the whole LA sample, it is seen that the 'efficient' plants have averages very similar to those of the complete LA group in age and number of kilns, use of the wet process, percentage of cement shipped in bags, share of electricity purchased from outside the plant, and wages per employee. Indeed, when the LA sample is divided into frontier and non-frontier plants, and differences in the means of both groups for each variable are tested for significance, the variables whose means are significantly different include only capacity utilization and variables related to the size of plant (output, employment, etc.), for both of which the efficient plants have higher values, and capital–output ratios, prices per ton of cement, and share of portland cement in total output, for which the efficient plants have lower values.[16] For the NLA sample, significant differences between the means of frontier and non-frontier plants emerge in a different group of variables; here the frontier plants have higher capital–labour ratios, newer kilns, higher average labour productivities, higher shares of employees with technical and university degrees, and pay higher average wages (but have lower shares of wages in sales) than other NLA plants.[17]

[16] For the LA efficient plants, the share of portland cement in total output was 84 per cent, capacity utilization was 92 per cent and average sales price was \$19·5 per ton of cement. The corresponding figures for non-frontier LA plants were 99 per cent, 82 per cent and \$24·3 per ton, respectively. The standard significance tests for difference of two means using t-statistics were carried out at the 95 per cent confidence levels. Steve Kadish, who urged me to perform these tests, also pointed out that they involve the assumption of equality in the variances for the two groups. When this assumption is dropped, approximate tests can be devised, such as that outlined in Paul G. Hoel, *Introduction to Mathematical Statistics*, 3rd edn (New York, Wiley, 1962), pp. 278–9. With that approximation to t-statistics, for example, the difference in the mean share of portland cement in total output for frontier and non-frontier LA plants becomes insignificant.

[17] While non-frontier LA plants have a very similar share of wages in total sales as non-frontier NLA plants (18·7 per cent v. 18·3 per cent), the corresponding

VI CAPITAL-INTENSITY AND PRODUCTIVITY AS A FUNCTION OF WAGES

The analysis so far has proceeded using non-monetary variables. An alternative approach would be to ask how do plants in different countries react to differences in factor prices. The questionnaire data provide information only regarding wages per employee in the different plants. This will be used in what follows, on the assumption that variations in wages provide a lower limit estimation to variations in factor prices. That is, variations in factor prices between NLA and LA will be no lower than observed variations in wage rates, as it can be supposed that LA capital costs will typically be no lower than those in NLA, and are likely to be higher.

With these considerations in mind, one can ask whether the observed variations in capital–labour ratios (which we have seen influence average labour productivity) are in turn related to underlying economic conditions, as reflected in wage rates. Besides wage rates, it may be hypothesized that other variables influence the capital–labour ratio used in each plant, including scale or plant capacity, as well as the age of the equipment. If LA and NLA plants are on different production functions, this could also affect the capital–labour ratios of plants. Table 16.12 presents regressions which explore these relationships, using several definitions for the dependent variable, the capital–labour ratio. The independent variables are labelled as in previous tables, except a new one, LAWR, which refers to the logarithm of annual wages and salaries paid per person employed in the plant (the basic wage data were all converted into US dollars).

For the pooled and the LA data, all wage rate coefficients are significant; for NLA regressions (not shown), they were all insignificant. On balance, these results provide further evidence of some capital–labour substitution in the cement industry. The value of the wage rate coefficients may be taken as rough approximations to the (upper limit of the) elasticity of substitution between labour and capital, and are very similar in both pooled and LA regressions, ranging from 0·30 to 0·70. It may be noted that when in the pooled regression the LA dummy is not included, the corresponding estimates were higher, ranging from 0·55 to 0·84, and their t-statistics were also higher.

figure is relatively higher for LA frontier plants (16·7 per cent) than for NLA frontier plants (12·3 per cent). This conflicts with the empirical generalization that the labour share is higher in high wage countries than in low wage ones.

TABLE 16.12 *Regressions 'Explaining' (log. of) Capital–Labour Ratio*

| | Pooled data | | | LA data | | |
	LKL1	LKL2B	LKL3	LKL1	LKL2B	LKL3
Constant	3·008	5·433	5·034	2·438	5·439	4·371
	(4·65)	(6·07)	(6·12)	(2·94)	(4·30)	(3·58)
LAWR	0·298	0·677	0·417	0·339	0·704	0·436
	(2·71)	(3·99)	(2·80)	(2·73)	(3·56)	(2·36)
LCAP	0·120	0·158	0·267	0·147	0·105	0·245
	(1·47)	(1·41)	(2·51)	(1·40)	(0·70)	(1·60)
AGE	−0·008	−0·003	−0·001	−0·011	0·000	0·005
	(1·35)	(0·29)	(0·14)	(1·22)	(0·00)	(0·42)
LA	−0·626	−0·353	−0·739	—	—	—
	(3·36)	(1·20)	(3·10)			
R²	0·68	0·71	0·67	0·32	0·41	0·26
Observations	50·00	48·00	60·00	32·00	25·00	34·00
F-test	23·50	25·90	27·70	4·30	4·90	3·50

TABLE 16.13 *Average Labour Productivity as a Function of Wages and Capacity*

| | Pooled data | | | LA data | | NLA data | |
	(1)	(2)	(3)	(1)	(2)	(1)	(2)
Constant	9·725	7.366	6·942	8·193	6·241	9·813	7·593
	(34·93)	(11·79)	(12·00)	(17·28)	(9·26)	(8·85)	(4·83)
LAWR	0·841	0·702	0·427	0·488	0·410	0·816	0·622
	(10·71)	(9·07)	(4·14)	(4·18)	(4·03)	(2·01)	(1·56)
LCAP	—	0·331	0·300	—	0·304	—	0·280
		(4·11)	(4·07)		(3·62)		(1·90)
LA	—	—	−0·610	—	—	—	—
			(3·64)				
R²	0·66	0·74	0·79	0·35	0·55	0·14	0·26
Observations	60·00	60·00	60·00	34·00	34·00	26·00	26·00
F-test	114·70	81·50	70·40	17·50	18·60	4·00	4·10

With one exception, the t-statistics for the coefficients of the capacity variable are all substantially below 2. (Note that the simple correlation between capacity and wage rates, for the pooled data, is +0·49.) The age variable again does poorly, but its sign indicates that the older the kilns, the lower the capital intensity of the plant. The LA dummy variable performs worst in the regression with the highest estimated elasticity of substitution; the simple correlation coefficient between the LA dummy and the wage rate is −0·82. Again the separation of the true elasticity of substitution from efficiency differences (which may be neutral or biased) proves to be difficult.

The literature on production functions has also attempted to estimate elasticities of substitution by examining the relation between average labour productivity and wage rates. Table 16.13 presents the results of similar experiments using the questionnaire data. The first group of results, using pooled data, shows how the coefficient for wage rates drops as other relevant variables, scale and the LA dummy, are introduced in the regressions where average labour productivity (still measured in tons of cement per employee) is the dependent variable. In the pooled and LA regressions all coefficients have t-statistics far above two; the complete regressions for both groups yield very similar coefficients for the wage rate (0·43 and 0·41), consistent with previous estimates of the elasticity of substitution.[18]

Finally, a bothersome negative result should be reported. Regressions making the capital–output ratio a function of wage rates and other variables (as in Table 16.12) yielded poor results. In no case did the t-statistic for the wage rate coefficient reach two; it climbed

---

[18] The data were also used to estimate price equations, where (the log of) price was made a function of selected cost and productivity variables, as follows:

$$\text{LPRICE} = -0{\cdot}584 + 0{\cdot}314 \text{ LAWR} - 0{\cdot}369 \text{ LOE}$$
$$(0{\cdot}37) \quad (3{\cdot}41) \qquad\qquad (3{\cdot}63)$$
$$+ 0{\cdot}018 \text{ LCALTN} + 0{\cdot}057 \text{ LKO3}$$
$$(0{\cdot}10) \qquad\qquad (0{\cdot}32)$$

$$R^2 = 0{\cdot}30$$
$$\text{Observations} = 48{\cdot}00$$
$$\text{F-test} = 4{\cdot}63$$

The variable LCALTN stands for (the log of) calories of fuel consumed per ton of cement; LOE refers to (the log of) average labour productivity; other variables are defined as before. Similar results are obtained when the sample is divided into its LA and NLA components.

For LA plants, the variable LCALTN shows a significantly negative correlation with plant capacity, while the NLA data show significantly negative correlation with CAPU.

to 1·42 when horsepower of electrical motors was used as the capital proxy, and pooled data were used in the regression. However, if only the frontier plants identified in the previous section (using horsepower of electrical motors as capital proxy) are entered into a regression pooling LA and NLA efficient plants, one emerges with a significant and positive coefficient for the wage rate, as explanatory variable for the capital–output ratio.[19]

VII CONCLUSIONS

Major conclusions can be summarized as follows: gaps in average labour productivity between LA and NLA plants can be explained only in part by differences in capital–labour ratios and scale. The two groups of plants appear to operate in what for the sake of brevity can be called different production functions. The elasticity of substitution, although not very high, seems to be significantly different from zero for the cement industry. This result is obtained even though the capital proxies used may fail to pick up equipment used in quarries and for materials handling, as well as computers, which are more widely used in NLA than in LA.

The data leave unclear for what kinds of capital labour can be substituted. A closer look at labour allocation within cement plants, as well as a more detailed inventory of capital goods is the next step in clarifying this point. Such an investigation may also shed light on what other factors, besides scale and capital per worker, account for the much higher average labour productivity of NLA plants. It should also help to establish whether efficiency differences are neutral regarding labour and capital, or whether systematic biases exist. A last point, which could be cleared up with those detailed data, concerns the degree to which the LA plants incorporate within

[19] The sample made up by pooling LA and NLA frontier plants was also used to estimate regressions similar to those shown in Tables 16.12 and 16.13. The results, as measured by t-statistics and F-tests, were not generally as good as those in the tables. The coefficients for LAWR were lower (about half) and those for the LA dummy were higher than those in Tables 16.12 and 16.13 for pooled data. For the ten LA frontier plants a relatively high simple correlation ($+0·76$) was registered between the capital–output ratio (horsepower of electrical motors as proxy) and average age of kilns. Within this group (LA frontier plants), very high simple correlations were also obtained between average wage rates and capital–labour ratios ($+0·86$, $+0·97$ and $+0·96$ for the three different proxies), between wage rates and average labour productivity ($+0·93$) and also between labour productivity and all proxies for the capital–labour ratio ($+0·95$, $+0·94$ and $+0·99$, respectively). The corresponding correlations were much lower for the LA non-frontier group.

themselves (or around themselves) a larger amount of processes and social overhead facilities, including not only bagging and electricity but also housing and repairs, which are excluded from NLA cement plants.

Another line of research would be to complement this cross-section study with one contrasting the performance of LA and NLA plants through time. Our snapshot has captured plants at different points in their learning curves, and sheds no light on that process nor on other dynamic changes. Yet a glance at available time series for both LA and NLA shows rapid changes in plant sizes, labour productivity, etc.

CHAPTER 17

Some Evidence on the Short-Run Productivity Puzzle [1]

R. M. SOLOW

The 'puzzle' I have in mind has been described often enough in the literature[2] so only a bare sketch is necessary here.

When output stagnates or falls away from a peak, productivity (output per man-hour) tends to fall, or to rise slower than trend; when output recovers, productivity rises faster than trend. All this happens in intervals so short that changes in the capital stock and in technology must be very small. The crude observations seem, therefore, to contradict diminishing returns to labour in the short run. When increased employment works on a given stock of capital goods, output per man-hour 'ought' to fall.

One can try to interpret the data with the help of a production function

(1) $$Q = F(K,L,t)$$

even if, in quarterly data, the stock of capital has to be represented by a time trend. In the short run, the stock of capital is predetermined by past investment and output is determined by effective demand. One then inverts (1) and estimates

(2) $$L = G(Q,K,t), \text{ or, more usually,}$$

(2') $$L_t^* = G(Q_t, K_t, t), \; L_t/L_{t-1} = (L_t^*/L_{t-1})^{\theta}.$$

The puzzle arises because, even after allowance for lagged adjust-

[1] My thanks go to the National Science Foundation for financial support and to John Reily and Leland Dorman of MIT for efficient and perceptive research assistance.

[2] N. J. Ireland and D. J. Smyth, 'The Specification of Short-Run Employment Models', *Review of Economic Studies* (April 1970), pp. 281–5.

ment of L to L^*, 'normal man-hours', it invariably turns out that the permanent partial elasticity of L with respect to Q is less than 1, so that the elasticity of Q with respect to L in (1) substantially exceeds 1 (in fact runs to 1·3–1·4 in Ireland and Smyth's Table I). I find this hard to believe.

There is one explanation that surely accounts for some, possibly for most, of the puzzle. Some employment is 'overhead' in character, essentially unresponsive to short-run fluctuations in output. It would be better to replace (1) by

$$Q = F(K,L-L_0,t)$$

and (2) by

$$L = L_0 + G(Q,K,t).$$

Increasing average product is then compatible with decreasing marginal product of labour, at least for a range of levels of employment. It is easy to approximate the quantitative effect of this amendment. If a fraction, h, of total man-hours is overhead, then a 1 per cent variation in total man-hours corresponds to a variation in variable man-hours of $100(1-h)^{-1}0\cdot100$ per cent (that is, 1 per cent on a base of $100(1-h)$ per cent). Thus the estimated elasticity of L with respect to Q should be multiplied by $(1-h)^{-1}$ and the estimated elasticity of Q with respect to L should be multiplied by $1-h$ to make them refer to variable man-hours. If $h = 1/4$ is a fair approximation to the fraction of overhead labour, then the figure 1·3–1·4 mentioned earlier for the elasticity of Q with respect to L is to be marked down to 1. That is a great improvement, though perhaps still 'too high'.

This explanation is not entirely satisfactory. Overhead labour adjusts more slowly than variable labour, but presumably it does eventually adjust to changes in output. The superposition of a distributed-lag adjustment process as in (2′) ought to account, even if imperfectly, for some of the overhead-labour effect. There remains something to be explained.

The standard approach via (2) presupposes that all the existing capital stock is fully utilized all the time. Changes in production are met by changes in employment alone. This would be the natural presumption if all capital costs were sunk and the capital–labour

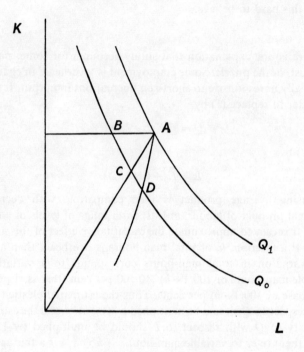

Figure 17.1

ratio were sufficiently flexible.[3] In that case, the expansion path (or 'contraction path') would run horizontally from A to B in Figure 17.1 as output falls from Q_1 to Q_0.

It is the contribution of Ireland and Smyth to remind us that there are user costs of capital, so that cost-minimization might call for idle capital even when factor-proportions are variable. (It is equally to the point that many costs associated with employment are not fully escapable when employment is reduced, so that labour has some of the characteristics of a fixed factor.) In the absence of any evidence or presumption to the contrary, Ireland and Smyth suggest that capital and labour inputs fall equally when output is reduced, so that the contraction path AC lies on the ray from A to the origin. Then, they point out, the estimated 'elasticity of Q with respect to L' is really a scale elasticity, since each 1 per cent change in L is associated, by assumption, with a 1 per cent change in *utilized K*.

I think this is a step forward, but probably not the end of the story. In the first place, I find scale-elasticities of 1·3–1·4 for large aggregates almost as unconvincing as labour-elasticities of that size. In the second place, casual observation of fluctuations in the reported 'capacity utilization' rate suggests that it may fall even faster than employment in the face of declining output.[4] The rest of this note is devoted to some limited evidence that the 'contraction path' may actually look like AD, with the ratio of utilized capital to man-hours falling as output falls. If further research should confirm this position, then the cyclical behaviour of output per man-hour

[3] Obviously, this argument does not apply literally to a model in which different layers or vintages of capital equipment have fixed but different labour requirements. In that context, I would give a different set of reasons why one might observe more or less the same thing. For example: firms own capacity of various vintages and efficiencies, and the age distribution varies among firms. When industry output falls, reductions in sales are distributed unevenly among firms because of geographical advantages, customer-relationships, and other imperfections of the market. So older capacity may be in use in one firm while newer and more efficient capacity is idle in another. Furthermore, the usual reasoning ignores user cost. The combination of use- and time-depreciation with the usual obsolescence of successive vintages means that it may be preferable for a firm to operate older and about-to-expire capacity while newer and more efficient capacity is idle, because the opportunity-user-cost is zero if the older capacity is about to expire anyway for other reasons, while the newer capacity can be preserved to produce another day.

[4] Since measured capacity utilization is moved mainly by output in the short run, this sentence amounts to the tautology that output falls faster than employment in downswings, that is, that productivity decreases. The rest of this paper is an attempt to escape the tautology.

becomes consistent with diminishing returns to labour and with near-constant returns to scale.

The issue could be settled easily by direct observation of capital-utilization rates and employment. The trouble is that there are no directly observed quarterly series of capital-utilization. (The one annual series available, though it is hardly direct observation, plays an important role in what follows.) Capacity utilization is in principle an output measure, not a capital measure. There is no alternative, then, to indirect inference about capital utilization in the short run. I begin by analyzing the relation between capacity utilization and the utilization of capital.

Rewrite (1) as

$$(3) \qquad Q = F(vK,L,t)$$

to allow explicitly for varying utilization of the available stock of capital. In principle, there is no reason to confine v between zero and 1; it can exceed 1 if there is long-run improvement in the rate at which services are extracted from a given capital stock. Now what capacity shall we associate with (3)? A natural definition is $F(v^*K,\infty,t)$, where v^* represents 'full utilization' under the conditions of time t. (In the absence of a trend, one would normalize at $v^* = 1$.) Here a not-very-serious problem arises. Unless the elasticity of substitution of F is bounded below unity, unlimited output can be produced from any given K. (The Cobb-Douglas is an example.) There would appear to be no finite 'capacity'. But of course no one seriously supposes that an unlimited amount of employment can be generated from a finite capital stock; and even if it could, there is only a finite number of people in the world. Let L^* be the practical maximum employment of man-hours at time t. ($L^*(t)$ presumably depends on K, but I shall ignore that nicety.) Then we can define capacity as

$$(4) \qquad C = F(v^*K,L^*,t).$$

The capacity utilization rate, u, is then simply

$$(5) \qquad u = Q/C = F(vK,L,t)/F(v^*K,L^*,t).$$

One can make various reductions of (5) on the assumption that F is homogeneous of some degree in its first two arguments. The most interesting conclusion is that u is a function of time explicitly unless technical progress is Hicks-neutral. But I shall jump, for empirical purposes, all the way to the assumption that F is Cobb-Douglas. Then (5) becomes

$$(6) \qquad u = (v/v^*)^a(L/L^*)^b,$$

where a and b are the constant elasticities of output with respect to utilized capital and employment, and v^* and L^* are to be treated as functions of time.

Now there does exist one attempt to construct an (annual) time series for v, the intensity of use of capital. It is due to Christensen and Jorgenson,[5] and covers the private US economy from 1929 to 1967. To estimate (6), I have matched this series with the Wharton School index of capacity utilization (which covers manufacturing, mining, public utilities, contract construction and services). The Wharton School index is published quarterly, and I have averaged the four quarters of each calendar year to give an annual series for u. L is represented by a special BLS tabulation of man-hours employed in private non-farm industry (monthly data averaged over the year). These two time series are available only since 1947. The sample available for estimating (6) thus consists of twenty-one annual observations covering the period 1947–67.

For this purpose, I replace v^* and L^* in (6) by exponential functions of time and take natural logariths to get

$$(6a) \qquad \log u = a \log v + b \log L - ct + \text{constant}.$$

Here c is to be interpreted as a weighted sum of the growth rates of v^* and L^* with weights a and b, and the size of the additive constant is unimportant. Least squares yields

$$(6b) \qquad \log u = 0{\cdot}168 \log v + 0{\cdot}815 \log L - 0{\cdot}015t - 5{\cdot}475$$
$$\qquad\qquad\quad (9{\cdot}0) \qquad\quad (8{\cdot}8) \qquad\quad (13{\cdot}9) \quad (5{\cdot}6)$$

$$R^2 = 0{\cdot}9643 \quad DW = 1{\cdot}52$$

with t-statistics written under the estimated coefficients.

This is almost too good to be true. The estimates of a and b add up to 0·98, which is to all intents and purposes a finding of constant

[5] L. R. Christensen and D. W. Jorgenson, 'The Measurement of US Real Capital Input, 1929–67', *Review of Income and Wealth*, vol. 15 (1969), pp. 293–320. Their attempt is based on electricity consumption relative to the installed horsepower of electric motors.

returns to scale.[6] Moreover, they are individually very close to their traditional Cobb-Douglas values, despite the fact that the data are quite different from those underlying the traditional estimates of aggregate production functions. Finally, in the Christensen-Jorgenson data, v seems to have a trend-increase of about 0·5 per cent per year; and in the BLS data, man-hours grow at about 1·5 per cent a year. On the assumption – as good as any, I suppose – that v^* and L^* grow at about the same rate as v and L, one may calculate 0·168 $(0·005) + 0·815(0·015) = 0·013$ and compare this with the estimated coefficient 0·015. The agreement is fairly good.

Obviously, a result like this needs confirmation more than it needs close interpretation. I propose to use it only to get a grip on the contraction-expansion path of Figure 17.1. Nevertheless, I have no wish to hide the precariousness of my interpretation of (6b). In particular, one must not forget that what I am calling 'capital utilization' is actually electricity consumption. It might be the case, for example, that electricity consumption is correlated mainly with manufacturing activity, and that the apparent reduction in capital utilization when output falls is in large part an aggregation effect reflecting the fact that manufacturing output falls more sharply than output as a whole. The only way to test this would be to reconstruct the analysis for manufacturing alone. It might be worth a try.

The trouble is that the Christensen-Jorgenson v-series is available only annually, whereas the productivity 'puzzle' involves shorter-run behaviour. To get around this difficulty, I have inverted the estimated equation (6b) to give v as a function of u, L and t. Since u and L are available quarterly, I can use them (and a quarterly time-variable) in (6b) to generate a hypothetical quarterly time series for v, the rate of utilization of capital. This procedure begs the question of quarterly timing: even if there were quarterly leads and lags among u, v and L, their annual relation might look synchronous. Nevertheless, so long as one does not take the timing too seriously, there may be something to be learnt about the shape of the contraction-expansion path.

For this purpose, I have limited myself to the four recession subperiods since 1947. In each case I start with the quarter in which man-hours reaches its peak, follow the downswing and the succeeding

[6] The standard error of $a + b$ is 0·08, so a 90 per cent confidence interval runs from 0·841 to 1·125.

upswing, and end with the first quarter in which man-hours reaches or exceeds its level at the preceding peak. The four sub-periods comprise the following intervals: 1948-IV to 1950-III, 1953-III to 1955-III, 1957-I to 1959-II, and 1960-II to 1962-II.

In each sub-period, I plotted a diagram intended to look something like Figure 17.1. In order to cancel out the trend in man-hours and put all four sub-periods on a roughly comparable basis, I measured along one axis L/L_P, where L_P is the input of man-hours in the peak quarter preceding a recession. Along the other axis, I measured the constructed quarterly series for v (without normalization, since the trend in v is small after 1947). The result did, indeed, in all four sub-periods look generally like the curve through AD in Figure 17.1. There was, however, a definite clockwise loop, suggesting a lag of L/L_P behind v in the course of each recession and recovery.

Regression of the natural logarithm of L_t/L_P on the natural logarithms of v_t and v_{t-1} gave the following results (with standard errors written under coefficients):

Sub-period I $\log(L_t/L_p) = 3 \cdot 71 + 0 \cdot 095 \log v_t + 0 \cdot 090 \log v_{t-1}$
                              $(0 \cdot 03)$ $(0 \cdot 007)$ $(0 \cdot 008)$

$$R^2 = 0 \cdot 9946 \quad DW = 2 \cdot 09$$

Sub-period II $\log(L_t/L_p) = 3 \cdot 83 + 0 \cdot 054 \log v_t + 0 \cdot 105 \log v_{t-1}$
                              $(0 \cdot 06)$ $(0 \cdot 014)$ $(0 \cdot 018)$

$$R^2 = 0 \cdot 9651 \quad DW = 2 \cdot 09$$

Sub-period III $\log(L_t/L_p) = 3 \cdot 80 + 0 \cdot 07 \log v_t + 0 \cdot 10 \log v_{t-1}$
                              $(0 \cdot 05)$ $(0 \cdot 01)$ $(0 \cdot 02)$

$$R^2 = 0 \cdot 968 \quad DW = 1 \cdot 56$$

Sub-period IV $\log(L_t/L_p) = 3 \cdot 97 + 0 \cdot 044 \log v_t + 0 \cdot 086 \log v_{t-1}$
                              $(0 \cdot 11)$ $(0 \cdot 026)$ $(0 \cdot 025)$

$$R^2 = 0 \cdot 8893 \quad DW = 1 \cdot 73.$$

There are some small but obvious variations among the coefficients in different sub-periods (and the slow deterioration of fit suggests that further fishing might catch something). But the differences are not very large relative to standard errors, nor do they appear to be systematic. It seemed sensible, therefore, to pool the observations for the four sub-periods, with the final result:

(7) $\log(L_t/L_{pt}) = 3\cdot80 + 0\cdot072 \log v_t + 0\cdot093 \log v_{t-1}$

$$R^2 = 0\cdot96 \quad DW = 1\cdot53.$$

With due account taken of the lag, then, it appears that the cyclical elasticity of L/L_P with respect to v is about one-sixth. A reduction of 6 per cent in the utilization of capital in the downswing is associated with a 1 per cent reduction in employment. And, again with the indicated lag, the pattern is retraced in the other direction as output rises back towards its previous peak. This rather remarkable result has to be tempered to allow for the overhead component in man-hours. If, for example, one-third of all man-hours are essentially fixed, then the 1 per cent change in total man-hours is a change of $1\cdot5$ per cent in variable man-hours, and the elasticity with respect to v is closer to one-quarter than one-sixth. Nevertheless, the strong impression remains that labour is more nearly the fixed factor in the short run, and variations in output are reflected substantially in the changing intensity of use of existing plant and equipment.

This has to be, unfortunately, a very tentative conclusion. The chain of reasoning and empirical inference that leads to it is necessarily indirect and sketchy, mainly because the data are not available for a more direct investigation. If the conclusion stands up under further research, then it would seem to call for some attempts to measure the user costs of plant and equipment, and the costs associated with changing employment, which must be substantial.

The elasticity of L with respect to v implied by (7) – one-sixth after the lag has gone by – strikes me as small. Nevertheless, I shall conclude with an example showing the implications of (7) and (6b) for the behaviour of productivity in the short run.

Suppose output, and therefore capacity utilization, were 1 per cent lower at some fixed time, t. Then according to (6b), the accompanying variations in v and L would satisfy

$$\frac{dQ}{Q} = -0\cdot01 = 0\cdot168\frac{dv}{v} + 0\cdot815\frac{dL}{L},$$

since v^* and L^* are unchanged. Imagine that this virtual movement occurs below a cyclical peak, so that L_P is also unchanged. Then, from (7), $dv/v = 6dL/L$, apart from the lag. Therefore

$$-0\cdot01 = [6(0\cdot168)+0\cdot815]\frac{dL}{L} = 1\cdot823\frac{dL}{L}.$$

Associated with the 1 per cent reduction in output is a reduction in man-hours of $1/1\cdot823 = 0\cdot55$ per cent. Output per man-hour would be lower by $0\cdot45$ per cent. The lag in (7) means that productivity would fall even more initially, but would then recover partially in the second quarter.

We actually observe changes from quarter to quarter, not virtual changes. The corresponding statement in real time would presumably say something like: if output rises at an annual rate 1 per cent slower than its trend, productivity will rise at an annual rate $0\cdot5$ per cent slower than its trend. This seems to be very close to what actually happens.[7]

[7] See, for example, R. J. Gordon, 'The Recent Acceleration of Inflation and Its Lessons for the Future', in *Brookings Papers on Economic Activity*, no. 1 (1970), especially equations (3) and (4) on page 39.

VII

VALUE THEORY

CHAPTER 18

A Quantum-Theory Model of Economics: Is the Co-ordinating Entrepreneur Just Worth His Profit?[1]

P. A. SAMUELSON

I INTRODUCTION

If an industry consists of symmetric firms with rising marginal costs, its total output is produced at minimum total costs when industry output is divided evenly among the firms. The optimal number of such firms will grow in jumps as industry output increases smoothly; but asymptotically, as industry output Q becomes large relative to the scale of each firm's U-shaped cost curve, the optimal number of firms, n^*, will be proportional to Q and the curve of industry's average cost will become asymptotically horizontal, no longer rising and falling perceptibly as each new firm is added.

All this has been well known for a third of a century.[2] But it pays no explicit attention to the need to pay the co-ordinating entrepreneur, if only for reason of his opportunity cost. Why does the firm's marginal cost curve ever rise if it can have *all* the inputs at fixed prices and can replicate processes in scale and also sub-divide them in scale? Why should it then not have a horizontal long-run marginal and average cost curve? Often, tacitly or explicitly, economists assume that the 'firm' needs a co-ordinating manager (or management), whose time and attention devoted to it involves some indivisible, minimum quantum of time and energy. Moreover, as more and more inputs are directed by him, his effective command

[1] Financial aid from the National Science Foundation and editorial assistance from Mrs Jillian M. Pappas are gratefully acknowledged.
    [2] See M. F. W. Joseph, 'A Discontinuous Cost Curve and the Tendency to Increasing Returns', *Economic Journal*, vol. 43 (1933), pp. 390–8; P. A. Samuelson, 'The Monopolistic Competition Revolution', in R. E. Kuenne (ed.), *Monopolistic Competition Theory: Studies in Impact – Essays in Honour of Edward H. Chamberlin*, (New York, Wiley, 1967), pp. 105–38, particularly pp. 129–35.

or span of attention gets stretched, so that the marginal cost of output from those inputs rises in much the same fashion that MC rises when any continuously-divisible fixed factor is held constant.

The essence of the present case of a co-ordinating entrepreneur is that it involves a granular factor that, by hypothesis, can change only in integral steps: you can contemplate $1, 2, 3 \ldots n, n+1$ of such agents; but not $1/2, \sqrt{2}$, or π.

To be sure, our case does not cover all models of co-ordinating management. In compensation, its results will apply to any integrally-lumpy factor – as when homogeneous land, for some reason, can be re-allocated only by the acre or by the square inch rather than completely continuously. Also, this analysis throws light on the valuation of taxi-cab medallions or other variants of artificial permits needed for a new business or new plant.

II PREVIEW

Suppose any 'manager' will leave the industry if his residual profits from production, after paying the hired factors, systematically falls below π. How high π is above zero depends on a general equilibrium analysis not here discussed; however, the present partial-equilibrium analysis is an important strand in that general equilibrium story. Suppose new managers will be attracted into the industry when there is a reasoned expectation that managers will earn in it residual profit of π or more.

Then, pretty clearly, as industry demand grows large enough to support numerous competitive firms, its healthy long-run equilibrium will involve price marked up above non-management unit cost by the π amount of needed-manager profit. What is the 'function' that any one representative manager is providing, to his firm or the industry or the consumer or society, that can 'justify' his profits being levied against the consumer?

Thanks to the writings of such Cambridge economists as Joan Robinson,[3] students of competitive price have realized that the lumpy entrepreneur usually gets his lumpy marginal productivity just as a divisible factor gets its smooth marginal productivity. But this has never been properly demonstrated.

Specifically, entrepreneur's profit becomes ('virtually') π in long-

[3] J. V. Robinson, 'Euler's Theorem and the Problem of Distribution', *Economic Journal*, vol. 44 (1934), pp. 398–414, particularly p. 409.

run equilibrium and π is the loss to society of having industry's output produced by one less (or, one more) firm out of many firms. What society loses when the entrepreneur is removed is his competitively determined profit. Charging that profit is needed to get production in each firm the optimal amount *beyond* the lowest point on the curve of hired-factor unit cost!

This lumpy, or quantum theory of marginal product is a remarkable case. Mathematically, we know that the production function which is smoothly differentiable in real variables

$$Y = F(X_1, X_2, \ldots)$$

and which is concave and homogeneous to the first degree, leads simply to marginal-productivity, imputation relations

$$\begin{cases} W_i = \partial F(X_1, X_2, \ldots)/\partial X_i & (i = 1,2) \\ Y = \sum_i W_i X_i. \end{cases}$$

All this holds by virtue of Euler's theorem.

But $\partial F/\partial X_1$ is not the same as

$$(\Delta F/\Delta X_1)_{X^2} = F(X_1 + 1, X_2) - F(X_1, X_2),$$

and Euler has no theorem to compel

$$X_1(\Delta F/\Delta X_1)_{X^2} + X_2(\Delta F/\Delta X_2)_{X^1} \equiv F.$$

Yet, as we shall see, for large enough X_i, $\partial F/\partial X_i$ and $\Delta F/\Delta X_i$ become identical. Indeed, it can be easily shown that even for $F(X_1, X_2, \ldots)$ 'almost homogeneous', satisfying

$$F(\lambda X_1, \lambda X_2, \ldots) = \lambda F(X_1, X_2, \ldots)$$

only for λ integral, this same asymptotic equivalance will hold.

III STATEMENT OF THE BASIC ASYMPTOTIC THEOREM

Although it is evident that Joan Robinson in her heuristic discussion of Euler's theorem has a clear understanding of the relationships involved, I cannot recall a rigorous statement or demonstration of the following basic quantum theory result

$$(1) \operatorname*{Lim}_{Q = \infty} \left\{ \{n^{**}(Q) - 1\} C[Q/\{n^{**}(Q) - 1\}] - n^{**}(Q) C[Q/n^{**}(Q)] \right\}$$
$$= \pi = C'(q^{**})q^{**} - C(q^{**})$$

where the total cost paid out optimally by the industry to the hired factors is denoted by $n^{**}(Q)C[Q/n^{**}(Q)]$ and $n^{**}(Q)$ is defined by

$$(2) \qquad \underset{n}{\text{Min}}\left\{nC[Q/n]+\pi n\right\} \overset{def}{\equiv} n^{**}(Q)\left\{C[Q/n^{**}(Q)]+\pi\right\}$$

and where $C[q]$ is each manager's total cost curve of hired factors (exclusive, of course, of any entrepreneurial profit, whether of the opportunity-cost, the short-run quasi-rent, or the long-run competitively-determined type).

What the fundamental relation (1) asserts is that, if a firm is selling at a competitive price equal to its marginal cost and that marginal cost is competitively above the average cost outlay to hired factors, then the profit doled out to it as a residual rent is equal to its opportunity cost and, more interestingly, is asymptotically for large enough scale precisely equal to its marginal product, even though that marginal product is of *finite* quantum type rather than of smooth-partial-derivative type.

IV PROOF

Here I shall briefly sketch the salient relations. The heavy curves in Figure 18.1 merely reproduce my textbook diagram (*Economics* (1970), p. 457) of the cost curves when entrepreneur's opportunity cost or profit is ignored; marginal cost curves have been added here. The upper curve superimposes the profit magnitude π, so that the curve represents cost-cum-profits that must at least prevail if each Q were to hold for ever and each firm in the industry were content to stay in it and, at the same time, no larger numbers of firms would be able to cover in profits their needed opportunity costs, π.

To anyone who understands the lower curve diagram and its logic, this new diagram should be self-explanatory. Let me comment on its features.

1. Because of need to pay profit to hold managers, every firm produces *beyond* the bottom of the lower hired factor U-shaped curve. This 'overproduction' in each firm is optimal and approximates to the amount $q^{**}-q^{*}$, where q^{**} is the point at which the excess of MC over hired-factor AC just equals the needed profit-per-unit, π/q^{**}.

2. The competitive industry acts *as if* the upper curve of cost-plus-needed-profit were its actual cost curve. Residual profits are,

par excellence, short-run rents or (in Marshall's terminology) quasi-rents; but they are truly long-run costs.

3. What the unit-cost diagram cannot show clearly is that the profit π equals the saving in industry cost from not losing the last

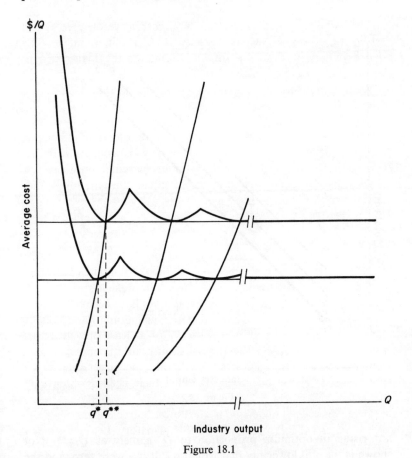

Figure 18.1

entrepreneur. Figure 18.2 sketches the total-cost aspect of this. Now the scale is tremendously reduced so that the initial less-than-100 firm stage is only a speck near the origin. The straight lines show that we are at a scale involving a really large number of firms, and it is only then that we get our asymptotic results with strictly parallel lines. Also, the vertical distance depicting π has been grossly exaggerated so that the diagram can be understood; naturally, the profit of one firm is very small compared to the total cost of the whole industry.

The ray marked q^{**} represents fixed-factor outlays (exclusive of π!), growing in proportion to industry output with number of firms

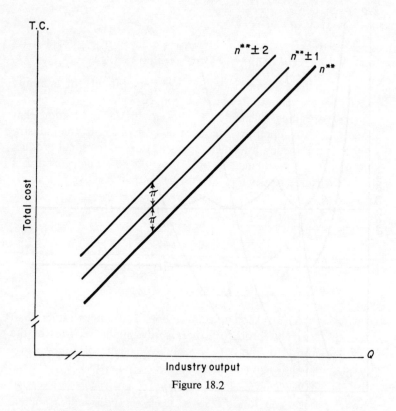

Figure 18.2

n^{**} rising in optimum proportion to Q, namely as Q/q^{**}. Not shown is the still lower ray that would result if π were zero, and the bottom-of-the-lower-U output, q^* rather than q^{**}, was achieved by each firm.

The rays marked $n^{**}\pm 1$ and $n^{**}\pm 2$ are parallel to the n^{**} ray and are equally-spaced above it. The essence of the present demonstration is that the space between the $n^{**}\pm 1$ ray and the n^{**} ray must be precisely π as $Q\to\infty$ and all curves become strictly straight lines.

Writing $n^{**}(Q)$ as n for short, we have

$$(n-1)C[Q/(n-1)]-nC[Q/n]$$

$$= n\frac{C[Q/(n-1)]-C(Q/n)}{[Q/(n-1)-Q/n]}Q\frac{1}{n(n-1)}-C[Q/(n-1)]$$

$$= [\triangle C/\triangle Q][Q/(n-1)]-C[Q/(n-1)]$$

(3) $$= C'(q^{**})q^{**}-C(q^{**})$$

as

$$Q/n^{**}(Q)\to q^{**} \text{ for } Q\to\infty.$$

This proves that asymptotic finite marginal product of a lumpy factor does converge to its remuneration. QED

Strictly speaking, I should append to this demonstration that entrepreneur's residual profit equals the cost saving to the industry his presence provides, a related demonstration on marginal product itself. Since the mathematical proof[4] would be straightforward, I shall leave to the reader the demonstration that

(4) $$\lim_{\lambda \to \infty}\left\{Q[\lambda x_1+1, \lambda x_2, \ldots]-Q[\lambda x_1, \lambda x_2, \ldots]\right\}$$
$$= \partial Q[x_1, x_2, \ldots]/\partial(x_1)$$

if Q is any smooth homogeneous-first-degree function. That is,

$$\lim_{\lambda \to \infty}(\Delta Q/\Delta x_i)x_j = \partial Q/\partial x_i$$

even though Δx_i is kept at a large positive number rather than going to zero. This property causes jigsaw-puzzle versions of the economic world to approach hydraulic versions of the world – provided that sufficient *replication* in scale is possible.

Moral: *Large numbers smooth!*

[4] Allyn Young, Frank Knight and Joan Robinson assume in their heuristic proofs that the factors hired by the withdrawn firm or acre of land go to work at sensibly *unchanged* marginal productivity for other firms or at the external margin: hence society loses the infra-marginal product of the withdrawn factor, which is its residual rent. I have merely made this rigorous by careful lim $n\to\infty$ argumentation. See Robinson, op. cit., p. 409; F. H. Knight, 'The Ricardian Theory of Production and Distribution', *Canadian Journal of Economics and Political Science*, vol. 1 (1935), pp. 3–25, 171–96, particularly p. 181 where Knight attributes the argument to Allyn Young's section of R. T. Ely, *Outlines of Economics*, 4th edn (New York, Macmillan, 1923), p. 410.
Hint: rewrite (4) as

$$\{Q[\lambda x_1+\lambda\lambda^{-1}, x_2,\ldots]-Q[\lambda x_1, \lambda x_2, \ldots]\}\{\lambda\lambda^{-1}=\{Q[x_1+\lambda^{-1}, x_2, \ldots]-Q[x_1, x_2, \ldots]\}\lambda^{-1}$$

which clearly goes to $\partial Q/\partial x_1$ as $\lambda^{-1}\to O$.

P. N. Rosenstein-Rodan: Bibliography

BOOKS

Capital Formation and Economic Development (Studies in the Economic Development of India, 2), editor and contributor (London, Allen & Unwin, 1964; Cambridge, Massachusetts, MIT Press, 1964).

Pricing and Fiscal Policies: A Study in Method (Studies in the Economic Development of India, 3), editor and contributor (London, Allen & Unwin, 1964; Cambridge, Massachusetts, MIT Press, 1964).

with I. M. D. Little. *Nuclear Power and Italy's Energy Position*; Reports on the Productive Uses of Nuclear Energy (Washington, D.C., National Planning Association, 1957).

with S. Chakravarty. *Development through Food: A Strategy for Surplus Utilization* (Rome, Food and Agriculture Organization of the United States, 1961).

Philosophy and Practice of Latin American Development (Cambridge, Massachusetts, MIT Press, 1972).

CONTRIBUTOR TO

A Study for the Committee on Foreign Relations (Cambridge, Massachusetts, Center for International Studies, MIT, 1957 and 1960).

The Emerging Nations: Their Growth and United States Policy, M. F. Milikan and D. L. M. Blackmer, eds (Boston, Little, Brown & Co, 1961).

Investment Criteria and Economic Growth (Bombay Asia Publishing House, 1961); Spanish edn (Madrid; RIACP, 1965).

ARTICLES

'Grenznutzen' (Marginal Utility), *Handwörterbuch der Staatswissenschaften* (1926). Italian version in *Nuova Collana d. Econ.*, vol. 4 (1937). Japanese translation in 1930. English translation in *International Economic Association Papers* (New York, Macmillan, 1960).

'Das Zeitmoment in der Mathematischen Theorie des Wirtsch Gleich-gewichtes' (The Element of Time in the Mathematical Theory of Economic Equilibrium), *Zeitschrift F. Nationalokonomie* (1929).

'Complementarieta: Prima delle Tre Fase del Progresso dell'Economia Pura' (Complementarity: The First of Three Phases of Progress of Pure Economics), *Riforma Sociale* (1934).

'The Role of Time in Economic Theory', *Economica* (1934). A modified version in Italian: 'La Funzione del Tempo in Teoria Economica', *Annali de Economia Estatistica* (Geneva, 1936).

'Co-ordination of the General Theories of Money and Price,' *Economica* (1936).

'Problems of the Industrialisation of Eastern and South-Eastern Europe', *Economic Journal* (1943). Reprinted in Agarwalla and Singh, *The Economics of Underdevelopment* (Oxford University Press, 1963; also other anthologies).

'How Much Can Germany Pay?', *International Affairs* (1945).

1947–1953 in the International Bank for Reconstruction and Development, Washington, D.C.; various unpublished reports on the Marshall Plan, the Doctrine of Development, Development of Southern Italy, Program-Approach versus Single Project-Approach, etc.

'Notes on the Preliminary Study of the Technique of Programming Economic Development', Part 1, 2 and 3 (Santiago, Economic Commission for Latin Affairs (ECLA), 1953), mimeographed.

'Theory of Economic Backwardness' (Spanish), *Panorama Economica* (Santiago, 1954).

'The Need for International Financing of Exports' (Cambridge, Massachusetts, Center for International Studies, MIT, 1954).

'Le Tre Indivisibilita . . .' (The Three Indivisibilities . . .), *SFIO* (Rome, 1955). 'Fabbisogno del Capitale dei Paesi Sotto Sviluppati', *SFIO* (1955); in French in *ISEA* (1956).

'Rapporti fra Factori Produttivi nell'Economia Italiana' (Factor Proportions in the Italian Economy), *Industria* (1954).

'Programming in Theory and in National Practice' (Cambridge, Massachusetts, Center for International Studies, MIT, 1955).

'Disguised Unemployment and Underemployment in Agriculture' (Cambridge, Massachusetts, Center for International Studies, MIT, 1956); and *Monthly Bulletin of Agricultural Economics and Statistics* (1956).

'Notes on the Theory of the "Big Push"' (Cambridge, Massachusetts, Center for International Studies, MIT, 1957); and in *Economic Development in Latin America*, IEA (Macmillan and Co., 1963).

'How to Industrialise an Underdeveloped Area' (Cambridge, Massachusetts, Center for International Studies, MIT, 1959); and in Italian in *Industria* (1960).

'Contribution of the Atomic Energy Power Programme in India' (Cambridge, Massachusetts, Center for International Studies, MIT, 1959); and in *India Studies*, vol. 3 (MIT Press, 1964).

'Alternative Numerical Models of the Third Five Year Plan of India' (Cambridge, Massachusetts, Center for International Studies, MIT, 1959); and in *India Studies*, vol. 2 (MIT Press, 1964).

'International Aid for Underdeveloped Countries', *The Review of Economics and Statistics*, vol. 43 (1961), no. 2. French translation in *Revue de l'action populaire* (Paris, November 1961).

'El Desarollo Economico de Italia Durante la Decada de 1950' (Economic Development of Italy in the 1950s), *Rev. de Economia Latin Americana* (Caracas, 1961).

'Technical Progress and Post-War Rate of Growth in Italy', *Il Progresso Tecnologico e la Societa Italiana*, vol. 1 (Milan, Giuffre, 1962).

'Reflections on Regional Development' (Cambridge, Massachusetts; Center for International Studies, MIT, 1963); and in *Scritti de Economia in Memoria de Alessandro Molinari* (Milan, Giuffre, 1963).

'Determining the Need for and Planning the Use of External Resources', *Science, Technology and Development*, vol. 8; *Organisation, Planning and Programming for Economic Development* (Washington, D.C.; US Government Printing Office, 1962). German translation in *Konjunktur Politik* (1964).

'Planning within the Nation', *Annals of Collective Economy* (1963) (English and French edition).

'The Alliance for Progress' (Symposium on Latin America, Wellesley College, Wellesley, Massachusetts, 1963).

'Inquiry into Problems of International Investment in the Second Half of the Twentieth Century', *Capital Movements and Economic Development* (International Economic Association Proceedings edited by J. Adler, New York, 1967).

'I Problemi della Sicilia alla Luce delle Modern Teorie dello Sviluppo Economico Regionale' (Sicily's Problems in the Light of Modern Theories of Regional Economic Development), *Notiziario IRFIS* (Palermo, April 1964).

'The Role of Income Distribution in Development Programmes', *Essays in Honour of Marco Fanno*, vol. 2 (*CEDAM*, Padova, 1966).

'The Modernisation of Industry', *Modernization: The Dynamics of Growth* (New York, 1966).

'The Consortia Technique', *International Organisation*, vol. 22; and in *Global Partnership*, R. Gardner and M. F. Millikan, eds (New York, 1968).

'Latin American Development: Results and Prospects', *Challenge* (1967).

'La Marcha de la Allianza para el Progresso', *Progresso* (Vision) (1966).

'A Study on Independent International Evaluation of National Development Efforts', *UNCTAD* (New Delhi, 11 December 1967). TD/&/ Suppl. 15.

'Multinational Investment in the Framework of Latin American Integration', *Multinational Investment in the Economic Development and Integration of Central America* (Washington, D.C., Inter-American Development Bank, 1968).

'The Crossroads and the Choice: Economic Alternatives for Full Employment Growth' (Conference CSDI in Mexico City, September 1969). Published in: *One Spark from Holocaust: The Crisis in Latin America* (Santa Barbara, Center for Studies of Democratic Institutions, 1970).

'Assitencia Financiera Exterior' (External Financial Aid), *Rev. de Economia Latin Americana* (Caracas, 1971).

'Problems of Unemployment' (in Spanish), '*Rev. de Economia Latin Americana* (Caracas, 1971).

'The Have's and the Have-not's Around the Year 2000' (Report, Conference of World Law Order, June 1969). Published in *Economics and World Order*, ed. Bhagwati, (New York, Macmillan, 1972).

'Latin America in the Light of Reports on Development' (Cambridge, Massachusetts, Economics Department, MIT, 1970).

'Criteria for Evaluation of National Development Effort', *Journal of Development Planning*, vol. 1, no. 1 (New York, United Nations, 1970).

'Planning for Full Employment' (Washington, D.C., CIAP, 1971).

'Employment and Growth in the Strategy of Development of Latin America' (Comments on CIES Report No. 1641; Washington, D.C., CIAP, 1971).

'Transfer of Technology' (Spanish) (Report presented in February 1971 in Lima, Peru; OAS, 1972).

LIST OF AUTHORS

JOHN H. ADLER, International Bank for Reconstruction and Development, Washington, D.C., U.S.A.

HANS W. ARNDT, Professor of Economics, The Australian National University, Australia.

PRANAB BARDHAN, Professor of Economics, Indian Statistical Institute, India.

JAGDISH BHAGWATI, Professor of Economics, Massachusetts Institute of Technology, U.S.A.

JORGE CAUAS, Professor of Economics and Director, Instituto de Economia, Universidad Catolica de Chile, Chile.

CARLOS DIAZ-ALEJANDRO, Professor of Economics, Yale University, U.S.A.

RICHARD S. ECKAUS, Professor of Economics, Massachusetts Institute of Technology, U.S.A.

BENT HANSEN, Professor of Economics, University of California at Berkeley, U.S.A.

EVERETT E. HAGEN, Professor of Economics, Massachusetts Institute of Technology, U.S.A.

BENJAMIN HIGGINS, Professor of Economics, McGill University, Canada.

ALEXANDER KAFKA, Executive Director, International Monetary Fund.

CHARLES P. KINDLEBERGER, Professor of Economics, Massachusetts Institute of Technology, U.S.A.

LOUIS LEFEBER, Professor of Economics, Brandeis University, U.S.A.

I. M. D. LITTLE, Professor of Economics of Underdeveloped Countries, Oxford University, and Fellow, Nuffield College, U.K.

JAMES A. MIRRLEES, Professor of Mathematical Economics, Oxford University and Fellow, Nuffield College, U.K.

FRANCO MODIGLIANI, Institute Professor, Massachusetts Institute of Technology, U.S.A.

PAUL A. SAMUELSON, Nobel Laureate and Institute Professor, Massachusetts Institute of Technology, U.S.A.

PASQUALE SARACENO, President, SVIMEZ, Rome, Italy.

ROBERT SOLOW, Professor of Economics, Massachusetts Institute of Technology, U.S.A.

JAN TINBERGEN, Nobel Laureate and Professor of Economics, Rotterdam, Netherlands.

INDEX